W9-CBV-592

An Improbable Life

An Improbable Life

MY SIXTY YEARS AT COLUMBIA
AND OTHER ADVENTURES

ಞ

Michael I. Sovern

A Columbia University Publication

A Columbia University Publication

Copyright © 2014 Michael I. Sovern
All rights reserved

Library of Congress Cataloging-in-Publication Data
A complete CIP record is available from the Library of Congress.

This book is printed on paper with recycled content.
Printed in the United States of America
c 10 9 8 7 6 5 4 3 2 1

Cover Design by Catherine Casiliano
Cover image by Joe Pineiro, courtesy of Columbia University.

For Pat

୨୦

CONTENTS

ILLUSTRATIONS

FOREWORD

WALTER F. MONDALE

When I ran for president in 1984, I was opposing one of the most popular chief executives in American history. Long before his election, Ronald Reagan, "The Great Communicator," had been a Sunday-night fixture in millions of homes as the television spokesman for General Electric and host of the GE Theater, the springboard to his winning the governorship of California. And Reagan had established his comfort with the Hollywood camera and his ability to win audience sympathy through memorable portrayals of such tragic characters as the epileptic John Galen in Philip Wylie's *Night Unto Night*, Drake McHugh in *Kings Row* ("Where's the rest of me?"), and George Gipp in *Knute Rockne, All American* ("Win one for the Gipper").

Clearly, it would be a major challenge to face this accomplished actor-orator and presidential incumbent on a television stage. As the time approached for the presidential debates, I knew I would need plenty of rehearsal time with the best possible stand-in for my opponent.

To play Ronald Reagan, I chose a faculty member I first encountered when I was a student at the University of Minnesota Law School. His name was Michael I. Sovern.

Mike Sovern taught at Minnesota for two years after graduating first in his class from Columbia Law School. Though he was the teacher and I was on the receiving end, I was three years older, having served in the army during the Korean War. As virtual contemporaries, we became not simply student and teacher but also friends.

When I asked Mike Sovern to play Ronald Reagan in rehearsals for the debates, he and I were nearly three decades away from those law school days in Minneapolis. He was now in his fifth year as the highly successful president of Columbia University.

Our debate rehearsals are among the many highlights of this book. Mike played the part well. He was better informed than Reagan, and several times he even managed to get under my skin. Of course he was preparing me to stay calm when my opponent tried to provoke me.

Mike's memoir covers a lot of territory. He grew up in a Bronx household near Yankee Stadium. His father died young, and the family was held together by a valiant working mother. He graduated from the prestigious Bronx High School of Science and then from Columbia College summa cum laude.

This book can be read as the story of a poor boy who made good by dint of intellect and skills. It is also the story of a great university, under siege in the 1960s, and of how Mike Sovern helped restore its integrity and reputation, first, as a faculty leader, the youngest full professor in Columbia history, then, as dean of the Law School, provost of the university, and finally as president.

During his administration, President Sovern opened undergraduate Columbia College to women students for the first time since its founding as King's College in 1754. He quadrupled the university's endowment, in large part by selling the land Columbia owned under Rockefeller Center. And I leave it to the reader to assess the scores of other accomplishments during his thirteen years as president.

This book is also a story of New York City in the last half of the twentieth century, from labor unrest among police, firefighters, and subway workers (Mike was a mediator in contract negotiations) to backstage Broadway, where he is president of the Shubert Foundation.

After he left the presidency of Columbia to rejoin the law faculty, he was called in to assume the board chairmanship at Sotheby's following the notorious price-fixing scandal with Christie's. Though he has written it with economy and brisk suspense, that fascinating chapter is a book in itself.

Mike Sovern's concern for the future of higher education and our national strength is reflected in his proposals to strengthen educational opportunity in America and require colleges and universities to practice greater fiscal discipline and hold down runaway tuition costs.

The young professor I first met in Minnesota has come a long way. I introduce him to you with the hope that you will enjoy his story and give thought to his ideas about where our country should be heading.

FOREWORD

LEE C. BOLLINGER

If you assume a world in which merit is recognized and rewarded, then there is nothing in the least bit improbable about the incredible array of roles, involvements, special assignments, and remarkable successes and achievements of Mike Sovern, which he recounts with such verve in this remarkable personal memoir. Mike's truly extraordinary talents and capacities were abundantly evident from his early years to virtually everyone (he became the youngest tenured member of the Columbia faculty at age twenty-eight), so it was indeed probable that over the course of his life he would be drawn into just about every part of the human drama of his era. That he views his life as "improbable," however, is an interesting fact, not least in how it brings an essence of pure delight to his telling of the stories in this book. It's as if everything here has an element of surprise in it, which means everything is all the more vivid to us, the readers.

Every life offers us insights into a particular moment in time as well as into the overall age. The breadth of Mike Sovern's experiences takes us many places over the last three quarters of a century—to race relations in America, to the development of freedom of speech at the dawn of the age of globalization, to labor issues in New York and beyond, to presidential elections, to arts and culture, and to dissent and conflict on America's campuses in the late 1960s.

Ultimately, though, this is a book about Columbia University and about one of its offspring, to whom the institution turned in perhaps its greatest hour of need and who responded with wholehearted dedication and the highest intelligence. It is perhaps too much to say that Mike Sovern saved Columbia, but surely his skills of leadership, of mediation, brilliance, and humor were essential to the rescue. Like all institutions that survive over centuries (roughly two-and-a-half now for Columbia), ours has had its good and bad times. But in the last century the swings of fortune were greater for the university than any other in America I can think of. During the period following the Second World War, Columbia was unquestionably the greatest university on the planet, measured by sheer academic brilliance. It was as well-endowed (financially speaking) as any of its peers, and in field after field it towered over them as well. But the controversies at Columbia of 1968 and their aftermath, combined with the desperate decline of New York City in the 1970s and the failures of institutional leadership in the university over this period, left Columbia nearly drained of resources of all kinds. Mike Sovern took over as president in 1980. He set about healing and repairing the institution while also reforming it, and collectively the successes rebuilt the foundation of this great university. It gave those of us who have followed him and his courageous colleagues the chance to recapture Columbia's unique role in higher education.

Mike Sovern says he thinks of himself as first and foremost a teacher. There is something deeply noble in that mission, and Mike exemplifies it. He was my teacher once, and he continues to be. A truly great teacher stays in your mind long after the course and continues to be a voice in your head leading you to places far beyond the original subject. Mike is such a teacher and will be that for you, too, when you read this book.

An Improbable Life

I

A SHARED STORY

Columbia began to affect my life when I was seventeen,
but the most dramatic impact came almost twenty years later.

Why do I call my life improbable? No savvy gambler would
have bet that a fatherless adolescent from the South Bronx,
the first in his family to graduate from high school, would grow up to
become president of one of the world's great universities.

My story is also a story about that university. I arrived at Columbia
more than sixty years ago, and I am still here. Columbia and I have been
together for almost a quarter of her 259 years. We have shared the best
of times and the worst of times.

One cannot lead a university without encountering the big issues
posed by our system, or nonsystem, of higher education. For example,
how can we make a Columbia education available to students capable
of benefiting from it but unable to pay for it? And a related issue: is affirmative action fair?

Financial issues abound. Among the challenges: what is the right
balance between spending today and saving for tomorrow? And then
an overarching issue that we addressed in the wake of the 1968 student
riots: how should Columbia be governed? Who is responsible for answering these and other critical questions?

One issue that most colleges had long since resolved: should we admit women to all-male Columbia College? The question would have been easy but for the potential effects on our sister college, Barnard.

In my quest for answers, I had to learn to dog-paddle in the swamp of academic politics. I encountered far more accomplished swimmers there than I. According to an apocryphal tale, Dwight Eisenhower, Columbia's thirteenth president, was asked why he left the presidency of Columbia for the presidency of the United States. "I couldn't stand the politics," he replied.

But I also had the exhilarating experience of working with brilliant scholars, gifted artists, pioneering scientists, and talented administrators to attack the problems faced by higher education.

I was no longer addressing issues as a scholar, as much as I enjoyed and valued that life. Now my responses were helping to shape my university's future.

One deserves priority: our answer to the question of how to keep Columbia's doors open to those who could not afford to pay. I could not bear the thought that under my leadership Columbia might become inaccessible to students like me. I raised tens of millions of dollars to support our financial aid programs, testified before Congress urging increased support for Pell grants—the national financial aid program for those at the bottom of the economic ladder—and regularly opted for additions to our financial aid budget. Happily, both my successors—George Rupp and Lee Bollinger—have shared my commitment to welcoming the best to Columbia irrespective of their financial condition.

The issues never go away. One hardy perennial: do great research universities undervalue teaching? We talk a good game about teaching, but the researchers get the grants and the competing offers that drive their salaries up. I tried to ameliorate the problem by creating new professorships for outstanding scholars committed to teaching undergraduates—chairs that honor the art of teaching.

We also worked to cultivate teaching skills in graduate school through more specific preparation for college teaching than tradition had dictated, assigning a higher priority to helping faculty beginners, and calling upon faculty mentors to devote more effort to helping their graduate students improve their teaching.

Many of our best researchers are in fact excellent teachers not because of institutional efforts but because that's what they want to be. And I need that consolation since neither at Columbia nor at the other great research centers have institutional efforts been all that productive.

On a university campus, more than in most places, issues of free speech are central. Free-speech issues took two main forms at Columbia during my presidency. One is heard frequently—the cry to ban an obnoxious speaker. I found this easy. The answer to objectionable speech is not suppression but more speech. When Khalid Abdul Muhammad, a spokesman for Louis Farrakhan, appeared on campus, I was proud to see that our Jewish students had gotten my message. Despite the fact that Muhammad had spoken of Columbia "Jew-niversity" and "Jew York City" and that, almost unthinkably, he was appearing on the anniversary of *Kristallnacht*, the Jewish Student Union did not ask that he be barred. Instead they held their own event to protest him and his message.

The other major threat to freedom of expression was the pressure to adopt a "speech code," a development that had become fashionable on college campuses during my presidency. For example, Brown banned "verbal behavior" that produces "feelings of impotence, anger, or disenfranchisement." The University of North Dakota defined as harassment anything that intentionally produces "psychological discomfort, embarrassment, or ridicule." Colby College outlawed speech that causes "a vague sense of danger" or a loss of "self-esteem." I challenged those who wanted Columbia to adopt a speech code to come up with a draft that did not curtail protected speech. No one met the challenge.

My university responsibilities did not keep me from off-campus adventures. My story would be incomplete without accounts of my representation of the victims of the Tuskegee Syphilis Experiment, my appearance before the U.S. Supreme Court, and my near miss at virtually every lawyer's dream—appointment to the Supreme Court. Nor could

I possibly omit my role as Walter (Fritz) Mondale's sparring partner as he prepared for his presidential campaign debates with Ronald Reagan.

There were other exciting challenges—helping to end a life-threatening strike by New York City's firemen, responding to a riotous dispute involving New York's policemen, avoiding work stoppages by the city's bus and subway workers, and answering the call from New York's governor and mayor to lead an anticorruption commission.

Though Columbia was the center of my working life, all did not end with my retirement from Columbia's presidency. Fun and fulfillment attended my becoming chairman of, first, the Japan Society and then the American Academy in Rome as well as president of the Shubert Foundation with its role in the world of theater. The greatest challenge of my post-presidential years was the chairmanship of Sotheby's as that venerable auction house struggled to survive the effects of anti-trust violations by its previous chairman and president.

But I get ahead of myself. Columbia began to affect my life when I was seventeen, though the most dramatic impact would come almost twenty years later, when the spring of 1968 changed both of our stories.

2

RIOT

*My life was about to change. Until this point I had been a
bemused observer of events that had little to do with me.*

I n the spring of 1968, at Columbia young men's fancies were not
turning to thoughts of love. Anger was in the air. For almost two
years, the Columbia chapter of Students for a Democratic Society had
been trying to rally students against the war in Vietnam, the draft, and a
cluster of related targets. More recently, protesting what they characterized as the university's racism, they had sought black student support. In
March, SDS led more than one hundred students in a noisy, disruptive
demonstration through the halls of Low Library, Columbia's central administration building. The university responded by putting Mark Rudd
and several other campus leaders of SDS on disciplinary probation for
violating a recently promulgated rule against demonstrations inside university buildings.

In early April, with great theatricality, Rudd interrupted a memorial service for the recently slain Dr. Martin Luther King Jr. Thrusting

---

In this and the following chapter, when I recount events I did not witness, I have drawn heavily
on the *Spectator*'s excellent account in Jerry Lewis Avorn et al., *Up Against the Ivy Wall: A History
of the Columbia Crisis* (New York: Atheneum, 1968). Unless otherwise indicated, the quotations in
these chapters are also attributable to that book.

himself between the university's vice president, David B. Truman, and the lectern at which Truman was about to deliver a eulogy, Rudd declared: "Dr. Truman and President Kirk [Grayson Kirk, Dwight D. Eisenhower's successor as president of Columbia] are committing a moral outrage against the memory of Dr. King." After a harangue against the university, Rudd led about forty followers out of the chapel.

This was only prelude. On Tuesday, April 23, SDS scheduled a noon rally to protest, among other things, the disciplining of their leaders. For the first time, Students' Afro-American Society, which had, until then, been uninterested in collaborating with their white radical classmates, agreed to participate. There ensued a chaotic demonstration marked by confused marches, colliding countermarches, scuffles with the police, and bumbling improvisation until an unidentified student protester shouted, "Seize Hamilton!"

Rudd took the hint and led his troops to Hamilton Hall, the stately McKim, Mead, and White building that houses Columbia College's administration and many faculty offices and classrooms. Soon Hamilton's lobby was bulging with four hundred chanting students. Acting Dean Henry Coleman arrived at the entrance to the building; Rudd invited him in and directed the mob to make way. Coleman accepted the invitation, never considering the possibility that it was a one-way ticket.

At first the protesters allowed free movement in and out of the building, though they maintained that they would remain where they were until all their demands were met. As articulated by a newly created steering committee, the demands were:

1. All disciplinary action now pending and probations already imposed upon six students be immediately terminated and a general amnesty be granted to those students participating in this demonstration.

2. President Kirk's ban on demonstrations inside University buildings be dropped.

3. Construction of the Columbia gymnasium in Morningside Park cease at once.

4. All future disciplinary action taken against University students be resolved through an open hearing before students and faculty which adheres to the standards of due process.

5. Columbia University disaffiliate, in fact and not merely on paper, from the Institute for Defense Analyses; and President Kirk and Trustee William A. M. Burden resign their positions on IDA's Board of Trustees and Executive Board.

6. Columbia University use its good offices to obtain dismissal of charges now pending against those participating in demonstrations at the gym construction site in the park.

America's student unrest in the late 1960s and early 1970s—at Columbia and on countless campuses elsewhere—drew from a menu of four issues. Protests began against the Vietnam war and racial injustice; if the protesters were disciplined, their treatment became the third issue; and in many instances "restructuring" of the university in the direction of greater democratization was added.

The Hamilton Hall list was archetypal, though restructuring of the university had not yet surfaced. The gym in the park was Columbia's big race issue. Beginning in the late 1950s, the university and New York City had worked out an agreement to let Columbia build a gymnasium in adjacent Morningside Park in return for Columbia including separate facilities for members of the neighboring community. My colleague Bill (William L.) Cary, later chairman of the Securities and Exchange Commission, doubted the wisdom of "building your house on your mother-in-law's land," but the agreement was widely applauded and approved by both the City and the State of New York.

The prevailing mood changed, however, over the years it took to raise the necessary funds. A new parks commissioner didn't like the idea of giving up park land, even though the once elegant Olmstead-designed Morningside Park had become a virtual no-man's land. Separate facilities for mainly white Columbians and mainly minority community residents no longer seemed such a terrific idea. The topography didn't help.

Columbia's entrance would be on Morningside Heights, through what would doubtless be seen as the front door, while the neighbors would enter down at the bottom, through the back door.

Dean Coleman communicated the protesters' demands to Vice President Truman, who offered to meet with the group in another building. The demonstrators were willing to send just their steering committee and then only if Truman first granted them all amnesty. He refused. By now—late afternoon—the demonstrators had also told Coleman that he was not free to leave Hamilton Hall, an assertion that Coleman chose not to test. He may well have been the first university official taken hostage on an American campus. Though President Kirk wanted to call the police at this point, Vice President Truman persuaded him to wait, a judgment in which Dean Coleman concurred.

During the course of the evening, more than a dozen black residents of Harlem joined the demonstrators in response to a plea from the Students' Afro-American Society. It was rumored some were carrying guns. Before dawn broke, the SDS-SAS alliance lay in shards. The definitive moment came when the black group told the white, "We want to make our stand here. It would be better if you left and took your own building." Though that may sound like a cartoon caption, these were not groups given to self-mockery. The white students straggled out, and the black group, in a fresh escalation, barricaded Hamilton's doors behind them. Still improvising, about two hundred students headed for Low Library, where they smashed through the glass portion of a door and dashed for President Kirk's and Vice President Truman's suite of offices. After breaking another glass panel, they were in. (I later spent almost fifteen years in those offices, but not even my mother could have imagined that in 1968.) It was not yet seven a.m., Wednesday, April 24.

Truman was no longer reluctant to use the police, but he and Kirk wanted to proceed only against those who had broken into Low Library. The racial rioting that had followed Dr. King's assassination was still fresh in memory, and Coleman's circumstances as a prisoner in Hamilton Hall were problematic. Arrest those in Low but not those in Hamilton, they told the police officials who had joined them in the part of Low not occupied by students.

The police demurred: the Columbia administration, they believed, was asking them to discriminate on racial grounds, and they could not do that. They were, however, willing to dismantle the barricades to Kirk's office erected by the invading students. Believing they were about to be arrested, most of the students fled through the windows, successfully navigating a ledge to safety, climbing down gratings or jumping to a patch of grass fifteen feet below. By the time the barricades were removed from Low Library, only a handful of students remained. But the police would not arrest them and leave Hamilton Hall a sanctuary, and Kirk and Truman were not willing to move against Hamilton. When it became apparent that there were to be no arrests, many of the fleeing students clambered back in through the windows. A golden opportunity to end the Low takeover had passed.

Columbia's administration was not alone in fearing that the Hamilton Hall occupation might get seriously out of hand. Mayor John Lindsay dispatched an assistant to help. Several leading black politicians joined him in fruitless shuttle diplomacy between Columbia's administration and Hamilton Hall. They did enjoy one success. After Human Rights Commissioner William Booth, State Senator Basil Paterson, and the Lindsay aide, Barry Gottehrer, warned the black students that they could be charged with kidnapping if they continued to detain Dean Coleman, he was set free. It was three-thirty Wednesday afternoon. Twenty-six hours had gone by since Coleman accepted Mark Rudd's invitation to enter.

A glutton for punishment, Coleman hurried to join an emergency meeting of the Columbia College faculty that had begun moments before his release. With President Kirk in the chair and after extended debate, the faculty voted to condemn the coercive actions of the protesters, to reject amnesty for them, to urge that the police not be used to clear the buildings, to ask the administration to suspend work on the gym pending reconsideration of the whole idea, and to set up a tripartite committee composed of faculty, students, and administrators.

The committee would "discuss any disciplinary matters arising out of the incidents yesterday and today, the issue of the gymnasium and any other matters which are subjects of legitimate concern to the University community."

Faculty were not the only ones meeting. Counterdemonstrators were heckling the Hamilton occupiers and milling about near Low. SDS held yet another rally. And faculty and administrators were meeting with students in small groups. Yet much of Columbia was conducting business as usual. So far, the takeovers were essentially an undergraduate affair. Students and faculty in Columbia's graduate and professional schools—more than two-thirds of the university—were engaged in their normal teaching and learning, research and writing.

That was about to change. At one a.m. Thursday morning, students in Columbia's Graduate School of Architecture declared their building—Avery Hall—a "Liberated Zone," endorsed the protesters' six demands, and added a few of their own. At two a.m., another group of graduate students took over Fayerweather Hall, which housed the economics, political science, and sociology departments. Students arriving for their classes later that morning were met by impassable barricades.

Thursday afternoon Vice President Truman, former dean of the College and heir-apparent to President Kirk, accepted an invitation to meet informally with more than one hundred faculty members in Philosophy Hall. He was a great favorite of the faculty, but that was not to last. On this day, he seemed a man in over his head. Professor Robert Belknap, a colleague who would one day fill the dean's chair himself, observed, "It was what he didn't say that bothered us. He hadn't said that negotiations were proceeding. He hadn't drawn up a statement saying what could or could not be done. He hadn't appointed a faculty group to advise him. . . . He lost his cool."

After Truman left, the faculty members present, by no means a representative group but still substantial in number and including more than a few respected scholars and teachers, decided to act on their own, thereby matching the students in reckless improvisation. They adopted the following resolution:

We, the undersigned members of the Columbia University faculty and teaching staff, make the following proposal to resolve the present crisis:

(1.) We request the Trustees to implement the immediate cessation of excavation on the gymnasium site, by telephone vote if necessary.

(2.) We request the administration to delegate all disciplinary power on matters related to the present crisis to the tripartite committee, consisting of students, faculty, and administration.

(3.) We request the students to evacuate all buildings now, and we pledge our faith and influence towards a solution. Should the students be willing to evacuate the buildings, we will not meet classes until the crisis is resolved along the above lines.

(4.) Until this crisis is settled, we will stand before the occupied buildings to prevent forcible entry by police or others.

(5.) No matter what has happened, we consider these students members of our community. We do not contemplate their being dismissed and we would oppose violently any such action.

Three hundred faculty would ultimately subscribe to this statement. But the students in the buildings were unmoved. Despite earnest efforts to persuade them by members of what became known as the Ad Hoc Faculty Group, the occupants resolved to stay put.

The Ad Hoc Faculty Group regrouped Thursday evening, with Professor Alan Westin in the chair. Among the speakers was a representative of students opposed to the demonstrations, who had collected 1,700 signatures for their side and who warned that their impatience would lead them to take matters into their own hands. Not long thereafter a group of students did in fact try to force their way into Fayerweather to remove the demonstrators. Several Ad Hoc Faculty Group members managed to persuade them to back off. But the level of anger and frustration among many hundreds of students denied access to their classrooms remained dangerously high.

At the same time the threat of racial conflict was reinforced by a group from Harlem who, after some inflammatory rhetoric, insisted on marching across campus. A serious clash with counterdemonstrators was narrowly averted when Dean Coleman cleared a path for the black marchers.

Truman and Kirk felt they could wait no longer. At about one a.m., Truman walked the few steps from Low Library to Philosophy Hall and announced to the Ad Hoc Faculty Group that President Kirk was about to ask the mayor to send in the police. He did not wait for a reply, which may have been just as well. The room filled with boos and denunciations. While the Ad Hoc Faculty Group was denouncing Truman and Kirk, the radicals were seizing a fifth building—Mathematics Hall. That did not keep members of the Faculty Group from honoring their pledge "to stand before the occupied buildings to prevent forcible entry by police or others." The sweet spring night was soon witness to the extraordinary sight of professors of all ages scrambling to station themselves before the occupied buildings to ward off the police.

As I learned later, summoning the police to clear out trespassing protesters is far more complicated than just calling 911. Forms must be signed, large numbers of officers have to be gathered and deployed, and even then the police may hesitate to act. And so it was that members of the Ad Hoc Faculty Group had ample time to try to persuade Truman and Kirk to reverse their decision. A group of plainclothes police officers unwittingly helped. Forcing their way into Low's security headquarters, a part of the building not held by the students, they bloodied a young faculty member who blocked their way. Truman had been warned only a few moments before that he had embarked on a course that would shed faculty blood. The swift fulfillment of that prophecy was too much. At three-thirty a.m. Friday, Truman emerged from Low and read a statement to the multitude assembled there:

> The faculty committee has persuaded the University administration to postpone the request for police action on campus while the faculty and administration continue their efforts to effect a peaceful solution to the situation.

Necessary security arrangements will of course be maintained. To encourage these efforts, the University will be closed until Monday. At the request of the Mayor and without prejudice to continuation at a later time, we have suspended construction on the gymnasium pending further discussion.

Undeterred by their total lack of experience and preparation for the role they were playing, the Ad Hoc Faculty Group had forced the administration to allow them to continue trying to mediate.

Friday was a busy day for the Group. Shifting subgroups maintained a cordon around Low, kept students from fighting one another, and talked virtually nonstop in Philosophy Hall while members of the Group's steering committee met with the black students in Hamilton Hall and with representatives of the white students holding the other four buildings.

At about two a.m. Saturday morning, Alan Westin, the Group's chairman, reported to a packed house in Philosophy Hall that negotiations with Mark Rudd and his team were making progress. He then called upon Rudd for confirmation. That was not what he got: "We had exploratory talks . . . very exploratory, more in the line of bullshit," Rudd informed the audience. He went on to insist on amnesty, a step that the administration would not take and that the Ad Hoc Faculty Group had steadfastly refused to urge.

Mark Rudd's choice of words to tell the assembled faculty what he thought of their efforts to mediate between student protesters and Columbia University's administration did not sit well. His terse dismissal of his elders shattered their fantasies. Alan Westin declared the meeting adjourned. Even members of the Group's steering committee had to acknowledge that they had run into a wall. They decided to suspend negotiations.

On Saturday President Kirk dispatched telegrams calling all of Columbia's assistant, associate, and full professors to a meeting in the law school on Sunday. Kirk's guest list differed in a critical respect from the

Ad Hoc Faculty Group's: it did not include Columbia's youngest teachers—instructors, preceptors, and teaching assistants. No one doubted that they were generally sympathetic to the protestors' point of view and that their exclusion would make the meeting more receptive to the administration. The Ad Hoc Faculty Group's request to add them was rejected.

In a triumph of hope over experience, a subcommittee of the Ad Hoc Faculty Group resumed negotiations Saturday evening with Rudd and several others. There was no movement, and the Ad Hoc Faculty Group again had to face the reality that there wasn't likely to be any.

The Group's steering committee spent the hours between midnight and dawn on a new course, the drafting of a public proposal for settlement. If both parties accepted it, the dispute would be over. If the students were willing but the administration was not, in essence the Group would side with the students. Conversely, if the administration agreed but the students did not, the Group would "refuse further to interpose ourselves between the administration and the students." The statement did not say what the Group would do if neither side accepted. The proposed terms were: acceptance of the tripartite commission as final arbiter of university discipline, uniform penalties for all the five hundred or so protestors (that is, the leadership could not be suspended or expelled unless everyone was), a veto power over the gymnasium plans to be vested in community representatives, and an end to the building occupations. At eight-thirty Sunday morning the Ad Hoc Faculty Group gathered again in Philosophy Hall and endorsed their steering committee's proposal.

At ten a.m., all the faculties of the university gathered in formal session for only the second time since World War II. The faculty of Columbia College was there, but so were the faculties of Columbia's fifteen other schools. Entering the meeting room, I chose a seat not far from the lectern at which I usually taught. My classroom had a capacity of 205 students, but by removing a wall it could be joined to its neighbor to form an auditorium twice that size. This was one of the rare occasions on which that was done, and the room was still filled to overflowing.

The administration was obviously seeking to preempt the Ad Hoc Faculty Group by having this duly constituted body act. The administration did not, however, seek explicit blessing for a call to the police. Instead, it had arranged for Peter Kenen, a respected young economist, to offer a resolution that, among other things, condemned the building occupations, blessed the idea of a tripartite commission, commended the cessation of gym construction, thanked the administration for its patience and the Ad Hoc Faculty Group for its efforts, and called "upon the students who continue to occupy University buildings to recognize that failure to resolve this crisis rapidly and peaceably may result in irreparable damage to all members of this community." The administration presumably believed that was enough of a warrant.

To ensure the resolution's passage, President Kirk called upon several Columbia greats to support its adoption—Polykarp Kusch, Nobel laureate in physics; Ernest Nagel, arguably America's greatest living philosopher; William Leuchtenburg, a preeminent historian of the New Deal; and Eli Ginzberg, a highly respected economist and adviser to Presidents Eisenhower, Kennedy, and Johnson. The resolution passed overwhelmingly. But then Professor Alan Westin was recognized and informed the assembly of the Ad Hoc Faculty Group's resolution. Unlike the resolution that had just passed, the Group's resolution would, most importantly, transfer from the university to outsiders the final word on the gym, assure that the demonstration's leaders would not be seriously punished, and align the faculty with the protestors if the administration did not agree. Though Westin did not seek action, the inconclusive discussion that followed left everyone free to claim that the assembled faculties did or did not agree with the Ad Hoc Faculty Group. The administration had been trumped.

On Monday the Ad Hoc Faculty Group set out to sell their package. Neither side was buying. Monday evening's meeting of the Group was dispirited and desperate. After hours of ineffectual discussion, the Group adjourned shortly after midnight.

I worked late that night in my Claremont Avenue apartment three blocks from Low Library. Though the evening was warm and I had the windows open, I heard nothing unusual. Later, while I was sleeping, the police arrested 695 students and hangers-on. My first word of the "bust" came in a phone call from my friend and colleague Monrad Paulsen. He told me not only that Kirk had summoned the police but that the Ad Hoc Faculty Group had convened a meeting for ten a.m. My immediate reaction was: "They're likely to do something foolish. Get as many faculty from law, business, and engineering there as possible."

My life was about to change. Until this point I had been a bemused observer of events that had little to do with me. I enjoyed my teaching and was basking in the glow of the responses to my book on employment discrimination. An offer from Harvard had boosted my Columbia salary, and the editors of *Time* were paying me well to serve as their legal advisor. Though my tastes were simple, I seemed to have a talent for procreation, and so to support my four children I would also arbitrate occasional labor-management disputes. I hadn't managed to save any money, but I had no debts, my income matched my outgo, and I loved my work.

I was only thirty-six, while in 1968 Columbia was in her 214th year. She had survived the British occupation of New York, two World Wars, the Great Depression, and much else. It never occurred to me to think she might be at risk, but it was a time for good citizens to rally round. And so, shortly before ten, I set out for the meeting called by the Ad Hoc Faculty Group. As it turned out, we did not get started until closer to noon: so many people responded that the meeting room had to be changed. We gathered at last in McMillan Theater, a single-balcony auditorium with a capacity of well over a thousand. It quickly filled.

Alan Westin entered stage left, leading the steering committee in to sustained applause. After a solemn invocation by the university chaplain, we heard from a physician who had treated students and faculty injured during the bust. By this time we had all heard reports of police misconduct as over a thousand officers forced their way into buildings and cleared the campus in predawn darkness, but this fellow professed to have witnessed Götterdammerung. In high rhetorical style he told us he had been on the bridge in Selma, Alabama, when civil rights marchers had been clubbed and gassed. "Never in my life did I think I would live to see such an occurrence in these halls of ivy. Last night I saw the naked face of fascism at Columbia University." It was his moment, and he was making the most of it. In the end he recounted all the cases of "abrasions and contusions" he had treated. I may have broken my mother's heart when I told her I wasn't going to be a doctor, but I still knew that just meant cuts and bruises. This physician may have seen the naked face of fascism, but he hadn't seen any serious injuries.

Westin followed him to the microphone to read a statement the steering committee had prepared that morning. It built to a condemnation of the administration and a call to action:

> A large and representative part of the Columbia University student body has called for a student strike. Normally we would regard the use of a strike by students as academically unwise, and by professors as professionally dubious. In the present situation, however . . . we believe we are fully within our professional responsibilities in urging our colleagues to respect this strike.

Deafening applause welled up.

3

REBUILDING

We learned in 1968 how fragile an enterprise a university is.

The administration had won the buildings, but at an enormous price. Some of the most radical leaders of the uprising had looked forward to this day from the beginning. The radicals' ideology was humbug, but their tactics drew on a brilliant perception: confront authority in such a way as to force it to give in or repress. If it gives in, you've won your substantive demands. If it represses, it alienates—in the jargon of the radicals, it radicalizes—those whose support the radicals seek. It took sensitivity and skills—skills the administration lacked—to duck this dilemma.

But that did not seem to me and some others to be a reason to support a strike. A series of speakers—for and against the Ad Hoc Group's resolution—addressed the audience. I asked to be recognized. The occasion was intimidating: I had no prepared text, and most of a very emotional crowd of over a thousand people favored the position I was about to oppose. The *Columbia Daily Spectator*, the student newspaper, reported my debut in university politics:

Michael Sovern, a young law professor, had played a negligible role during the crisis. Now his words, spoken with ease and self-assurance, had great effect:

"We're here in a mood of outrage this morning because the University administration set in motion forces that led to physical injury to ninety-six of our students. We deplore the effects of the forces they set in motion. I suggest to you that there is a grave risk that we're about to do the same. The Ad Hoc Faculty Group's claim to legitimacy from the beginning has rested on its moral force, its commitment to no coercion, its commitment to reason and avoidance of polarization of this community. We are abandoning those objectives this morning. I do not deny that there has been provocation for that abandonment, but there are hundreds, presumably thousands of our students who will not support the strike, who will want to attend their classes."

"No, No!" several professors shouted from the floor.

"Don't deny the fact, face the fact—you're talking about a strike!" Sovern responded, raising his voice. There was scattered applause. "You know from the noises you hear that many of the faculty will not support a strike." He continued to increasing applause: "Our students are entitled to succumb to the emotions of the moment—we are not. The statement drafted by the committee was necessarily drafted hastily," he went on, his support growing, "under enormous pressure and emotional stress. . . . Let's do this job in an air of reason, peace, and not a divided and potentially violent University campus!" Westin now looked out over the audience and realized that the proposal was running into more opposition than he had expected. Some respected senior members were turning against him, and the points they raised were proving more persuasive than those of the leftists.

The debate was nearly over. After Fritz Stern, a much admired historian, added his voice to those objecting to the Ad Hoc Group's position, Westin had enough. Turning against the still strong strike sentiment, he announced: "I don't think that this faculty should become split just as the radical element of the student body would like to see. I think it would be very wise to have this resolution withdrawn. . . . I think you may have a majority to pass this resolution, but if you do so, I will have nothing to do with it." The audience went wild: faculty seeking the floor tried to out-shout one another; points of order were hurled at the beleaguered chair. Finally, Westin declared: "I am going to walk off this stage, and I call on all the members of the steering committee to do so. We as a steering committee would like to reconsider, at least I would. . . . I am not going to put this to a vote to the group. That is simply my act. I am going to leave." And they did.

Leaving the chaotic scene, my friend and fellow law professor Ken Jones and I went to lunch at the nearby West End Cafe. We had learned that President Kirk had called another meeting of the university's faculties for that afternoon. Musing over our sandwiches, I predicted: "The Ad Hoc Group will steal this meeting from Kirk, too." Jones, who had also been at the administration's previous attempt to win faculty support, agreed.

In what began as purely academic speculation, we asked ourselves what the administration should do. The key elements emerged clearly. First, preempt the strike move by setting aside a day for reflection. Second, since the administration could not possibly repair the damage done to the university on its own, a strong faculty committee enjoying the confidence of both the administration and the faculty had to be created. And, third, fair disciplinary procedures had to be set up to deal with all those accused of violating the university's rules. Having outlined, almost in a spirit of play, the steps the administration should take, Ken and I began to get serious. Neither of us had more than a nodding acquaintance with Kirk and Truman. Though they presumably would recognize our names, we doubted they could associate them with our faces. We decided to see if Bill Warren, the dean of the law school, was available.

We found Bill in his office and read him what we had blocked out. Ken and I had conceived an executive committee of the university's faculties that would be composed of four heavyweight supporters of the administration, four members of the Ad Hoc Faculty Group's steering committee, and our most luminous Columbia colleague—Lionel Trilling. The administration supporters were easy to identify: we simply picked the four titans who had spoken on the administration's behalf at the meeting in the Law School the previous Sunday—Eli Ginzberg,

Polykarp Kusch, William Leuchtenberg, and Ernest Nagel. From the Ad Hoc Group we picked Westin, Daniel Bell, Alexander Dallin, and Walter Metzger. Dallin was a distinguished Sovietologist; Metzger was an American historian whose classes were immensely popular. Bell's stature as a famous sociologist rivaled that of the administration group, though he was perhaps best known for his response to Henry Luce when Luce asked why Bell would leave a great job as a *Fortune* editor for a professorship. Bell replied: "For three reasons—June, July, and August."

Warren's response to the roster startled me: "You should be on that list, Mike. They need someone with real experience." I am not given to false modesty, but I had not thought of myself for the role and had no idea whether I was well suited for it. I kept my reservations to myself and became the tenth name on the list.

While we were talking, the law faculty was gathering, and Ken Jones left to explain the dean's delay in joining them. His place in our conversation was taken by another colleague, Maurice Rosenberg. Warren, Rosenberg, and I agreed on a final draft of a proposed resolution, which I was to sell to the Ad Hoc Faculty Group steering committee and Warren was to urge upon Truman and Kirk. Rosenberg would keep the law faculty fully informed.

Our resolution read as follows:

> In our University's hour of anguish, we members of its faculties must assume responsibility to help return this University to a community of reason. In this spirit we adopt the following resolutions:
> That the University set aside Wednesday for reflection so that without classes, students and faculty may meet and reason together about their University.
> That there be an Executive Committee with power to call the faculty together and to take other needed steps to return the University to its educational task at the earliest possible moment and that the committee be composed of such people as the following: Daniel Bell, Walter Metzger, William Leuchtenberg, Alexander Dallin, Eli Ginzberg,

Polykarp Kusch, Ernest Nagel, Michael Sovern, Lionel Trilling, Alan
Westin.

That the recently appointed tripartite committee of representatives
of the faculty, student body and administration immediately begin
functioning to assure due process and equitable treatment to students
facing charges.

That each member of the Columbia community act in a manner
showing respect for his colleagues and assuring the return to life and
health of this great University.

With text in hand, the three of us set out on our respective errands. I
tracked down a dispirited gathering of most of the Ad Hoc Group's
steering committee. They quickly accepted the proposal. Bill Warren, on
the other hand, ran into a stone wall: Truman would have nothing to do
with our resolution.

We saw nothing more we could do at the moment. Warren, Rosenberg, and I agreed to sit together and adapt as best we could as the
meeting unfolded. Our colleagues on the law faculty would try to sit
nearby and follow our lead. We left the law school for St. Paul's Chapel,
chosen this day not for its spiritual possibilities but for its size. St. Paul's
could accommodate the more than five hundred faculty assembling for
the occasion. But the building was obviously designed for religious ob-
servances, not for faculty meetings. In an unintended irony, an administration charged with insensitivity had chosen to meet in a place where
it could be heard well from the rostrum but faculty speaking from the
floor would be all but inaudible.

As in the law school two days before, the meeting began according
to the administration's plan: Truman reported on the decision to call the
police and the ensuing events; and Professor Richard Hofstadter, a great
and influential historian, offered an administration-approved resolution
that would have no immediate effect on the status quo. And then, once
again, the administration lost its hold.

Professor Morton Fried of the anthropology department offered as
a substitute the strike resolution abandoned by the Ad Hoc Faculty

Group earlier in the day. Under standard parliamentary procedure, the strike resolution became the pending business of the meeting. Since that resolution also condemned the administration and declared "a vote of no confidence from the faculty," Kirk felt that in fairness he should not continue to chair the meeting. Who should? The dean of the law school seemed a natural, and so, at Kirk's behest, Bill Warren left his seat in the front row and took the chairman's place on the podium. He left Rosenberg and me, our minicaucus shrunk by one-third.

This was not an easy meeting to conduct. The largest official faculty meeting in the history of the university, an extraordinarily charged atmosphere, and a hall in which faculty speakers could not hear one another, even when they wanted to, would have challenged the most skillful chairman. Bill Warren had many estimable qualities and abilities; leading meetings wasn't one of them. After several moments of confusion, Warren called me to the podium to help him as parliamentarian. Rosenberg was now a caucus of one.

The debate on the strike resolution proceeded in a relatively orderly manner until, it seemed to me, a vote would kill it. As parliamentarian, I was in no position to call for the vote, so I mouthed the suggestion to Rosenberg in the front row and whispered to Warren to call on Rosenberg. He did, and then Rosenberg startled us both by introducing our resolution. Warren thought I had double-crossed him, but Rosenberg later explained that he had decided to offer the resolution and was about to ask to be recognized when I signaled him.

The parliamentary situation was a mess, with a substitute being offered for a substitute, but we muddled through to a voice vote that overwhelmingly approved our resolution. The meeting adjourned. I was now a member of the Executive Committee of the Faculties. Since I had ready access to the microphone on the podium, I asked the newly elected members of the Executive Committee to gather at the front of the chapel. Almost all of us were soon there. Eli Ginzberg's first words to me were: "You should be chairman." My initial reaction to that idea was mild panic, which was as far as I'd gotten when Walter Metzger arrived and urged that Alan Westin chair the committee. He was quickly echoed by his fellow Ad Hoc members—Dallin and Bell—and Westin was not shy about wanting the job. The administration adherents were, however, firmly opposed to Westin, and I emerged as their candidate. They really didn't have much choice: Ginzberg, Kusch, Leuchtenberg, and Nagel were too wise to want the job for themselves, and Trilling wasn't the executive type. I wasn't particularly keen on the assignment myself, but effectively turning ourselves over to the Ad Hoc Group after their performance was not an acceptable course.

I suggested that Westin and I serve as co-chairmen. Though neither he nor the administration supporters were enthusiastic about the idea, that is what we did. The task our committee faced was formidable. In the words of the resolution that created us, we were to take the necessary steps "to return the University to its educational task at the earliest possible moment." There was no point in seeking agreement that Tuesday evening on what those steps might be. The tension between the two factions was an obvious difficulty, and I did not feel well enough informed to act.

Time would presumably help solve those problems. The situation outside the chapel was far more problematic. The university was scheduled to reopen Thursday morning following the one-day pause for reflection called for by our resolution, but it was not at all clear that it could. Hundreds of radicalized faculty and students were now supporting the original demonstrators in their call for a strike. Police were out in force, patrolling the campus and guarding its entrances. For many, their presence was a provocation. Most importantly, our community's collegiality had been shattered. Students had confronted students, large segments of the faculty had never been so angry at one another, and the administration was the object of rage and derision. I was deeply saddened when I saw David Truman accompanied by a bodyguard.

We decided to begin by inviting students to meet with us: we might learn something, and we would be sending a message of concern. Metzger and Westin led the selection process, and by late Tuesday evening we were joined in a Fayerweather Hall classroom by about twenty student leaders, including editors of the *Spectator*. We sat randomly, straddling desks and chairs. Not all the students were friendly, but then Metzger, in a pedagogical tour de force, went to the blackboard on some pretext or other and everybody reverted to role. The students faced front and listened attentively as their professor held forth. The physical dictated the psychological.

The conversation was mainly about restructuring the university and was not seriously encumbered by discussion of how the university actually works. Nonetheless, we seemed to have accomplished something, for the *Spectator* editors in attendance told their readers: "We now have the opportunity to do something creative and exciting with this University—our University—that we may never have the chance to do again. Appalled at the past, we are confident for the future." It was past midnight when we recessed. We agreed to reconvene the following morning, and I sent word that I would like to meet with Mark Rudd.

He and I met for the first and only time the following day—May Day, as it turned out. It was the press coverage of Rudd that prompted me to think that you can determine a newspaper's attitude toward a public figure by the photographs they choose to use. *Spectator* depicted him in a variety of poses, but the professional press typically showed an open mouth, with lots of teeth and jaw, poised as if to bite.

Later, when angry alumni asked how we could have admitted such a monster, I replied by asking: "Suppose you were an admissions officer and had a choice of two students: one an honor graduate, Eagle scout, son of a retired military officer; the other an indifferent student, expelled from one school, in difficulty at another. Which would you choose?" Though wary, my interlocutor could make only one choice, which enabled me to say: "Congratulations. You just chose Mark Rudd over Harlan Fiske Stone."

My meeting with Rudd was civil enough, though like duelists we were each accompanied by a second. When he presented me with his list of non-negotiable demands, I told him: "Look here, Mr. Rudd, I just got power yesterday. If you think I'm giving any of it to you, you're crazy." We talked for a while longer. I could see that nothing could be accomplished with him, but I did not want to seem to be closing any doors and so agreed to further meetings with other members of the Executive Committee.

I had another fascinating encounter that day. The Executive Committee was meeting virtually nonstop in a cramped room. At one point a note was passed in to me, asking that I step outside to meet with Eric Bentley, a man I knew only by reputation as a great interpreter of Bertolt Brecht and an exciting teacher of drama. I asked Dan Bell, whose judgment I respected, how to respond. He scribbled a "No" across Bentley's note, and I followed his advice. When we took a break some time later, I found Bentley still waiting. Fixing me with a furious glare, he shouted, "Fuck you, Sovern! You're just like Kirk."

The most important meeting for our new committee still lay ahead. Shortly after ten o'clock on the evening of May 6, we joined Columbia's trustees in the Men's Faculty Club (there was still a separate Women's Faculty Club next door) for a mutually respectful but wide-open discussion lasting several hours. The gathering was unprecedented. Except for Eli Ginzberg, who knew several of the trustees, we were strangers. After sounding us out, the trustees seemed relieved to find that we were sensible people and deeply committed to our university. I was greatly heartened when the chairman of the trustees, William Petersen, having told us who would co-chair a committee that would work with us, changed his mind and replaced one of the two co-chairs who had shown himself too inflexible for the assignment. It was a wise and courageous move and, I thought, quite stunning, occurring as it did in full view.

The two co-chairmen—Alan Temple, a banker, and Robert Lilley, the president of AT&T—proved to be excellent choices. And the university was lucky in Petersen's leadership too. Head of the Irving Trust Company, he had succeeded to the chairmanship of Columbia's trustees only a few months before the buildings were taken over. Here was the rare case of a banker who was not thrilled at having gotten a lot more than he bargained for.

Our committee did not believe the university could be put back together with hundreds of students facing prosecution for criminal trespass. One of our first decisions was to recommend that those charges be dropped, leaving the offenders to disciplinary action by the university. The trustees did not much like that idea, but they accepted it nonetheless. The final decision would rest with the district attorney, Frank Hogan, also a Columbia trustee, and the court, but the trustees' recommendation would carry considerable weight. In the end, except for a few students charged with resisting arrest and other offenses more serious than criminal trespass, the charges were dropped.

In the meantime, the university was in chaos. The law and business schools resumed classes on Thursday, following the one-day moratorium, but most of the university's divisions remained closed for the rest of the week. Many students decided to join the radicals in striking; others were enjoying the circus. Virtually licensing the disarray, the College faculty voted to permit any student who didn't wish to be graded in a course to elect a "P" for pass. No further class attendance was required.

Our committee was meeting every day, groping for ways to be useful. In the same spirit that had moved us to urge that the criminal charges be dropped, we decided to appoint a fact-finding commission. The general confusion was being amplified by a welter of charges and countercharges as to who was to blame for bringing the university to this pass. The appointment of a responsible commission would create a forum where those issues could be hashed out while the rest of us tried to get back to work.

The perceived importance of the Columbia events enabled us to recruit an outstanding panel. My friend Archibald Cox, a former solicitor general of the United States and professor of law at Harvard, agreed to serve as chairman. (His Watergate role was still five years away.) He was joined by former federal judge Simon H. Rifkind; Dana L. Farnsworth, the head of Harvard's health services; Professor Hylan G. Lewis, a sociologist from Brooklyn College; and Anthony G. Amsterdam, a professor of law at the University of Pennsylvania. We announced their appointment on May 5. Cox later told me: "You gave me a tiger on my left and a tiger on my right." He was referring to Amsterdam, an academic wunderkind and deeply committed civil rights lawyer, and Rifkind, once a liberal wunderkind himself and now a leader of the legal establishment. As a courtesy, I called Grayson Kirk to let him know that we were going to announce the commission's appointment the following day. "Take your damned witch-hunt and go to hell," he said. In only forty-eight hours, I had brought Eric Bentley and Grayson Kirk to agreement.

The Cox Commission took its assignment very seriously. During the late spring and early summer it held twenty-nine days of hearings, at which seventy-nine witnesses appeared; conducted countless interviews; and produced a 222-page report. Fred Friendly asked his friend Bob Bernstein, the head of Random House, if he could rush the report into print so it could be broadly available before classes resumed. Bob obliged with a paperback entitled *Crisis at Columbia*. Its overall conclusion was sobering. "The fabric of the University's life is now twisted and torn. The violence has now yielded to bitterness and distrust. Only heroically open-minded and patient efforts can repair the injury."

Thorough and thoughtful, the report contained a detailed account of what had happened and an analysis of contributing factors. Though it was appropriately critical of those "consciously seeking to subvert and destroy the University," it also concluded that "the hurricane of social unrest struck Columbia at a time when the University was deficient in the cement that binds an institution into a cohesive unit." It buttressed that conclusion with an unflattering chapter entitled "Conditions Special to Columbia," underscoring, among other factors, the "inferior quality of student life," as exemplified by run-down residence halls and "the total inadequacy" of student counseling; the lack of faculty participation in institutional decisions, leading to a wide gulf between faculty and administration; and Columbia's abysmal relations with its neighboring community. Many Columbia loyalists were not happy, believing that the events of the spring could have happened anywhere. When Harvard erupted two years later, schadenfreude could be detected among Columbia alumni.

While the commission was working, the Executive Committee was concentrating on our most important task. Early on, we recognized that while we could help clean up the mess, there was little prospect that the university would return to anything approximating normal in the few weeks remaining until Commencement. We had to focus on the future and ask what changes in the university's governing arrangements would both enable her to function better and generate confidence in the fairness and wisdom of her decisions.

The Kirk administration had already made an important concession. Bowing to pressure to appoint a committee composed of seven faculty, seven students, and three administrators to recommend disciplinary procedures, the administration effectively acknowledged that the university could no longer discipline students with as much or as little process as it chose. The Columbia tradition was not unusual. Attendance at a college was deemed a privilege, one that could be revoked at will by those who ran the institution. No more.

The Joint Committee on Disciplinary Affairs, as the new body styled itself, and the Executive Committee stayed in close touch. With radicals stirring the pot, we could lose the next academic year if hundreds of students were still facing disciplinary action and the university had not, by some means deemed legitimate, adopted a set of fair rules for adjudicating their cases as well as future breaches of discipline.

And so the Executive Committee was keenly interested in the work of the Disciplinary Committee. Indeed, one meeting between the two in which we went over their work line by line for more than twelve hours was epiphanic for me. Ken Jones was a member of the Joint Committee, and after that seemingly interminable session finally ended, he said: "Mike, wasn't that awful"? "I have a terrible confession to make," I replied. "I enjoyed it." My days as a working scholar were numbered.

Disciplinary arrangements were only a small part of the governance of a university. We resolved to address much of the rest.

Our committee changed itself a bit in the days after our election. To gain the benefit of their perspective and broaden our base of support, we invited two nontenured faculty to join us. Though Alan Westin and I were getting along well, I arrived at a meeting of our committee to find unanimous sentiment for his removal as co-chairman. He had angered the entire group by criticizing David Truman in a *New York Times* interview. I prevailed upon them to leave things as they were—the appearance of stability was important. Alan Westin could step down later, and he did, though he remained a productive member of the committee.

The peculiar circumstances of our election left us vulnerable. Had those who voted for us known what they were doing in that madhouse? We decided to find out by offering ourselves up for a fresh election, albeit a very circumscribed one. We were working well together, and this was no time to reconstitute the group. Faculty could vote our entire roster up or down. More than 70 percent of the faculty voted for us. We would hold an open election later, one in which each school was entitled to choose a representative. We lost several of our original complement but gained, among other luminaries, Richard Hofstadter and Fred Friendly.

The academic year ended with another departure from tradition. Unlike most colleges and universities, Columbia calls upon her president to deliver the principal address at Commencement, a tradition I came to treasure. But everyone agreed there would be no practical way to maintain discipline during a public address by President Kirk. This year the Commencement speaker would be Richard Hofstadter.

As spring turned into summer and as the Cox Commission, the Joint Committee on Disciplinary Affairs, and the Executive Committee earnestly attacked their agendas, Columbia's trustees were not idle. Losing confidence in President Kirk, they arranged for his retirement with as much grace as could be mustered under the circumstances.

Who would serve as acting president during the search for Kirk's successor? Truman wouldn't do for two contradictory reasons: he was still a candidate for the permanent job, and he had been discredited by his involvement in the events of the spring. As we prepared for a meeting with the trustees' leadership, the Executive Committee found itself without a strong choice. We offered Polykarp Kusch, a Nobel laureate and dedicated teacher, but he was also a somewhat quirky colleague whose only administrative experience was as chairman of the physics department.

Over the course of our meeting, Bill Petersen asked for our opinion of a number of people. The trustees seemed particularly interested in Andrew Cordier, dean of the School of International Affairs. Cordier had come to the university six years before after a career at the United Nations that culminated in his service as undersecretary to the legendary Dag Hammarskjold.

All of us on the Executive Committee agreed he wouldn't do. There may have been some among us who were moved by the charge that Cordier had conspired in the assassination of Patrice Lumumba when Cordier headed the United Nations' operations in the Congo, but if so, nobody admitted it. I regarded the charge as farfetched and in any case clearly not proven. The problem with Cordier was that he was not a real academic. He had taught as a young man, but he was recruited to Columbia as a professional administrator, not as a scholar or teacher. At this moment in Columbia's history, she needed a leader who was emphatically one of us.

On August 23, the trustees appointed Andrew Cordier acting president. It was a gutsy move. Had we on the Executive Committee opposed the appointment publicly, Cordier would have had a very difficult time of it. But the trustees gambled on our behaving responsibly, and they won the bet. More importantly, they were right and we were wrong: Cordier indeed was the man for the job. Self-confident, open, flexible, patient, intelligent, experienced, and possessed of enormous stamina and a pleasant avuncular style, he was the perfect healer. (He would overspend the university budget by massive amounts, but that is another part of the story.)

Cordier asked to meet with me almost immediately after Bill Petersen let me know the trustees' choice. Though he was sixty-seven, old enough to be my father, we quickly became Andy and Mike. From then until the Executive Committee declared itself done at the end of the '68–'69 academic year Andy and I talked almost every day. We often met first thing in the morning—first thing for me, that is. Andy took great pride in the fact that he slept only four hours a night. At eight a.m. meetings he would boast of having been up and dictating for hours.

Andy took an immediate interest in the work of both the Executive Committee and the Joint Committee on Disciplinary Affairs. In fact, he attended the entire marathon session that produced my epiphany. He didn't say much, and I began to suspect that he could get by with only four hours' sleep at night because he had mastered the art of sleeping with his eyes open during committee meetings.

But he obviously had paid enough attention. The Disciplinary Committee's rules of conduct were not as tough as he or the Executive Committee would have liked, and their enforcement procedures left something to be desired, but they accepted some of our suggestions for improvement, and we went along with the rest. The resulting draft was surely better than nothing, and we had pushed the Disciplinary Committee as far as it would go.

To make the rules work, though, we needed wider assent. We agreed that the Executive Committee would convene a meeting of the entire tenured faculty on September 12, 1968, to debate and, we hoped, adopt the rules. There had never been a meeting like this at Columbia or perhaps anywhere. Eight hundred professors of every conceivable political hue were to consider a detailed code of conduct, debate particular provisions, and offer amendments as they wished, and, if all went reasonably well, adopt what would be a coherent body of law.

Calling the meeting to order, I asked President Cordier to address us. After reviewing the parlous condition of the university, Andy expressed his confidence, saying, "I have been in tougher spots." Following him to the lectern, I confessed that, unlike our president, I had never been in a tougher spot. The debate began. I insisted that amendments be offered in writing. They were then immediately duplicated, distributed to everyone in the auditorium and, in due course, voted upon.

At one point, while an amendment that would have eased the rules was under discussion, we heard a pounding on the auditorium doors. A security officer whispered to me that SDS was using a battering ram to try to get into the auditorium. I so advised the assembly. Professor Penn Kimball leapt to his feet, shouting: "That is a McCarthyist charge. How do you know SDS is trying any such thing"? "Well," I replied, "SDS distributed leaflets before this meeting saying that they would try to break in, I hear pounding on the doors, I have just been informed that SDS is trying to break in, and so I jumped to the conclusion that they are trying to break in." (Charles Frankel reproduces this exchange in his novel *A Stubborn Case*.) Kimball wasn't altogether wrong. The thought had occurred to me that mentioning the SDS assault at that point might affect the vote on the softening amendment. In any case, it was defeated.

After about four hours, we had a code, duly adopted. SDS would challenge it on the ground that students hadn't participated, but they didn't have much success. The rules we adopted that day would be amended many times over the years, sometimes quite substantially, but they were good enough for our purpose—a successful reopening of the university. We had yet to resolve the critical question of how the university might improve its governance.

For almost all of the nineteenth century, the trustees and president of an American college or university were its actual governors. Professors were employees. Over the ensuing decades, authority devolved upon faculties over such key matters as curriculum, faculty hiring, and requirements for graduation. Although trustees typically retained final authority in all of these areas, in fact they had little or nothing to say about them. By 1968, the president of a respected university would not dream of firing a full professor, as Columbia's Nicholas Murray Butler had done during the First World War.

This transformation received legal recognition in the case of *National Labor Relations Board v. Yeshiva University*.[1] The National Labor Relations Act requires employers to bargain with unions representing a majority of their employees, subject to certain exceptions. One of those exceptions exempts managers from the right to be represented by unions. The *Yeshiva* case held that the university did not have to bargain with a union of its professors: faculty had so much authority over the affairs of the institution that they were in fact managers.

But a number of important matters remained beyond faculty reach. At Columbia, for example, faculty had no authority over budgets. The president and his colleagues in the central administration decided how much should be allocated to each school, and the respective deans carved it up from there. (There were variations on this theme, but that's the basic idea.) Similarly, decisions to build new buildings or renovate old ones were centrally made at Columbia, with the trustees tending to take an active role—in no small part because large expenditures were usually involved.

The filling of vacant deanships was also a presidential prerogative, in the exercise of which faculty might or might not be consulted. Justice William O. Douglas told me that, as a young member of the Columbia faculty, he resigned in protest against President Butler's failure to consult the faculty before appointing a new dean of the law school.

What might be called issues of public policy also fell outside the ambit of faculty authority. Not long before the troubled spring of '68, Columbia was embarrassed by the decision of her president and trustees to endorse the Strickman cigarette filter. This foray into the commercial world proved doubly embarrassing: not only did we have no business in the tobacco industry, even if the filter was supposed to cut carcinogens, but the thing didn't work—no one could comfortably pull any smoke through it.

Faculty played no part in that debacle, nor were they involved in Columbia's decision to build a gym in Morningside Park, a decision that contributed to Columbia's trouble in 1968. Similarly, the president and the trustees were responsible for Columbia's decision to undertake classified research for the government—a decision in tension with a university's role as open disseminator of knowledge. Indeed, the theme of Columbia's bicentennial celebration in 1954 had been "Man's Right to Knowledge and the Free Use Thereof."

These were matters that went to the heart of the university's reputation. For those who believed as I did that universities should stand as moral exemplars, the process by which these decisions were reached seemed too closely held, too likely to overlook important values. Opening up the process might well lead to wiser decisions. It would surely increase the chances that all relevant considerations would be aired. And it could enhance spirit and commitment by assuring faculty and others in the community that, whatever an issue's outcome, their views were heard and considered. How to achieve this without politicization or even possible paralysis was the challenge. Columbia had a University Council, a body that included all the deans of the university plus elected representatives from each faculty. Over the years, however, the only matter it seemed to act on was the university calendar. It was not the answer.

When I became dean of the law school, student-power advocates made much of my statement that "A law school is not a democracy." Nor is a university. But we were, quite pragmatically, trying to find a level of participation that would help the institution function better. Being scholars, we launched a substantial research project. My colleague on the law faculty, Frank Grad, agreed to lead the effort. A wise and experienced man, he had overseen the drafting of statutes at every level of government. He mobilized a task force of faculty and students and proceeded to learn how decisions were actually made at Columbia, how those processes were perceived by Columbians, how other universities dealt with questions like ours, what options the Executive Committee might consider, and so on.

Frank reported to the Executive Committee on a regular basis, and he and I spoke almost daily. Over the summer and much of the ensuing academic year, Frank and his group would reflect, consult broadly, and ask new questions. By late winter, we were ready to recommend the addition of a new instrumentality to Columbia's government—a University Senate.

In 1968, many universities had faculty senates, though they often functioned like Columbia's University Council. The Senate we proposed was quite different, to the best of our knowledge unique. It would include not just faculty and administration but representatives of Columbia's other constituent elements as well—students, alumni, and staff. To be sure, faculty would dominate, and some representation could fairly be called token. Columbia's more than one hundred thousand alumni, for example, received two seats in our proposed body of one hundred.

Our policy of inclusiveness was carefully worked out. We did not want a separate student government. Though such bodies could play a useful role in particular schools, Columbia's experience with a University

Student Council was unhappy: remote from most students' interests, it could easily fall under the control of unrepresentative and potentially troublesome groups. We believed that student representation in a faculty-dominated body was good educational policy. As we put it in our supporting statement, "It forces them to make difficult choices instead of simply criticizing the hard choices made by others. Such participation also offers especially fruitful contact with their elders."[2]

By the time we made our recommendations, most of the schools of the university had already added students to their principal committees, and the innovation seemed to be working well. As for staff representation, we said: "A University . . . depends to a very considerable degree on the contributions made by professional library, research, and administrative staff. The research and library groups, especially, include many persons of . . . an eminence comparable to that of numbers of the tenured faculty." All three groups could bring useful insights to the Senate's deliberations.

We thought a Senate of one hundred was small enough to be able to function and large enough to accommodate at least some representation from each of the university's constituent groups. The faculty and student delegations had to be large enough so that each of Columbia's sixteen schools had at least one of each. We recommended the following apportionment: Faculty—59; Students—20; Administration—7; Affiliated Institutions (Barnard, Teachers College, School of Pharmacy, Union Theological Seminary)—6; Librarians—2; Research staff—2; Administrative staff—2; Alumni—2. Actually, the affiliated institutions would not have made it into our big tent (they had their own governance arrangements), but the university's agreements with them were construed by counsel to require their inclusion, so we complied.

The alumni association wanted more seats, but we pointed out that no university had ever given alumni any. Some students thought we should have offered one-person-one-vote, but we pointed out that the alumni would swamp them. By holding rigidly to our cap of one hundred, we forced any group seeking more seats to tell us from whom we should take them.

The other big question was: What powers should the Senate have? We were not writing on a blank slate: whatever role the Senate was to play had to fit with those of the trustees and central administration and the existing powers of schools and faculties in Columbia's federal system.

In form, the Senate had to be subordinate to the trustees, as were all parts of the university. But just as the trustees' ultimate authority over faculty appointments did not keep the faculty from exercising actual authority in that sphere, so the Senate's de jure subordination to the trustees need not deny it real power.

In general, the Senate was to "be a policy-making body which may consider all matters of University-wide concern and all matters affecting more than one faculty or school." In particular, it could take up such matters as the ownership of patent rights on inventions developed with university resources, the university's relations with outside agencies like those funding research, amendments to the rules of conduct, and changes in the tenure code. For some matters trustee concurrence would be required—the president and trustees would decide which those were—but even in those instances the trustees could be expected to give great weight to Senate action.

The trustee selection process itself would be opened to Senate participation: six of Columbia's twenty-four trustees would have to "be mutually acceptable to the Nominating Committee of the Board of Trustees and to the Executive Committee of the Senate."

Even where the Senate's role would be solely advisory, we broke new ground. Before a future president or provost of the university could be chosen, the Executive Committee of the Senate had to be consulted. And the Senate's Budget Review Committee was to "review the annual budget of the University after its adoption to assure its general conformity with short-range and long-range priorities of the University and expressions of policy by the Senate." The limitation on this grant of authority—the budget was to be reviewed *after* its adoption—was as important as the grant of authority. We believed in broad participation in the university's affairs, but we weren't zealots. To have allowed

University Senate participation in the actual making of a budget would have produced results as unedifying as those of the U.S. Congress.

The trustees were not in full accord with all of our ideas. They would have preferred, for example, to have all sixteen deans as members of the Senate, but we believed this would bear too close a resemblance to the discredited University Council. They did persuade us to make the president of the university the presiding officer of the Senate, a bit of leverage I would come to value.

After innumerable drafts and countless meetings and hearings, we submitted our proposal to separate referenda of faculty and students in March 1969. It was endorsed by affirmative votes of more than 80 percent.

The trustees were not pleased that we had gone to a vote before working out all the details of the proposed Senate with them. But we had stayed in close touch all through the year, and not that much remained to be agreed upon. Charles Luce, an extraordinarily able lawyer and executive who had been brought to New York to straighten out Consolidated Edison, directed the end game for the trustees. In June, while I was attending an international conference in Mexico on student unrest around the world, I received a telegram informing me that the trustees had approved our proposal with minor modifications. As we observed at the time: "The preparation of these recommendations has in our view contributed to an atmosphere of reflection conducive to a peaceful campus; adoption of a new system of University government would be a further contribution to that environment."

And so it proved to be. We learned in 1968 how fragile an enterprise a university is. A small group of the disaffected could bring a great institution to its knees if they could persuade others that it was behaving arbitrarily. In the years to follow, with rare exceptions, that case could no longer be made at Columbia. The university offered a representative forum where all issues could be fairly heard. There was no tinder waiting to be ignited, no disgruntled legions ready to march, just a somewhat boring deliberative body effectively defusing potential explosions and generally making wise policy.

4

AFTERMATH

Bill McGill became president of Columbia and joked about
how the university's treasurer had turned him down for a
mortgage when he was a young faculty member. I told him
that the treasurer was probably right about his lack of financial
responsibility. After all, he had now accepted a job that began
with a $16 million deficit on a budget of $130 million.

The year 1968 was wonderfully satisfying for me. I had helped accomplish something important, and I didn't mind that my contribution was appreciated by my fellow Columbians. I had learned a great deal—about the university, to be sure, but also about myself. I discovered skills in dealing with people that I didn't know I had. I remember with pleasure the Executive Committee meeting at which Bill Leuchtenburg, agreeing with an argument I had made, said that I was the most persuasive person he had ever met. And, of course, I discovered my taste for administration.

The year also left me with enduring friendships—most notably, Eli Ginzberg, unquestionably the most important member of the Executive Committee for his wisdom and relationships with Columbia trustees; Fred Friendly, who before joining the journalism faculty had been Edward R. Murrow's producer and then president of CBS News; and Andy Cordier, whose openness and willingness to listen were just what Columbia needed.

Andy and I came to respect and trust each other to an extraordinary degree. The best example of that occurred one evening when Andy was hosting a dinner at the president's house. A group of employees led by Sidney von Luther, a labor organizer for Local 1199 of the Hospital Workers Union, had attempted to enter Low Library. The only entrance open at that time took them to an area that served as a center for Columbia's security forces, who quickly barred the employees from going any further. A group of SDS adherents, seeing an opportunity for worker-student solidarity, soon joined them.

A security supervisor, thinking that I might be helpful, asked me to come over. I found a potentially dangerous mess: several security officers blocking a chained door giving access to the rest of Low. They were facing about forty people jammed into a confined space, and interested spectators were beginning to gather outside the building. The union was protesting the university's refusal to recognize it as the representative of a subset of employees, and I inferred that Sidney von Luther saw the possibility of occupying Low as a wonderfully dramatic way to make his point.

The group was in high spirits, not yet made testy by their confinement. I asked von Luther for a private chat but was shouted down by the mini-mob. I soon found an opportunity. One of von Luther's group had been injured by a security guard during a brief scuffle, and von Luther was allowed entry to check on him as he rested on a couch in the ladies' room. I followed.

"Sidney, how are you going to get us out of this?" I asked. I didn't have to spell out for him that he was effectively stalemated and that the situation could get very ugly. His solution: let the mini-mob in, and he would tell the SDS contingent that this was the employees' struggle and that SDS must leave; he would then explain to his troops that they had accomplished what they had set out to do, namely focus attention on their cause, and march them out.

The offer would have been tempting if von Luther didn't have a reputation for untrustworthiness. And, of course, if he double-crossed me, I would have been responsible for letting SDS take over Low again. It was time to talk to Andy. I called and interrupted his dinner party. After briefing him and emphasizing the risk of accepting von Luther's proposal, I told him I was inclined to trust von Luther on this one. Andy authorized it, the doors to Low opened, and the group marched in. About twenty minutes later, the SDS contingent marched out with fists in the air, and, about half an hour after that, Sydney and his union group emerged, managing to look triumphant. Just another day at the university.

Andy had been appointed acting president in the summer of '68 in the expectation that we would find a new president during the '68–'69 academic year. The search process was complicated by the existence of three search committees, one consisting of trustees; another, a faculty group, to which I was appointed by the Executive Committee; and a third made up of students. But the trustees handled this masterfully, avoiding conflict by sharing the process with the other two committees. In fact, by the time the search was over, the three committees were meeting as one and concurring unanimously in the final choice.

The Columbia presidency was no longer a much desired post. Faculty members were still feuding, with some leaving; student applicants were frightened off by the stories of disrupted educations; finances were in disarray; and many alumni were disaffected.

The first candidate we all agreed on—Chancellor Alexander Heard of Vanderbilt University—turned us down. It became clear that we would need Andy for more than one year. He agreed to continue but asked the trustees to drop "Acting" from his title and, though his tenure was still temporary, he became simply president of Columbia.

He and my law school colleagues were surprised when I chose not to run for one of the school's University Senate seats, but I wanted to make it clear that I had served as I thought a good citizen of the university should and not out of a wish for power or administrative advancement. I was genuinely content to let others serve now and to resume a full schedule of teaching, which I had had to truncate during my Executive Committee year.

But then Bill Warren announced that he would step down as dean at the end of the 1969–1970 academic year. One evening as I was dining with my friend and colleague Curt Berger, our conversation turned to the impending vacancy in the deanship. He observed that a majority of the faculty would almost certainly make me their choice if I wanted the job.

Columbia had no tradition of allowing faculties to choose their own deans. Far from it: some members would be consulted, but the choice was the president's. At a law faculty meeting over which Andy Cordier was presiding, he asked that the faculty submit several names to him for consideration. Ken Jones asked what would happen if we submitted only one. Andy replied that it would depend on who the one was.

In a very civilized manner, without any overt campaigning, we polled ourselves, and I emerged as the winner. To no one's surprise, Andy was happy to accept me, and on July 1, 1970, I became the law school's seventh dean.

In the meantime, the presidential search process had yielded a very attractive prospect—William J. McGill, chancellor of the University of California–San Diego and a former chairman of the Columbia psychology department. Although Bill McGill was presiding over a well-funded, rising branch of the University of California system, Governor Reagan was making it difficult for the university's administrators, and McGill was willing to leave for Columbia. His credentials were imposing, and he charmed us all. He became president of Columbia on September 1, 1970. Like Andy Cordier before him, he thought it best to dispense with the sort of impressive inaugural that usually attended the beginning of a new presidency.

McGill joked about how the university's treasurer had turned him down for a mortgage when he was a young faculty member. I told him that the treasurer was probably right about his lack of financial responsibility. After all, he had now accepted a job that began with a $16 million deficit on a budget of $130 million with two months of the fiscal year already elapsed. Andy Cordier had been a healer, not a manager. He had also been a spender, and the trustees, perceiving the university as a perilously fragile place, had not been disposed to add to its stress by trying to rein him in.

5

CONDOMS AND
WRINKLE CREAM

Every time a couple made love using one of our condoms,
I would earn two-fifths of a cent. Visions of sugarplums
danced in my head.

S hortly before assuming my decanal responsibilities, I flew to Japan for the first of what would prove to be many visits. I accompanied my friend Al Rubin, the head of Rogosin Laboratory at the
Cornell Medical School and a distinguished clinician and researcher. Al
and I had become friends at *Time*: he as medical advisor and I as legal
advisor would usually come in late on Thursday afternoon to review
what had been written in our respective fields. We would often dine
together, along with Dick Seamon, one of *Time*'s top editors.

Al's interest in kidney transplants had led him to study solubilized
collagen, which he hoped could diminish the risk of organ rejection. He
also suspected that the collagen, which was made from animal hides but
closely resembled human skin, might have a number of other uses. The
possibilities included burn treatment, contact lenses, and condoms. Al
was collaborating with the Japan Leather Company, which produced
the collagen for him and was dissatisfied with an expiring contract it
had with the pharmaceutical giant Johnson and Johnson.

If collagen worked as a burn treatment, Al was committed to making
it available to all comers without royalty payments, but he saw no reason

to be similarly humanitarian with the profit potential in condoms. He invited me to be his partner in a new company formed to market collagen products; we were to go to Tokyo to negotiate a contract between our company and Japan Leather.

Collagen was already being used in Japan as a sausage casing; it might not take much to convert a casing into a condom. And if a collagen condom could be made, it would sweep the market. The competition consisted of basically two kinds: a latex condom and a more sensitive condom made from the lining of a lamb's appendix. A collagen condom would be more sensitive than the first and cheaper and easier to produce in standardized quantity than the second.

An all-expenses-paid trip to Japan would have been enticing enough, but Al was delightful company—and the prospect of earning a profit every time a couple made love was irresistible.

Somewhere between Honolulu and Tokyo, thousands of miles from land, a flight attendant came to our seats and said: "Please, Dr. Rubin, we have a passenger who needs your help." (Like so many physicians, Al treated "Dr." as virtually a part of his name, and thus the flight crew knew from the manifest that he was a doctor.) Al attended to the afflicted woman and soon reported back that she was simply hyperventilating, but the flight crew's gratitude was boundless: they couldn't give us enough to eat and drink. I felt as though I was traveling with a god.

The negotiations with Japan Leather were fascinating. We spent endless hours together—most of each day from a Monday through Friday—drinking green tea and talking. The Japanese thought it important to get to know us, and, of course, everything had to be said twice, once in English and once in Japanese. Al and I spoke no Japanese, and, though I suspected our new friends understood some English, everything we said was translated for them.

Each evening I would try to reduce to writing what we had agreed upon so far. The Japan Leather people were unhappy with the length and legalistic style of their Johnson and Johnson agreement, which ran to more than forty pages. Al urged me to try to sum it all up in two, which I managed. They signed the agreement without change and without an attorney ever having appeared during our five days together. The final clause, at their request, did provide that the agreement was subject to review by their attorneys, but they never asked for any changes. And so we all lived happily ever after with my two-pager.

As I reflected on this experience it occurred to me that every culture must have its own way of dealing with the anxiety that attends a business transaction. The American way is to rely heavily on lawyers, not just for legal advice, but sometimes for business advice and often just for psychological support. The Japanese way, I learned, was gallons of green tea to be consumed as the parties get to know one another.

Al and I didn't have much time to tour. On one evening we were taken to an old-style geisha house, a charming experience that I repeated at a similar establishment years later. On both occasions attractive young women served us excellent dinners, never leaving our sake cups empty, and sought to amuse us. For example, on my later visit, the geishas dressed a friend's wife in their traditional costume and taught her a few moves. On both occasions we were treated to a samisen performance and a whole lot of girlish giggling. (None of the geishas seemed to speak more than a few words of English, and they usually found our attempts at Japanese hilarious.)

We walked the crowded streets of Tokyo, where Al, who was a little over six feet, and I, a bit under, could see over the heads of the Japanese around us. (The Japanese have grown a great deal since.) I bought my first two woodblock prints by Hiroshige for a hundred dollars each. They are on the wall of my study, joined by several others I subsequently acquired. Though we never left Tokyo and didn't see much of it, I saw enough to know that I wanted to return to Japan.

Not long after our return to New York, Kenzo Tatsuno, our Japanese partner, arrived with huge sample condoms, proudly announcing, "They are Melican size." We negotiated a deal with the Schmid Rubber Company, a major condom manufacturer. They would pay us $100,000 for the right to test our condom for possible development, and if they proceeded, a royalty of two cents for every condom sold.

I could now quantify my prospective wealth. We had become five partners, so every time a couple made love with one of our condoms, I would earn two-fifths of a cent. And there was every reason to expect that Schmid would be able to sell tens of millions of our condoms. Visions of sugarplums danced in my head.

The shelf life of the collagen condom shattered my dreams. It would decay before it was sold. But we still had the $100,000. We were paid another $100,000 when Charles Revson, the head of Revlon, decided to try our collagen in his antiwrinkle cream. Unlike our condoms, we didn't really expect this to work, and we were right: Revlon soon dropped our product. Collagen also flunked as a disposable contact lens. It would shape very nicely, but it couldn't hold the prescription. My days as a putative billionaire were over.

Al did have some success with the burn treatment, but since no royalty was to be charged, he handled that without the participation of our little company.

6

BECOMING A DEAN

*One of my favorite innovations as dean was to take half of the
enormous men's room on the first floor and convert it into a
women's room. When asked what to do with the urinals,
I suggested we put flowers in them.*

I accepted the deanship knowing full well that I could not expect financial help from the university, but I also knew that the law school was in reasonably good shape. Bill Warren had succeeded in raising the funds for the new building we had moved into ten years before. We had a great library, though its budget was under stress, and, while the faculty salary and student financial aid budgets could also stand improvement, they were nearly adequate. Bill had also strengthened the alumni organization and built a development capacity that had never existed before. When I saw that the Annual Fund had raised almost $400,000 in Bill's last year, I wondered what would happen if I failed to raise as much.

We faced a more serious threat in the impending retirements of some of our giants, including Walter Gellhorn, Herbert Wechsler, and Telford Taylor. Law faculties are small—we were fewer than fifty at this time—and it was vital that we recruit worthy replacements for them.

I had two main goals. First, to ensure that we provided a superb education. As each class arrived, three hundred extraordinarily gifted people entrusted us with three years of their lives. Our premier mission was to be worthy of that trust. Second, by virtue of temperament and talent, the Columbia Law School faculty has the capacity to make large contributions to the understanding and development of the law. The second goal was to maintain an environment that maximized those contributions.

Though she was not yet a giant, we were confident that our first faculty recruit would become one, and Ruth Bader Ginsburg did. It is hard to believe that until Ruth joined us, the Columbia Law School faculty had always been all male. I had already promoted two administrative assistants to the rank of assistant dean, giving us our first female deans. We also broke the color barrier, recruiting Kellis Parker, our first African American. Sadly, Kellis died prematurely, never realizing his full potential.

Legal education was still a heavy dose of the Socratic method in large classes, with too little in the way of writing experience and not much in the way of seminar and small-group work. I believed it was professionally important and educationally useful for every first-year student to have at least one member of the faculty know him or her as an individual rather than as part of a large mass. Fortunately I was able to find the resources to make it possible for every beginning student to take a section with no more than thirty students.

New York City is extraordinarily deep in lawyers and judges with a didactic bent. I set about recruiting some of the best to enrich our curriculum with specialized upper-class seminars. We were already doing some of this, but expanding this aspect of our program was virtually cost free. Typically, I offered a nominal thousand-dollar honorarium on the theory that even the most responsible feel more responsible when they are being paid for their effort. I didn't suggest it, but I had no principled objection to any member of our adjunct faculty donating his or her honorarium back to the school.

We also established new clinical programs—offerings that gave our students the chance to confront tough intellectual questions in a practical context and begin to acquire some of the counseling, negotiating, and litigating skills that their predecessors had to pick up after graduation. The students worked in a wide variety of lawyering operations on and off campus, suing employers that discriminated, defending clients accused of misdemeanors, and serving as aides to New York City's counsel.

The one invariable aspect of all our clinical work, which distinguished our clinical commitment from many others, was the assignment to each clinic of faculty whose teaching load consisted mainly of supervising the student work in the clinical seminar. These programs were invaluable in making issues of professional responsibility real to our students. It is one thing to be high-minded in the classroom and quite another to behave ethically when it hurts a client or a cause to which student counsel is committed.

We pursued the holy grail of university administrators—interdisciplinary research and teaching that crossed boundaries to bring fresh insights from one field to another. We expanded the curriculum with offerings from a philosopher, historians, and a journalist. Cyril Harris, the professor of engineering and architecture who had overseen the acoustics at the Kennedy Center, shared a seminar in noise pollution. We added a Center for Law and Economic Studies and new joint degree programs with the journalism school and the Graduate School of Arts and Sciences to our programs with business, international affairs, and architecture. We reached out to Princeton's Woodrow Wilson School so that students could take a master's in public affairs alongside their law degree. That move persuaded Columbia to offer its own master's in public affairs, and our School of International Affairs soon became the School of International and Public Affairs.

We sought to enrich our students' experience with a host of visiting lecturers and judges who would preside over moot court arguments. Attorney General Edward Levi's visit coincided with serious threats against his life. As he and I were riding down in the elevator with his two bodyguards, the elevator made an unexpected stop and the back door opened: a startled assistant librarian was met with two drawn guns.

When Justice William Rehnquist—he was not yet Chief Justice—came to the law school, he and I took a walk to see the sculpture that adorned the school's plaza. In addition to Jacques Lipchitz's *Bellerophon*

Taming Pegasus, we are the proud owner of Henry Moore's *Three Piece No. 1: Points*, a large bronze mounted in such a way that it can be rotated on its base. I was much younger then, and Bill and I decided to have a go at it. To the best of my knowledge, that was the last time the Moore was rotated.

My accession to the deanship coincided with a trend toward ever-growing numbers of applicants to law schools. When I joined the faculty in 1957, we had about eight hundred applicants for three hundred places. Roughly half of those we accepted chose to go elsewhere or to forget about law school altogether; we were accepting six hundred to fill the entering class. In other words, it was easy to get into law school in those days, an assertion my students today find incredible: they were forced to compete in a pool of roughly seven thousand for four hundred places.

The law school's journey from that day to this was marked by a fairly consistent trend line beginning in the 1960s and lasting well into the first decade of the twenty-first century. Prompted originally by a military draft that awarded exemptions to those who stayed in school, fueled by youthful idealism coupled to a sense that lawyers could do good—and, on the other hand, by sharply rising salaries—and, not least, by roman-ticizing television programs with attorneys as their heroes, young people flocked to law school. Most importantly, the applicant pool nearly doubled as the profession became more welcoming to women. (One of my favorite innovations as dean was taking half of the enormous men's room on the first floor and converting it into a women's room. When asked what to do with the urinals, I suggested we put flowers in them.)

Talking to students, I discovered that a number of them would have preferred to take a break between college and law school but feared, correctly, that it would be even harder to get in the following year. That led me to institute a policy that granted admitted students the right to defer arrival for a year or two. They could alleviate their anxiety by find-ing out whether we would take them but defer the beginning of their legal education until they were ready.

We were also giving special weight in our admissions process to appli-cants who had done something else with their lives before coming to law school. The result was a significant number of students who were somewhat older and more experienced than the traditional student. Some of their experiences were particularly interesting. My favorite was a police captain nearing retirement who could attend class because he worked a night shift. He would enrich discussions in classes on criminal law and evidence; I spent a fascinating night accompanying him on his rounds.

Not long into my deanship I met Jerome Greene, a graduate of the College and law school who felt that the legal education he had received at Columbia had made possible his professional and financial success. In addition to being a named partner at a major law firm, Jerry was a very successful real-estate investor. Among the jewels he and his partners owned was the Carlyle Hotel. Jerry and I became close friends, and he would become one of the most generous donors to the law school, the College, and the university in Columbia's history.

Our first adventure together began with my belief that Columbia could not continue to have separate faculty clubs for men and women. Since the Men's Faculty Club was the larger and better equipped, I was pretty sure that it would be the integrated survivor and that the Women's Club would close. That club happened to be located immediately adjacent to the law school, so I wrote to Bill McGill to ask that when it closed, the law school be allowed to take it over as an annex.

When we got it, Jerry gave me $400,000 to renovate it for our use. On the recommendation of Jim Polshek, the dean of our school of architecture, I hired a promising young architect named Robert A. M. Stern, who did a beautiful job, giving us a student lounge, new placement facilities, and student offices. His ensuing phenomenal success came as no surprise. In later years, Jerry and I would reminisce about marching up and down Madison Avenue, shopping at art galleries for the prints with which we decorated our new annex.

I was still in my first year as dean when Ruth Traynor, our placement director, told me we faced a serious problem. The high student demand for interviews with visiting law firms and the school's limited space for interviews meant that she could allow each student only five interviews, a step guaranteed to make our students miserable. I asked whether it would be feasible to advance the fall hiring season to the week before regular classes started and devote virtually the whole building to job interviews. Ruth thought it would be worth a try, but we agreed that it would be prudent to limit the first year of the experiment to New York law firms. I didn't want partners from California flying across the country only to find a handful of students waiting.

What we came to call the Placement Fair was a huge success. Law firms from around the country complained that they were not included, but, of course, they have been ever since. By the time I left the deanship, we were holding eighteen thousand job interviews a year at the school. An unintended consequence of this orgy of interviews was that because law firms saw our students before those of any other school and because our students were very attractive, the firms decided to snap them up before waiting to see the others. We regularly placed more than 95 percent of the class before Commencement.

Another of the dean's responsibilities is to welcome a dozen or so alumni reunions each year. (Most classes return every five years.) I usually enjoyed these. People who attend reunions are, for the most part, people who feel good about themselves and about their school. And that obviously makes for an upbeat occasion.

These events yielded their share of laughs and surprises. When the Class of 1912 gathered for its sixtieth reunion, eighty-six-year-old Arthur Watkins, the courageous senator who had presided over the proceedings that censured Joe McCarthy, proudly announced that he had just married. Judge Harold Medina whispered to me very loudly: "He'll be dead within a year." And he was.

One law school reunion produced a family reunion. After I had exchanged greetings with an alum who, I knew, headed the CIA's covert operations division, he told me, "I'd like you to know that your cousin Mo is one of our best men." I assumed he was referring to my cousin Maurice Sovern, the son of my father's brother, Mac. Over the years following my father's death our families had drifted apart, and the last I had heard of Mo until that moment was his departure to attend Purdue

University. I did nothing with this fresh information until Mo's name came up again. I was visiting the CIA to look at portraits of James Schlesinger and William Colby to see whether I wanted the artist who had painted them to paint my obligatory decanal portrait. The functionary who greeted me said, "I bring you regards from your cousin Mo."

That did it. When I got home, I wrote to Maurice Sovern, c/o CIA, Langley, Virginia:

Dear Mo,

It seems to me that first cousins should get together at least once every 30 years. Please call.

When he did, he agreed to come to dinner and we have stayed in close touch ever since. He doesn't say much about what he did for the CIA, but my guess is that he was a spymaster in Berlin.

Shortly before leaving office, I addressed a longstanding irritant. The school's library was nearly unique among the great law libraries of the country in being managed not by the law school but by the central library administration. With characteristic humility, we thought we could do it better, and the university agreed to let us try. The new arrangement preserved full access to all university libraries for every member of the Columbia community while allowing the law school the autonomy it felt it needed to support the instructional and research requirements of its faculty, students, and alumni. The arrangement has stood the test of time.

As I left the deanship I couldn't help remembering my initial fears about fundraising. Aided by the creation of the Harlan Fiske Stone Fellowship, a donors' society named in honor of the great chief justice and beloved dean of the law school in the early twentieth century, we tripled annual giving and raised enough endowment funds to double our scholarship program and treble the number of endowed professorships.

Summarizing my eight-and-a-half-year experience as dean, I learned more than I hoped, laughed more than I expected, and probably contributed less than I think. Walter Gellhorn offered his own appraisal:

"Mike has a great ability to grasp the other fellow's point of view without losing his grip on his own." I hope he was right.

During my term as dean, I met and married my third wife, Joan Wit, a gifted sculptor, with whom I spent twenty happy years until she succumbed to cancer in 1993. (We traveled to Japan on our honeymoon, a fact that always delighted our Japanese friends.) I engaged in other extracurricular activities, but none as important as marrying Joan.

I worked on the second edition of a casebook on law and poverty that several of us had originally produced in 1969. For a time I continued to teach a portion of the law and poverty course as well, but eventually I gave up teaching. I could find the time to hold classes, but I couldn't keep up with my old fields of interest, and I didn't want to go in ill prepared.

I arbitrated a dispute between the Rolling Stones and their former manager, Allen B. Klein. I was not impressed with Klein, but he must have had something: he had managed to persuade both the Stones and the Beatles to let him manage their affairs for a time. Mick Jagger was on the witness stand for most of a week, and I let my daughter Beth, then fifteen, take a morning off from school to shake his hand. Her right hand remained unwashed for a long time thereafter.

The case was heard by a tripartite panel with each side appointing one member and agreeing upon me as the neutral, third member. The Stones' appointee was Lloyd Cutler, a very wise, engaging attorney from the prominent Washington law firm Wilmer, Cutler, and Pickering. He would later loom large in my life.

The parties disagreed about who had the rights to certain songs the Stones had written. Though neither party struck me as altogether credible, I was persuaded that the Stones had the better of the argument and so held.

I had another exposure to the world of celebrities when my friend and fellow Columbia alum Ira Millstein asked me to testify before the Senate Judiciary Committee on behalf of the National Basketball Association's players union. Ira's law firm, Weil Gotshal and Manges, represented the union, which was fighting an attempt by the NBA to persuade Congress to grant them an exemption from the antitrust laws. Under those laws team owners could not agree on such things as a player draft or a salary cap unless they did it via collective bargaining. It was obviously vital to the players and the union to preserve that protection.

I began my assignment with a conference at Ira's home with him; Larry Fleisher, the union's general counsel; and Bill Bradley, not yet Senator Bradley but then one of the stars of the New York Knicks' championship team. Since we were meeting on a weekend, I took along my teenage son Doug, who was thrilled when Bill offered to shoot hoops with him.

I had testified before a Senate committee before and understood that members of the committee would usually wander in and out of a hearing, with relatively few in attendance at any moment. Not this time. The union's members were out in force, with one star from each team and all of the Knicks' championship five in attendance. The senators may have been big fish in a big pond, but they behaved as though the players were whales. They wanted to meet the players and made sure they did by inviting our entire delegation to lunch. The proposed dispensation from the antitrust laws did not pass.

Washington beckoned on another occasion. The July 15, 1974, issue of *Time* had included a section entitled "200 Faces for the Future": "young (45 or under) American leaders who, in the editors' view, had noteworthy civic or social impact on their communities, their institutions or the nation." The list included Ralph Nader, Gloria Steinem, Barbara Walters, Donald Rumsfeld, Walter Mondale, Jerry Brown, John D. Rockefeller IV, Paul Sarbanes, Patrick Buchanan, a lot of other people who have been forgotten, a lot of others who have not been, and me.

A little more than two years later, *Time* invited all two hundred of us to a two-day conference on the subject of leadership. The acceptance rate probably set a record. We all wanted to meet one another. On the day I was to go, my son Doug showed some signs of appendicitis, but the symptoms quickly disappeared. Our internist said that was common and that he could not rule out an appendicitis attack; Doug should be seen by a surgeon. By this time Doug was feeling fine, but we set off for

Mt. Sinai Hospital, I with my suitcase, on the assumption that Doug would be given a clean bill of health and I would go on to the airport.

Not surprisingly, the surgeon advised that Doug should give up his appendix. (Never ask a barber whether you need a haircut.) He explained that there was about a 70 percent chance that the appendix was diseased and could burst. Though that also meant that there was a 30 percent chance that Doug was fine, we decided the consequences were too serious if we took the 30 percent bet and lost. The appendix came out—we won our bet; it was diseased—and we stayed to see Doug and kiss him goodnight, getting home around midnight. Though I had missed the beginning of *Time*'s conference, I took an early flight the next morning and enjoyed what remained of it.

I remained active in the labor field. I was asked to serve as one of the mediators in the biennial negotiations between the Transport Workers Union representing New York City's bus and subway workers and the Metropolitan Transit Authority. While a strike by the union would be illegal, with serious consequences for it and its members, it had happened before, bringing the city to a virtual standstill.

The press coverage was intense. We had special telephone lines run into our hotel suites so that reporters couldn't bribe hotel operators to listen in on our calls. The official deadline was midnight of New Year's Eve, but the negotiations typically went on into the early morning hours. In those days television watchers at midnight would see the Times Square ball drop followed on one network by Guy Lombardo's band. But people wanted to know whether there was going to be a strike. That year the dropping of the ball was followed by my press conference, one of many I had held by this point. These were typically unenlightening, since anything I might say could inadvertently affect the negotiations; it was better to say nothing of substance, offering platitudes like: "Everyone is trying hard to reach an agreement."

Mayor Lindsay, like his predecessors and successors, had no actual role in the negotiations, but he could hardly stand by while the fate of his city was being determined. (Though it is responsible for the city's transportation life lines, the Metropolitan Transit Authority is a state agency whose head is appointed by the governor, not the mayor.) And so John Lindsay followed tradition, moved into the hotel where the negotiations were taking place, and met with the parties, who treated him with great courtesy. With similar good manners, when we were ready to announce at about four a.m. that the parties had reached agreement, we woke the mayor so that he could make the announcement.

The second time I mediated a MTA-TWU negotiation, we were ready to announce a deal early in the evening, but the head of the MTA was worried that Mayor Beame would criticize him for giving away too much, so he insisted on running the agreement past the mayor and his advisors. They balked, and I protested, "If the union walks, what will you wind up offering to get them to come back to work?" It took most of the night for them to see the light, but the mayor and his team finally concurred, and once again the announcement came in the early morning hours.

Labor negotiations include lots of down time as parties caucus and breaks are taken for meals and other purposes. During one of those quiet times, a participant brought to life my knowledge of history. I knew that in 1920 the New York State Assembly suspended five of its members for belonging to the Socialist Party. I found myself talking to one of those five men, an attorney named Louis Waldman who was present at the negotiations representing a breakaway group of subway motormen.

Charles Evans Hughes, a hero of mine, had sought the Socialists' reinstatement, persuading the New York City and State Bar Associations to denounce the Assembly's action and chairing an independent committee that filed a brief on behalf of the Socialists with the Assembly's Judiciary Committee. Waldman told me that Hughes, who, as the Republican nominee, had narrowly lost the presidency to Woodrow Wilson in 1916, was warned that if he represented the Socialists, he would forfeit his chance at renomination in 1920. A man whose life was characterized by fidelity to principle, he was undeterred. And he was never renominated, though it's not clear that his advocacy on behalf of the expelled Socialists had anything to do with his being passed over.

I was also called to serve in what has so far proved to be a unique labor dispute—a strike by New York City's firefighters. It was terrifying while it lasted—hundreds of fire alarms were handled by patchwork crews made up of probationary firefighters, fire officers, and the relatively few firefighters who refused to strike. Luckily, by the time the strike ended, about six hours after it began, no one had died.

I was enjoying an excellent lunch with the French consul at a restaurant of his choice when the proprietor brought a telephone to our table. At the courthouse the firefighters' union and the city had just agreed to arbitrate their differences. The issues were to be presented immediately to three named arbitrators, including me. The strike was over, and so was my lunch.

I was also called upon when New York's police misbehaved. As the *New York Times* reported it,

> Hundreds of off-duty police officers, in direct violation of a court order, blew whistles and blocked traffic last night near Yankee Stadium and encouraged roving bands of youths in unsuccessful efforts to crash the gates to the Muhammad Ali-Ken Norton heavyweight championship fight.
>
> In some scattered instances, the policemen were joined in the whistle-blowing by colleagues in uniform. . . .
>
> Last night's demonstrations, in which the off-duty officers were frequently cheered by the uniformed policemen, were part of a continuing agitation by policemen to protest new work schedules and deferred raises.[1]

To resolve the dispute, the city and the police union asked me to arbitrate their differences. They were not that far apart, and I was able to render a decision quickly. Both parties accepted the result with good grace.

A final vivid memory I have of this period in my life is of a march in support of Soviet Jews whose efforts to emigrate were being frustrated by the Soviet government. My friend Nick Scoppetta, seeking to help the Jews, had asked me to put him in touch with Telford Taylor. The Russian procurator general had worked with Telford at the Nuremberg war crimes trial and Nick hoped that Telford might help persuade the Russian to use his influence to help the Soviet Jews. Tel made the effort, and it may have done some good. I was touched by this collaboration of my Christian friends.

The march was to begin at City Hall; each of was to carry a placard bearing the picture of a Jew seeking to emigrate. I was given the picture of Natan Sharansky, a well-known human rights activist, but a parade marshal asked me to give it back, saying Mayor Koch wanted to carry Sharansky's picture. In return I received the picture of a woman I had never heard of. As I sat on the steps of City Hall waiting for the march to begin, a woman approached me. I looked at her, then I looked at the picture I was carrying. It was she! She explained that she had just been allowed to leave Russia. It was a thrilling moment, but its seriousness didn't keep me from returning to the parade marshal and reporting: "O.K., I got her out. Who else do you have?"

7

LITIGATING: TUSKEGEE AND THE SUPREME COURT

*Joan and the kids took up most of the front row. Not long into
my argument before the Supreme Court of the United States,
Julie, our eleven-year-old, fell sound asleep.*

The Tuskegee Syphilis Experiment ranks among America's most cruel and inhuman cases of racial exploitation since the abolition of slavery. Its leading perpetrator was the U.S. government through its Public Health Service.

Following up on a Norwegian study, the U.S. Public Health Service wanted to learn more about how syphilis affected men who were not treated for it. To seek that knowledge, the PHS collaborated with the Tuskegee Institute and Alabama physicians to deny treatment for syphilis to black men in Macon County, Alabama. Physicians in Macon and neighboring counties who were not involved in the study were provided with lists of men they were not to treat.

The study began in 1932 with approximately four hundred black sharecroppers who had contracted syphilis; a control group of roughly two hundred uninfected blacks was soon added. All were promised free medical care, occasional meals, and burial insurance in return for participating. They were told they were being treated for "bad blood." Only the most minimal treatment was administered. In 1933, the acting director of the PHS's Division of Venereal Diseases wrote that "everyone is agreed that the proper procedure is the continuance of the observation of the Negro men used in the study with the idea of eventually bringing them to autopsy."[1]

When the study began, it might have been rationalized—and undoubtedly was—on the ground that there was no effective treatment for syphilis anyway. That would not, of course, excuse lying to the men, but at least the doctors could claim they were being faithful to their Hippocratic oath to "Do no harm."

Rationalization continued to work its magic when penicillin became the standard treatment for syphilis in the 1940s. It was thought that very large doses of penicillin would be needed to cure the late-stage syphilis infecting the men, and it was not clear whether doses of that size would cause seriously adverse side effects. And so the study continued. In 1958, those still alive were rewarded with twenty-five-year certificates signed by the Surgeon General plus one dollar for each year of the study. The research was not a deep dark secret: findings were periodically reported in medical journals.[2] But it was not covered by the mainstream press until a whistleblower brought them the story in 1972, forty years after the study began.

When the facts came out, surviving victims and descendants of victims sought redress. They turned to Fred Gray, an Alabama civil rights attorney well known in the African American community. Fred was eager to help, but the case was too big and complicated for his small law office, and the government is no pushover as an adversary. As a cooperating attorney with the NAACP Legal Defense Fund, he asked its head, Jack Greenberg, where he might find help. Jack tried a few law firms who occasionally assisted the Legal Defense Fund, but nobody wanted to take it on. That's when he called me.

I was not an experienced litigator, but I had helped try a case in federal court, assisting my colleague Maurice Rosenberg; the many arbitrations over which I had presided were trials, though usually less formal than the courtroom variety—in one unusual instance the parties had agreed that I was to conduct the hearing as though it were a trial in a federal district court—and for years I taught the law school's evidence class, the stuff of trials. I was willing to consider the possibility of helping Fred.

My next step was to consult my younger colleague and former student, Hal Edgar, our specialist in medical ethics and related topics. He knew about the study, of course, and thought we could help. We would need to get ready for trial, though we expected the government would ultimately settle rather than undergo the glare of a public contest. We would need to prepare expert witnesses and address the difficult issues of proof in recovering for the heirs of those who had died. Just finding some of the heirs was an enormous challenge in itself.

We decided to join Fred. By this time there was a sense of urgency: although most of the study participants were dead, one hundred or so remained alive and we wanted to help them before they too were gone. Fred had the Herculean task of finding the survivors and collecting their stories as well as tracking down the heirs and learning what they knew. A young historian, Jim Jones, mined the National Archives for critical records of the study. (He would later write *Bad Blood: The Tuskegee Syphilis Experiment*, the definitive book on the subject.) Hal went to work on the legal issues and the expert witness part of the case, and he and I consulted with Fred on tactics. We decided that our first witness would be a survivor who was repeatedly lied to and denied treatment even as he deteriorated from visit to visit.

Despite our sense of urgency, this all took time. When we felt ready to explore whether we could get a favorable settlement, we were surprised by how unyielding government counsel seemed. (The federal Centers for Disease Control had already informed the participants that the federal government would pay their medical expenses for the rest of their lives.) There was no sign of repentance or remorse. But these, of course, were lawyers, not the offending physicians. They obviously conceived of their role as no different in this case from any other—to save the government money.

The legal issues were formidable. The issue of damages—how much should each victim be paid—was a major stumbling block. If we had to deal with this question on a case-by-case basis, we would be in court for a very long time.

In the end it was up to the victims who were serving as representatives of their fellow survivors and heirs to decide whether to accept a blanket settlement or go to trial. They chose the bird in the hand. The government would pay approximately ten million dollars, with $37,500 going to each infected survivor, $15,000 to heirs of the infected, $16,000 to survivors of the control group, and $5,000 to heirs of the deceased members of the control group. Though the dollars were significant to our impoverished clients, we had hoped to do better for them. But the only way to get more was to go to trial. Even if we prevailed, it would be too late to do our survivors any good.

All of this was subject to approval by the federal district court in which Fred had initiated our suit, so Hal and I traveled to Montgomery, Alabama, for the court hearing. Nobody objected to the settlement nor to Fred's petition for attorney's fees, although Judge Frank Johnson did cut Fred's request, reflecting the public interest nature of the suit.

While we were still working on the Tuskegee study, I took on another irresistible case in anticipation of a sabbatical leave. In 1974, New Jersey and New York enacted identical laws repealing legislation containing a bond covenant, effectively repudiating a promise to bondholders that limited the ability of the Port Authority of New York and New Jersey, an agency of the two states, to subsidize rail mass transit. By repealing the promise, the legislatures of the two states freed the Port Authority to deploy some of its substantial resources to aid commuter rail service. The representative of the holders of Port Authority bonds sued, claiming that the two states had violated Article I, Section 10 of the U.S. Constitution, which prohibits states from passing any law "impairing the obligation of contracts."

The covenant had been enacted at the insistence of Austin Tobin, the former executive director of the Port Authority. A powerful executive, Tobin wanted nothing to do with rail mass transit, a big money loser. He preferred bridges and building projects. In fact, the very legislation that contained the now repudiated covenant also authorized the Port Authority to build the World Trade Center, whose twin towers were roundly criticized when they first rose. The legislation also obliged the Port Authority to take over the Hudson and Manhattan Tubes, a deficit-ridden commuter rail line connecting New York and New Jersey. As part of the package, Tobin had gotten the two states to promise not to saddle the Port Authority with any more rail mass transit. To be sure they would keep the promise, it was enacted into law. This was the promise the two states had now repealed.

At the time of the repeal, Lew Kaden, a brilliant young lawyer I had invited to teach a seminar with me and who would later become a regular member of the Columbia faculty, was counsel to the governor of New Jersey. Lew asked me if I would defend the governor and state of New Jersey. Since the case might well go all the way to the U.S. Supreme Court and the prospect of arguing there was thrilling, I happily agreed.

Hal Edgar had proved an excellent partner. Since it wasn't clear that we would be paid for our work on the syphilis case, I invited him to join me in representing a paying client. I rounded out our team with another very smart former student, a New Jersey lawyer named Murray Laulicht.

A trial was the first step on a possible path to the Supreme Court. We were assigned to an able judge in Hackensack, New Jersey, where our opponents were represented by a whole phalanx of lawyers, including Robert Meyner, the former governor of New Jersey, and his law firm, Meyner, Landis, and Vernon, as well as the prominent Wall Street firm of Carter, Ledyard, and Milburn.

The courtroom was small. Our team fit comfortably at our counsel table, but our opponents spilled over into the spectator seats. At the beginning of the second week of the trial, the bailiff told me that each team had had its own carafe of water during the previous week because he had borrowed a carafe from another courtroom while the judge was away. That judge had returned. "Would you mind," he asked, "sharing a carafe with your adversaries?" "No," I replied, "as long as they understand that we get to drink half the water."

We had spent over a week negotiating stipulations of fact on which we could agree in order to simplify and shorten the trial itself. There remained our opponents' effort to prove that the repeal had caused the bonds to lose value. On cross-examination of their principal witness I sought to show that no such loss had followed. Since it is a safe bet that when a lawyer's memoir reports on his cross-examination of a witness, it will not be the witness who emerges victorious, the trial judge's conclusion should come as no surprise. He found that "the evidence fails to demonstrate that the secondary market price of Authority bonds was adversely affected by the repeal of the covenant, except for a short-term fall-off in price, the effect of which has now been dissipated."

The heart of the case, though, was not a factual issue but a legal one. Like so many of the Constitution's provisions, the clause prohibiting the impairment of contractual obligations is not applied literally. In the words of the Supreme Court, "the prohibition is not an absolute one and is not to be read with literal exactness like a mathematical formula."[3]

Our job was to persuade the court that this was one of those cases in which impairment was permissible. To do so, we argued that repealing the covenant permitted New York and New Jersey to respond rationally to their need for more mass transit, a need that was dramatically emphasized in 1974 when gasoline shortages produced vast disruptions of life in communities without mass transit alternatives. Moreover, we maintained, more mass transit was a powerful weapon against air pollution generated by automobiles, which federal regulations required New Jersey to reduce.

We contrasted the vital interests of the states in public health and energy conservation with the trivial harm to the bondholders, emphasizing that our adversaries didn't even claim there was any likelihood that the bonds would not be paid in full and on time. The trial judge was persuaded. Judge Gelman concluded: "It is the judgment of this court that the repeal legislation was a reasonable and hence valid exercise of the states' police power which is not prohibited by the Contract Clause."

As we anticipated, that result was promptly appealed to the Supreme Court of New Jersey. I had appeared there once before—in a dispute over the ownership of thousands of acres of New Jersey property. That case turned on the application of a centuries-old doctrine—that land covered by water at mean high tide belongs to the crown, latterly the state. A corollary to that doctrine holds that if the tide is kept out by artificial structures, as distinguished from natural accretion, the property line does not change. As a consequence, an individual holding title to land that had long been dry might find that title challenged by the state on the ground that it had been rendered dry by artificial means.

After briefing and argument by the parties, the Supreme Court of New Jersey found itself unable to decide who owned the land. It set the case down for reargument and turned for help to the Commission to Study Meadowland Development, a New Jersey state agency. The commission asked me to brief and argue the case. My instructions were very unusual: research the issues and urge the court to adopt whichever result I thought best. I came down on the side of the state, and so did the court.[4] Met Life Stadium, the home of the Giants and the Jets, would ultimately be built on a portion of that land.

Though not a member of the New Jersey bar, I received special permission to appear in the New Jersey courts, first in the Meadowland case and then again in the Port Authority case. This time the Supreme Court of New Jersey seemed to have no difficulty deciding. After receiving briefs and hearing argument, it unanimously affirmed Judge Gelman's decision.[5]

Though I had taken the case in the hope of arguing before the U.S. Supreme Court, when my opponents asked the highest court to review the decision of the New Jersey Supreme Court, it was my job to oppose their request, and oppose it I did. Like countless lawyers in litigation, I had come to believe wholeheartedly in the justice of my client's cause. I really wanted the Supreme Court to reject the appeal.

Each year thousands of litigants seek U.S. Supreme Court review of adverse decisions. Fewer than a hundred make it. The court chooses those cases it regards as, for one reason or another, especially important. As I anticipated when I took the case, ours was a likely candidate. And so it proved to be. After considering our submissions for and against review, the court set the case for full briefing and argument.

Though the U.S. Supreme Court accepted the case in June 1976, it would be November before I would stand in the well of the court. We used the intervening months to prepare as well as we could. We submitted our brief in September. In October, several colleagues were kind enough to serve as a moot court before which I could try out my argument. They could be counted on to test me with the toughest questions they could think of, simulating the sort of colloquy that a Supreme Court argument typically becomes. The occasion also gave me a chance to see how I might best use the half-hour the Supreme Court would allow me, focusing my argument as sharply as possible.

By November I felt ready and so yielded to my family's entreaties to let them all come hear the argument. We reserved a suite at the Washington Hilton. I flew down the afternoon before the argument, to allow myself time for a final review. After school that day my wife, Joan, drove to Washington in our station wagon loaded with seven kids: my son Jeff, almost twenty; my daughter Beth, eighteen; my son Doug, fifteen; my daughter Julie, eleven; my stepson David, fourteen; my stepdaughter Hannah, eleven; and our niece Ellen, sixteen. They arrived late and were still sleeping when I left for the court the next morning.

To make the most of its time, the Supreme Court maintains what I call the "on-deck circle." When the case before ours began, we had to be seated at tables directly behind the lawyers arguing that case. By happy coincidence one of the lawyers in that case was my old friend from law school Harriet Schapiro. We had a chance for hugs before she had to go to work.

Joan and the kids took up most of the first row, where they were joined by Judge Gelman, our trial judge. Not long into my argument, eloquent as I thought it was, Julie, our eleven-year-old, fell soundly asleep.

When our case was called, only seven justices were on the bench: Justices Powell and Stewart were nowhere to be seen. This was not unusual. Supreme Court justices need give no notice of their intention to recuse themselves nor any reason for their recusal. The most likely reason was that they owned Port Authority bonds, but that's just my guess.

As counsel for the appellant, my opponent, Devereux Milburn, went first. Since this was the third court in which we had squared off, his argument contained no surprises for me, nor did mine for him.

I opened with a simple statement of our view of the competing considerations: "Of all the hundreds of cases alleging contract impairment that have come before this court in two centuries, none has involved public ends as vital as those sought to be served by the State here, and few have involved contract infringements so inconsequential." I managed two more sentences before the questions started. We may have had only seven justices, but that didn't lower the court's activity level. In fact, Devereux Milburn was interrupted so often that the chief justice granted us each an extra five minutes. Nor was I allowed much uninterrupted flow. We were both asked questions about the facts of our case, about relevant precedents, about the powers of the states, about how bondholders might behave under various hypothetical circumstances, and more.

Hal Edgar and I thought I had done well, making our points and handling the questions successfully. We couldn't tell from the questions which way the court would decide, but, believing (as lawyers do) that our case was stronger, we thought we would win. We were wrong. On April 27, 1977, the Supreme Court handed down its decision in *United States Trust Company of New York v. New Jersey*.[6] By a vote of 4 to 3, the court held that New Jersey had violated Article I, Section 10 of the U.S. Constitution when it repealed the covenant.

Justice Blackmun, joined by Chief Justice Burger and Justices Rehnquist and Stevens, believed that the state had other means of discouraging automobile use and improving mass transit. He went on to say:

During the 12-year period between adoption of the covenant and its repeal, public perception of the importance of mass transit undoubtedly grew because of increased general concern with environmental protection and energy conservation. But these concerns were not unknown in

1962, and the subsequent changes were of degree and not of kind. We cannot say that these changes caused the covenant to have a substantially different impact in 1974 than when it was adopted in 1962. And we cannot conclude that the repeal was reasonable in the light of changed circumstances.

Justice Brennan wrote a dissenting opinion in which Justices White and Marshall joined. I took some comfort when I saw my argument reverberate in Justice Brennan's opinion:

> In my view, the Court's casual consideration both of the 1962 covenant, and of the relatively inconsequential burdens that resulted for the Authority's creditors, belies its conclusion that the State acted unreasonably in seeking to relieve its citizens from the strictures of this earlier legislative policy.

Needless to say, I also thought his opinion much the better reasoned.

We filed a petition for rehearing, with no real hope that it would be granted. Such petitions rarely are. Justice Cardozo, in response to such a petition, is alleged to have said: "We shall give it the benefit of our most prejudiced consideration." And so, although eleven judges on three courts voted for us and only four voted against us, my record in the Supreme Court of the United States remains zero wins, one loss.

8

PROVOST

On balance the tenure system, administered with rigor, has been a plus—which is not to say that we didn't have a few faculty I would love to have let go.

Shortly before the law school's faculty took the vote that led to my selection as the new dean, we resolved that a dean should serve no more than ten years. Toward the end of a six-year term, he could be elected for four more years.

At the beginning of my ninth year, Hans Smit, one of the original supporters of the ten-year rule, called upon me to say that my colleagues would be happy to waive the limit if I wished to stay longer. I thanked Hans, told him how pleased I was by the offer, but demurred. The faculty's original position, in my view, was correct: ten years is long enough. A deanship is not endlessly interesting; an extended tenure invites boredom or at least a slackening of the energy one brings to the job. The school would be better off with a fresh dean, one who saw new and exciting possibilities. Besides, I missed teaching and was looking forward to getting back to it.

Later that fall, Bill McGill told me that Ted de Bary was stepping down as provost, the chief academic officer of the university, and asked whether I was interested in the job. If not, he would put me on the search committee for a new provost. I said, "Put me on the search committee."

My fellow search committee members included Robert Merton, one of the most respected sociologists of his day. One afternoon, Bob called to say he was the rump subcommittee of the search committee charged with sounding out those members of the committee who had been nominated by others for the provostship. Would I come over for a drink? My first instinct was to thank Bob and tell him I was not interested, but to brush off an old friend and revered colleague seemed churlish to me, so I headed to his Riverside Drive apartment.

Over very dry martinis, Bob put the question to me, and I told him that I wasn't interested in the job, except for two remote possibilities. First, if they couldn't find an acceptable candidate, I would serve for a couple of years while they sought other candidates. Ted de Bary was a world-class scholar and a wonderful citizen of the university—he had helped found our Asian Humanities program decades before anyone else was even thinking about doing that—but I didn't think much of his performance as provost. I thought it important to have the job done right, was immodest enough to believe I could do it, and was willing to serve in what seemed to me to be the best interests of the university. Bob asked for the other possibility. "If Bill McGill were planning to step down as president," I replied.

This was the first time I had admitted to myself that I was interested in the presidency. The following morning Bill McGill called to tell me that he was planning to retire at the end of the next academic year. A series of meetings followed—with the search committee, with the chair of the Trustees Education Committee, and with Bill himself. At its January meeting, the trustees approved my appointment as executive vice president for academic affairs and provost of the university. On February 1, 1979, I left the law school and moved into Low Library.

The deputy provost was Norman Mintz, who had given up a promising career in economics for academic administration. He would become a good friend and trusted advisor. On this day he undertook to brief me on my new responsibilities. "The provost assigns faculty apartments," he began. I interrupted him: "No, Norman; the deputy provost assigns faculty apartments." I was mindful of President McKinley's complaint that for every patronage job he filled, he made nine enemies and one ingrate. Desirable faculty apartments were in short supply and high demand. I knew it well, having put in my own time on the apartment waiting list. I had much to do, I didn't want to get bogged down in apartment squabbles, and I knew Norman well enough to trust him to do the job about as well as it could be done.

The provost is the guardian of the intellectual quality of the university. His main instruments for preserving and enhancing that quality are his decisions affecting the budgets of the individual schools and his supervision of the process by which faculty are awarded tenure. With the chief financial officer, he also oversees the budgeting for the whole university, including expenditures for new construction and maintenance of the physical plant. The libraries also report to him.

Harvard's peer—some would argue its superior—before World War II, Columbia had begun to slip even before 1968. The fallout from the events of that year exacerbated the decline. We lost some very good faculty, many of the best students chose to apply elsewhere, and our finances were a mess. Columbia enjoyed a balanced budget for the first time in over a decade in the fiscal year ending June 30, 1979. (It was on its way to that happy outcome before I became provost.)

When I asked our vice president for facilities management to give me a prioritized list of needs so that we could deploy our limited resources intelligently (apparently a request that no one had ever made before), I ultimately received a list that had as its top priority "Life-threatening conditions." This was not hyperbole: on Commencement Day 1980, a Barnard student was killed by a piece of falling masonry. Columbia, like many universities, had woefully neglected its physical plant, operating on the principle that proper maintenance can always be deferred for another year.

Working with the deans on their budgets, I was empathetic, having been on the other side of those transactions myself, but there wasn't much to go around, making most of the allocations formulaic, namely, a small percentage increase over the previous year. The highly centralized process was frustrating for all concerned. It lacked incentives for the deans to increase enrollment or advocate for larger tuition increases to finance key initiatives. Fundraising was not subject to central capture, and so the deans of law, business, and medicine, who were good at it, could improve their lot. The rest suffered.

I thought I had demonstrated the folly of the existing system when I was still dean. At a time when the law school was admitting a class of 290, I wrote to the provost, explaining that we lacked the resources to staff that number responsibly and that unless my budget was increased, I would have to admit a smaller class in the future. My budget was not increased, and the following year I admitted a class of 265. Since there was no linkage between enrollment and budgets, my budget allocation was not adversely affected. I next offered an ad hoc deal: I would increase the next class to 290 if the law school could keep the incremental revenue each year—that is, twenty-five times the tuition each student paid for the indefinite future; otherwise we would remain at 265. My offer was accepted, and the law school's budget got a nice boost.

That was a silly way to run a university. Beginning as provost, in collaboration with the chief financial officer, and continuing as president, I helped move us to a more decentralized system, with appropriate incentives for the individual schools to manage their affairs efficiently.

Superintending the tenure system may have been the most interesting part of the provost's job. Many school districts award tenure to their teachers almost automatically after a stipulated period of time. At the great universities it doesn't work that way. Systems vary in their particulars, but those at the best look something like Columbia's. First and perhaps most important is the "up-or-out principle": a professor who does not receive tenure by, in most cases, the end of his or her seventh year must leave. When I was provost, roughly five out of six nontenured assistant and associate professors did not receive tenure. While the aspect of tenure that receives public attention is the lifetime security that the winners receive, a critical feature forces departments to review their junior cohorts and winnow them out. This is enormously valuable.

Without this sort of forced review, many departments would allow some of their junior faculty, who are by and large a pretty good group, to stay around indefinitely, with a likely erosion of quality over time.

Another advantage of the tenure system is budgetary. If colleges and universities did not offer lifetime security, they would almost certainly have to pay more to attract at least some of the talent they now attract. Some would add that tenure is also an important buttress of academic freedom: professors vulnerable to dismissal would hedge their bets and skew their work to avoid controversy. I am inclined to agree, but not everyone does.

Are these advantages worth the disadvantages—mainly those relatively few professors who once they achieve tenure slack off, some to the point of lazy teaching and little scholarship? My own view is that, administered with rigor, on balance the tenure system has been a plus—which is not, of course, to say that we didn't have a few faculty I would love to have let go.

The abolition of mandatory retirement may shift that positive balance. When Congress initially outlawed mandatory retirement, the statute included a five-year moratorium for tenured faculty. As the five years ran off, I tried to persuade my fellow university presidents to lobby for its extension. Under the retirement plans in effect at most universities, every year retirement is postponed adds materially to a professor's pension. If enough faculty are moved by this incentive, opportunities for new faculty, so critical to the regular reinvigoration of disciplines, will be foreclosed. And because senior faculty earn so much more than juniors, every senior who stays on precludes the appointment of two or three juniors. My presidential colleagues were unmoved by my arguments, maintaining that retirement expectations were well established and would not be much affected by the change in the law. At the time of this writing, the consequences have not been as serious as I feared, but I remain pessimistic about the longer run. In one of life's many ironies, however, I have been the beneficiary of my failure. Thanks to the abolition of mandatory retirement, teaching remains a prized part of my life.

Administering the tenure system with rigor was my job. When a school or department thought a candidate was ready for tenure, a dossier would be prepared containing the candidate's scholarly record, appraisals from within and outside the department, and whatever else the proponents thought would help. I would then convene a committee of five faculty members drawn from outside the department. We would review the file and then typically meet with the chairman of the department who would present the case for tenure.

I say this may have been the most interesting part of the provost's job because it was a wonderful way to learn about the university. The presenter would talk about the field, the way the candidate's work fit within it, and why that work was important.

A vote against the candidate would end the matter; a three-to-two vote in favor was not a guarantee of success. In theory, the provost was not bound even by a unanimous vote in favor, but I am not aware of any occasion when a provost overruled a favorable vote of more than three to two. There would typically be more than thirty tenure reviews each year, some of them promotions from within the university, some recruitments from elsewhere. The promotions from within were more likely to be contaminated by friendships, mentors looking after protégés and the like. In one case the candidate was the chairman's girlfriend.

After I settled in, I could usually identify cases that would be easy approvals and, given the press of other business, let Norman Mintz handle those. The process was time consuming, so I concentrated on the instances where I might actually have to make a judgment. I resolutely refused to accept an argument for a weak candidate that it was the best we could do. If we couldn't do better, we should make do with nontenured faculty until we did attract someone worth a lifetime bet.

In one case our inability to find a suitable candidate for tenure caused me to return a $500,000 endowment gift. A generous donor had given us that endowment to fund a tenured professorship in Chinese art. We do not let donors pick faculty, but we did have a nontenured faculty member in the field she thought was wonderful and worthy of tenure. He didn't make it. The gift was not conditioned on her favorite receiving tenure; we would not have entered into such an agreement. But the art history department's exhaustive search for a first-rate appointment in the field proved fruitless. The donor's patience wore out, and I saw no basis for denying her attorney's request for a refund.

Tenure denials are awash in potential for difficulty. The disappointed candidate may claim discrimination of one kind or another; the disappointed department may appeal to the president, who is free to reject the provost's recommendation, though no Columbia president in my experience has ever done so; and disappointed students (these cases sometimes involve first-rate teaching and second-rate scholarship) may protest vociferously.

It wasn't until I had been president for several years that the process turned on me. In 1988, a business school candidate for a professorship in marketing had received a three-to-two vote in favor of tenure. That narrow vote of confidence was even weaker than it seemed. As a professional school, business was entitled to place two members on the ad hoc committee; they cast two of the three positive votes. It would have taken great courage for them to vote against their school's candidate.

Bob Goldberger, the provost at the time, decided to recommend that I deny tenure. The dean of the business school came to see me and did his best to make the case for his candidate, concluding that if I denied tenure, he would have no choice but to resign in protest. Lost on the dean was the irony that I had been all set to fire him for his poor performance only months before but had yielded to his plea to give him a little more time to show me what he could do. After thoroughly reviewing the case, I decided to deny tenure. The dean resigned, to the applause of his faculty, who had generally been dissatisfied with his performance until then. I had converted a failed dean into a heroic martyr. The case received attention from the press, but that quickly faded, and when I appointed an outstanding successor to the deanship, the school began to blossom.

One school in the university—the law school—believing that its internal review process was as good as it gets and reluctant to accept the burden and risk of review by those unfamiliar with its discipline, had refused to submit to it, and we had made the refusal stick. Though responsible for that position as dean, I was willing to rethink the issue as provost and found myself, not surprisingly, ambivalent. I didn't see how I could persuade my old colleagues to change their minds anyway, so I let the matter drop. Since the law school faculty enjoys the highest rating in the university without participating in the ad hoc system, my original position may well have been the right one.

Among the visitors to the provost's office in 1979 were Richard Lanier and Elizabeth McCormack. Richard had assisted John D. Rockefeller III in his program of supporting arts exchanges between Asia and the United States, and Elizabeth was the Rockefeller family's philanthropic advisor. John Rockefeller had died, and they were looking for a way to institutionalize his exchange program. Would it be better to create a standalone foundation or bring the program to Columbia? Painful as it was for me, I advised against coming to Columbia, where they would be swamped by all the competitors for Columbia's fundraising resources. They took my advice, and what became the Asian Cultural Council is still going strong. In what struck me as a perverse reward for my candor, they invited me to join their newly created board. Believing in the value of their mission and liking them both enormously, I accepted.

The provost is also the officer charged with acting in the absence of the president, and I found myself called upon to fulfill that role shortly after taking office. Bill McGill was rarely unavailable, but he was out of reach for a few hours in late March 1979 when two groups of workers occupied the university's computer center and controller's office. They were members of Local 1199 of the Hospital Workers Union, which, despite its name, represented about five hundred of Columbia's office and clerical workers. Local 1199 and Columbia were engaged in difficult negotiations for a new contract, and the occupiers were protesting the lack of progress.

They had taken two vitally important centers; they could do enormous harm if they chose to. After consulting with colleagues who understood the potential for damage, my conclusion was that we could not leave the occupiers there. We had learned well that summoning police to campus is a risky business, but I thought we had little choice. The time it takes between the request for police and their actual appearance would be long enough to allow Bill McGill to overrule me if he thought I had acted imprudently. He didn't, and nearly one hundred police removed the protesters without incident, arresting thirty-three members of Local 1199 in the process. Bill later cited the incident to the trustees in case any of them thought I wasn't tough enough to be president. I didn't think of it as an exercise in machismo; it was something that had to be done.

Bill generously allowed me to take the lead on another, deeply moving, occasion. The trustees had resolved to award an honorary degree to Justice William O. Douglas, a graduate of the law school, a former member of its faculty, and the longest-serving justice in history. Unfortunately a stroke had left Douglas unable to travel, so we decided to take the degree to him. It would be only the second time Columbia had awarded an honorary degree off campus. (Abraham Lincoln received his in Washington when the Civil War had him fully occupied.) I made the presentation at the Supreme Court with all of its members in attendance. Justice Douglas responded very briefly. It was all this once extraordinarily vigorous outdoorsman could manage.

When Bill McGill announced in the spring of 1979 that he would be retiring at the end of the following year, it was widely known that I was a candidate to succeed him. That earned me some extra respect: everyone dealing with me knew that next year I might be their president. But it also intensified a debilitating temptation for me: do nothing that would turn anyone hostile before Bill's successor was chosen. I think that for the most part I succeeded in resisting that temptation, performing my provostial duties as I would have anyway.

My candidacy was a strong one. I had worked successfully with some of the trustees in 1968–1969, several were law school alumni who knew my work well, and, as provost, I had worked closely with the Trustees Committee on Education. I was known by faculty throughout the university because of my 1968–1969 experience. As dean I had demonstrated my ability as a fundraiser. And my civil rights record augured well for my ability to handle community relations.

I was never told what outside candidates the trustees considered, but the inside competition was obvious. Paul Marks had become dean of the medical school and vice president for health sciences the same day I had become dean of the law school. He had done an outstanding job, but I had at least one important advantage: Bill McGill knew us both well and would, I was almost certain, tell the trustees I was the preferable choice.

Though I usually attended trustees' meetings from the beginning, leaving only when they went into executive session, before their January 1980 meeting I was asked to wait until summoned. I spent the time thinking about my response if I were told that I would be the new president. Within the hour I was invited to join the meeting. I entered to warm applause; I had been elected president of the university effective July 1, 1980.

In the ensuing months I joked to friends that I had no place to hide. When faced with a troublesome issue, the president can sometimes buck it to the provost, and the reverse is also true. But as both provost and president-designate, I was stuck. And, of course, the authority of the president began to seep away from Bill the day my appointment was announced. Every idea he had rejected was dusted off by the originators and presented to me as if it were brand new.

Bill and I had always worked well together, and we continued to for his remaining months as president until June 13th, when he walked into my office and declared, "There's nothing for me to do here anymore. I'm appointing you acting president." Bill's wife Ann had hated New York and insisted they keep their home in California, so they moved back there. Bill said that keeping that property was the best investment decision he had ever made.

During his last weeks at Columbia, Bill generously offered to brief me on various aspects of the Columbia presidency. Our weekly tutorials were a richly rewarding experience. On one occasion, mindful of the fact that Arthur Krim, the chairman of the trustees, would soon be retiring, I asked Bill whether he would consider succeeding Arthur. He declined, citing both personal reasons and the threat to my presidency that his continued involvement would entail. He wisely observed that there would inevitably be occasions when one or another group would be dissatisfied with me and that I should not create a competing power center on campus for them to turn to.

I continued to do the work of the provost, though I delegated more of it to Norman and the other members of the provost's office, even as I began to build my administration. My first effort was to try to retain Paul Marks, who was being courted to head Memorial Sloan-Kettering Cancer Center. It was a hopeless quest, lasting only until Paul secured the terms he wanted from Sloan-Kettering. I won the contest for the Columbia presidency, but Paul moved across town at more than twice my pay.

I now faced vacancies in two top jobs—the leadership of health sciences and the provostship. I believed we also needed new vice presidents for development and for government and community relations. We were solid in finance, headed by Anthony Knerr, with whom I had been working productively as provost, and he had recruited a first-rate budget director in Diana Murray. The executive vice president for administration, Paul Carter, was a man I would come to depend upon.

9

BUILDING AN ADMINISTRATION

A great university is an idea as immortal as any mortals can conceive. It can be likened to a great cathedral—an enduring and soaring monument to the human spirit. The university differs, however, in that it is never finished. It is always being built.

It is one of the oddities of academic life that university presidents are typically inaugurated some months after starting work. Maybe this is because their terms usually begin on July 1, and nobody wants a ceremonial installation in the middle of summer.

I was inaugurated on a beautiful day in late September, with about 4,400 guests in attendance. I remember with pleasure the spontaneous applause of students as I appeared, capping an academic procession composed of Columbians and representatives of 160 academic institutions from all over the world appearing in the order in which they had been founded.

I had worked hard on my inaugural address and regard it as one of the best speeches I have given. Here are a few thoughts from it.

To us falls the special responsibility for keeping alive the spirit of inquiry. Basic science often turns out to have practical applications. But, at least some of the time, we in the universities should think of fundamental inquiry the way we think of art. The impulse to do it is not practical. The search for knowledge, for understanding, is an eternal quest, a powerful inspirational force. This above all else we must preserve and protect.

In 1768, our predecessors asked: "Is the main purpose of education to make us able and rich, or wise and good?" The question has not lost its force.

More than one wise man has observed: "I want to do good. I wish I knew what it is." Classrooms are not pulpits. Universities do not exist to preach. But we do offer earnest exploration of difficult questions in a disciplined way. In the right hands that method works as well for ethics as it does for less exalted subjects. Aristotle understood that. So did Socrates. And now and then a gifted teacher helps our students to sense the ineffable.

But we should aspire to more. Attention and commitment will take us a long way. Some curricular change, yes, but most important is the unembarrassed acceptance of the responsibility to try to lead to the good. That is the key to great teaching and inspired learning.

Each year, eighteen thousand people take the remarkable step of entrusting us with a central role in their lives. We should aspire to transmit to them the heritage of civilization; to unlock the treasures of the past; to bring fresh vision and new discipline to the ever-growing fund of human knowledge; to enliven curiosity, to cherish the freedom to explore and express; to encourage joy in the presence of beauty and appreciation in the presence of wisdom; to discover, in the words of William Saroyan, "that which shines and is beyond corruption."

I would add that the task of choosing is the toughest challenge facing the citizens of a free society. And I believe that we can do more to prepare them for it. If I am right in this, if we can help our students to do a better job of asking the right questions, assessing imperfect evidence and making balanced judgments, we shall not only have made a larger contribution; we shall also have taken a big step toward the teacher's ultimate goal—to make himself unnecessary to his student.

Today's ritual reaffirms our debt to the past and makes anew our promise to the future. We are part of an unending commitment; we share an institution, an idea as immortal as any mortals can conceive. A great university can be likened to a great cathedral—an enduring and soaring monument to the human spirit. The university differs, however, in that it is never finished. It is always being built. I hope that in the years ahead we may add a stone or two together.

The address was received enthusiastically, in part because of a narrowly averted disaster. The text each speaker would deliver was included in a binder on the lectern, where each of us would find it when his turn came. I had never before delivered a speech that I hadn't brought with me. In what was undoubtedly a neurotic moment, as we left for the ceremony I gave my wife, Joan, a copy of the text to hold for me.

When my turn to speak came, I began in fine form and was sailing right along when I finished page 10 and confronted page 12. This was not, of course, the first time I had read this text, and I had a pretty good idea of what I had written on page 11, but instead of muddling through, I said: "I might as well 'fess up. I'm missing a page. I thought of winging it, but we have a backup system." To rousing applause, Joan ran up with the text. We were later laughingly accused of having staged the whole thing, but I protested that I wasn't that good an actor.

With characteristic thoughtfulness, Arthur Krim, the trustees chairman, realized that Marge Montana, my superb executive assistant, would be wretched over having left a page out of the binder she had supervised. He sought her out and, finding her in tears, did his best to console her.

The inauguration was a great party, but it was time to return to work. My administrative team was almost complete. The provostial appointment had proved the most difficult. With the president coming from a professional school, I thought it important that the provost come from the arts and sciences, the group comprising Columbia College, the Graduate School of Arts and Sciences, the School of International and Public Affairs, General Studies, and, later, the School of the Arts. Yet the arts and sciences professor who seemed to me most qualified for the job couldn't be persuaded to take it.

I decided on two innovations. First, since the provost's portfolio had seemed to me to be too full, I separated the position's two titles and, letting the executive vice president for academic affairs stand alone, assigned that office responsibility for the libraries, athletics, and a miscellany of lesser matters. This had the additional advantage of creating a post for Norman Mintz. Now I could take him with me as I moved from provost to president.

Second, since no one in the arts and sciences willing to take the job seemed likely to succeed as provost of the whole university, I decided to have three provosts—one for the health sciences, one for the remaining professional schools, and one for the arts and sciences. We didn't complete the health sciences search until 1981, when we recruited Bob Goldberger, a distinguished physician and senior official at the National Institutes of Health. His job was unique among the three: it wasn't actually a new set of responsibilities, since he would have been in charge of the same schools—medicine, public health, nursing, and dentistry—as the vice president for health sciences, but as a provost he would report directly to me.

I appointed Peter Likins, dean of the School of Engineering and Applied Science, to be provost for the professional schools. He had done a first-rate job as dean, and I would have been happy to make him overall provost but for my unwillingness to have only former professional school deans in the senior administration. And I persuaded Fritz Stern, a widely respected historian and an old friend, to take the arts and sciences provostship.

I was obviously taking a calculated risk with the new arrangement, and I did get a few pointed questions about it, but it functioned well. The four of us met at least weekly, enabling us to handle any problems that might arise, but they all worked very well together; my intervention was rarely required. Interacting with three provosts rather than one meant that I was more hands on than I might otherwise have been, which I regarded as a great advantage in my early years as president.

After two years, Peter Likins was lured away to be president of Lehigh, and Bob Goldberger took over his duties. A year later, Fritz Stern decided he had had enough. I had promised him I wouldn't press him to stay when that moment came. Bob Goldberger then became sole provost, and for a while at least nobody seemed to care that neither the president nor the provost came from the arts and sciences.

Columbia's fundraising was woefully inadequate. I was lucky enough to recruit Terry Holcomb from Yale to take over as vice president for development. Yale had recently cut its development budget after the conclusion of a successful capital campaign. Terry believed the retrenchment to be a serious mistake and so was susceptible to my courtship.

When Terry didn't move his family to New York, I feared my success might be short-lived, particularly since he was a Yalie all the way. Sure enough, Bart Giamatti, Yale's president (later baseball commissioner), realized that letting Terry get away had been a big mistake and persuaded him to return. But Terry was with us long enough to get our fundraising on track, and I quickly found a worthy successor in Peter Buchanan, who had left Columbia a few years earlier because Bill Mc-Gill didn't want to undertake a capital campaign.

I had one more important position to fill. Columbia did not have a senior officer responsible for government and community relations, even though we intersected with government at every level. We received tens of millions of dollars in federal funding and millions more from the state and city of New York: all of them regulated us in one way or another. Fortunately, there was a deep pool of talent available. I picked Gregory Fusco, who had been a top aide to Senator Jacob Javits. Greg built a small but effective team, with Larry Dais handling community relations and Bill Polf managing our relations with New York State. Greg and Larry were my productive partners for all thirteen years of my presidency.

10

BEGINNINGS

Successful people who deny their roots are missing half the fun.

Many events during my presidency triggered memories of my long journey from the boy in the Bronx to the man I had become. Welcoming the College's entering class would stir recollections of my own first days at Columbia. Meeting the parent of a first-generation graduate on Commencement Day would evoke my mother's joy at my graduation. But I recall most vividly chatting with Joe DiMaggio at a dinner in honor of the guests upon whom we would confer honorary degrees the following day. DiMaggio was one of those guests.

He was telling me about the negotiations that brought him to the New York Yankees. Though he was already starring for the San Francisco Seals, the Yankees general manager, Ed Barrow, offered him only $5,000 a year. DiMaggio sought advice from Ty Cobb and, with his help, pushed the offer to $7,500. Barrow had said he would go no higher. But Cobb told DiMaggio, "tell Barrow that if they don't do better, you'll go play for the St. Louis Browns." DiMaggio said, "Mr. Cobb, I don't want to play for the St. Louis Browns." And that's how Joe DiMaggio became a Yankee for $7,500 in 1936.

So much had happened to both of us since, as a boy, I had watched that extraordinarily graceful athlete from a bleacher seat I could barely afford. He was now afflicted with arthritis, eating and drinking very little lest, without much exercise, he would balloon up. And here I was, president of Columbia University, the host of one of my boyhood idols.

Our conversation was a powerful reminder of my origins. Successful people who deny their roots are missing half the fun. I was not only enjoying my conversation with DiMaggio; I was also enjoying having come so far.

My parents were highly intelligent, but, in the fashion of the time for most children of immigrants, they hadn't spent much of their lives in school. My father attended DeWitt Clinton High School for two years; my mother never even started. They had high hopes for their children. My sister Denise and I would become the first in our line to attend college.

My father did not limit himself to hoping for the future. He was a natural teacher. When I asked him what batting averages meant, he taught me the decimal system. When I was adding a column of figures, he pointed out how easy it was to make a mistake if I failed to align the numbers in straight columns. He was a regular reviewer of my homework assignments. And he taught me a lesson about right and wrong in a way I have never forgotten and never will.

I was eleven when I took my sister along on a shoplifting excursion to the local Woolworth's. My friends and I were small-time thieves, and not just because that was all we could be in a five-and-ten-cents store. We stole items of little value for which we had little use. It was the excitement, not the prospect of profit, that drove us.

My sister, who was seven at the time, chose to take a small box of paste-on American flags. When, to my horror, she showed them off at the dinner table that evening, my father asked where she got them. "Ask Mickey," she said. (I was Mickey to friends and family.) I had no satisfactory answer, and so I confessed. More than sixty years later, my father's response still reverberates. We were disciplined, but mildly—sent to our rooms without the rest of our dinners. But the shaping experience was my father's seemingly heartbroken reaction of disappointment in me. I was devastated. I was never tempted to steal again.

Baseball was his favorite sport. He taught me to field grounders and judge fly balls. Yankee Stadium was only a few blocks away, and he would take me to games most weekends. At first I wanted just to be with him and to eat my fill of peanuts, but in time I would become a true fan. Soon I could hold my own when he and I were opining on such tactical issues as whether the batter should bunt, the base runner should steal, or the pitcher should be yanked.

In late summer of 1944, my father died.

We had already begun our descent from middle-class comfort. My father had been a partner in a small company that manufactured women's clothing. His success had brought us to a three-bedroom apartment in a relatively new building in the south Bronx, which was not yet a symbol of urban decay. But a few years after our move he and his two partners guessed wrong about what women would want next. He lacked the capital to survive the ensuing drought in orders.

He found work as a salesman, and we moved to a smaller apartment nearby. Planning to start a new business as soon as he could, he sought to remain creditworthy by paying off his debts rather than seeking their discharge in bankruptcy. To do so, he drew down the cash value of his life insurance. Three years later, after a short struggle with cancer, he was dead. It was September 12, 1944, less than three months before my thirteenth birthday.

Fifty years later my granddaughters Melanie, five, and Lindsay, three, lost their mother to cancer. I wrote a letter for them to read when they were older. It read in part:

A word of caution about this and the other remembrances you will be reading, a warning bred of my own experience. My father died when I was twelve years old. As a result, all my memories of him are those of a young boy vis-à-vis his seemingly quite old parent. I never had the maturing experience of coming of age and seeing him as a fellow adult with whatever flaws he may have had. He was locked in my memory as a near-superman, who helped me with my homework, taught me to play baseball, guided me and disciplined me with strength and wisdom.

In some sense I have tried all my life to match that matchless performance. That is a blessing and a curse. Watch out for it. On the one hand it is wonderfully inspiring to have a superb model to emulate. On the other, the goal is unachievable, even unrealistic, for the man I knew as a child was, of course, a myth. Nobody is that good, not even my father. Not even your mother.

My father had left my mother very nearly destitute at thirty-seven. She found a job as a bookkeeper for a storefront exterminating company that paid twenty-five dollars a week. Its great virtue from her point of view was that it was across the street from my eight-year-old sister's primary school and only a few steps from the streetcar stop to which I would return each day after junior high school.

She never married again, though she was still a very attractive woman. (When I was younger, in a classical Oedipal moment I wondered why such a good-looking woman would have picked my ordinary-looking father.) My sister and I were the center of her life. She managed to be loving and supportive without ever seeming to be controlling. In fact, as I look back from the vantage point of my own parenting years, I see that she allowed me a remarkable degree of freedom for an adolescent.

In addition to her salary, my mother received eighteen dollars a month under Social Security's widows and survivors benefit program. To make ends meet, she invited her sister Etta to come live with us and share the rent. Etta was the eldest of seven children, almost a full generation older than my mother, who was the youngest. Etta had recently divorced my Uncle Jack, and she was living alone. She would soon live alone again. She had no children of her own and little patience with my sister Denise and me. A two-bedroom apartment with a single bathroom required a considerable measure of mutual tolerance, a test we both flunked.

When she moved, we had to move again—this time to a small one-bedroom apartment on the second floor. My sister and I shared that bedroom, and my mother slept in the living room. Fortunately for us, the building in which we lived—1190 Shakespeare Avenue—was a neighborhood of its own, one in which other families looked out for my sister and me, taking some of the load off my mother. Several couples hired me to babysit for their children—at seventy-five cents a night. Two of the men in the building took me to baseball games and Friday night fights at Madison Square Garden. My sister's best friend lived just down the hall, and her family routinely included Denise in their activities.

We were certainly aware that money was short, but we didn't feel downtrodden or desperate. Our friends' families were not all that much better off than we. To be sure, the family of my best friend, Richie Goldenberg (later to be the distinguished psychiatrist and author Dr. Richard Gardner), owned a car, but not many people we knew did.

Being fatherless made me feel something akin to shame. At the public library near our home, we were entitled to move up from the children's section to the adult's upon completion of the eighth grade. I had looked forward to this giant step, and as soon as I was eligible I went to present myself to the librarian. There was a boy ahead of me, and, as I waited, she duly recorded his answers to her questions. When she came to "Father's name?" I turned and ran out. I couldn't bear the thought of telling her my father was dead.

In time the lure of the books overcame my dread. I read voraciously. My parents had bought books when my father was alive, but we could no longer afford to do that. The Highbridge branch of the public library was a godsend. My taste in books was eclectic: I ranged over mysteries, science fiction, mythology, coming-of-age stories, biography, and history, but I read for entertainment and escape rather than enlightenment. I attended an outstanding high school—the Bronx High School of Science—where we had excellent English teachers offering Shakespeare and other great writers. But requiring students of high-school age to read a particular work, as so many have found, converts what should be pleasure into pain. My taste remained relentlessly lowbrow.

From the age of thirteen, I held a variety of after-school and summer jobs. I was literally frightened out of my first summer job. New York's child-labor laws prohibited children under fourteen from working and, even at fourteen, required the young aspirant to obtain working papers as a condition of employment. By lying about my age to a none-too-punctilious employer, I obtained work assembling boxes to hold combs that would be worn in women's hair.

Several days after I began, I received a letter from the U.S. Department of Labor summoning me to appear at a local office. I had been caught! I was terrified. I quit immediately, and, after a reassuring conference with my mother and a supportive neighbor, the neighbor agreed to appear on my behalf. It turned out that hiring me was not my employer's only illegal action: he was violating the federal wage and hour law. I was being summoned as a potential witness, not a discovered culprit. Since he was paying me the required minimum—forty cents an hour—officialdom had no further interest in me.

When I turned fourteen, I could at last work legally. A friend of the family helped get me a job as a clerk at the company that manufactures Van Heusen shirts, and I returned there for the summer after my fifteenth birthday. At sixteen, another family friend helped get me a summer job as a busboy at a hotel on the New Jersey shore, where I could save virtually everything I earned.

When I returned to school that fall, my studies took a back seat. I had started out at Bronx Science like a house afire, having just graduated from junior high school at the top of my class. But by the end of my junior year the hormones were surging, and the social was trumping the academic. The teachers at Science were almost uniformly superb, and I actually enjoyed most of my classes, but girls and friends were more important. I was also president of my class, and during my senior year worked after school as a shipping clerk in the garment district four hours each day during the week and all day Saturday for the then munificent rate of ninety cents an hour.

When it came time to apply for college, I was no longer a shoo-in. I knew very little about the possibilities, and counseling then was no better than it appears to be now. No one ever told me about scholarship programs. I assumed I could not afford to go away to school. My friend Richie was a year ahead of me and very happy at Columbia, so that was my first choice. My safeties were City College and New York University, and it looked as though I would need one of them.

My Columbia interview was a disaster. My interlocutor was given to long pauses, leaving me to figure out whether I was to fill them in. The process was especially unnerving because he was cross-eyed, which robbed me of the usual cue afforded when an interviewer looks at you expectantly. It did not occur to me to tell him that I would one day be president of his university.

I was waitlisted. City College and NYU admitted me, and I paid the $25 deposit to NYU to hold my place. It was late June before Columbia admitted me to the Class of 1953.

Tuition was $600 per year, which was made more manageable for me when I won a New York State Regents Scholarship. This was a wonderful program that, on the basis of a statewide competitive exam, awarded hundreds of students scholarships that paid $350 a year to attend a New York college. My savings from my past jobs and earnings from future summer work covered the rest of tuition plus the cost of books and my other expenses. This meant that I was free to devote full attention to my courses without having to take a job during the academic year.

In that era high-school classes graduated at mid-year as well as in June. And so in February 1949 my friend Roy Nevans and I, with eight months to wait to start college, headed to Florida to look for work. We had prepared ourselves by obtaining driver's licenses in New Jersey which, unlike New York, permitted seventeen-year-olds to drive. One had to be a resident of New Jersey to take advantage of this privilege; that problem was solved by the driving school Roy found: we were to enter "West New York," a New Jersey town, on our application.

But the full measure of driving-school corruption in New Jersey had yet to be revealed to me. After I completed my driving lessons, the school scheduled my road test. Not owning a car, I had no chance to practice beyond the lessons and was almost certainly a danger to myself and others. My driving inspector seemed to think so too: when I was slow to hit the brake in response to a truck that pulled out of a driveway into my path, the inspector yelled, "Are you trying to kill me?" But the fix must have been in: I passed.

We wanted the licenses so we could drive when we got to Florida. We went there by bus. Passengers could leave the bus at any scheduled stop and get on a later bus without charge. Roy and I wanted to see something of Washington, which neither of us had ever visited. (I had never been south of New Jersey.) Before heading back to the bus terminal we managed to fit in visits to the Supreme Court, the Capitol, FBI Headquarters, the Air and Space Museum, and a burlesque theater.

Actually, the bus terminal is the most memorable of all the places we visited, for it was there that I first encountered Jim Crow. The restrooms and water fountains were marked "White" and "Colored," as were the waiting rooms. I saw a policeman chase a black man who had wandered into the white waiting room. Until our trip home, it would be segregation all the way. I wish I could say I reacted with the appropriate outrage, but at seventeen I tended to take the world as I found it. I didn't like segregation. It was an alien practice that made no sense to me, but it would be years before I felt I had to devote a part of my life to fighting it.

On arriving in Miami Beach, we answered a want ad for a cheap room and rented a car, which, of course, we couldn't drive very well. After a day spent mostly in second gear (automatic transmission was yet to come), we returned the car and spent the rest of our stay on foot and public transportation.

Roy and I easily found jobs as busboys in a cafeteria, and those financed our trips to the Hialeah racetrack and the dog races. As gamblers we were not going to get rich on either the horses or the dogs, but we came close enough to breaking even to treat the cost simply as an entertainment expense. Unfortunately, our jobs didn't pay very well, we couldn't find anything better, and our outgo was exceeding our income. After two weeks, it was time to go home.

Jobs in New York seemed to be scarce in the winter of 1949. I answered a slew of want ads before Mangel Stores finally hired me to work in their warehouse on lower Madison Avenue in Manhattan. When their business went slack, I was laid off. Mangel's personnel manager recommended me to a haberdasher on East Fifty-seventh Street, where I sold shirts, ties, and other men's accessories until it was time to start at Columbia.

II

COLUMBIA COLLEGE

College alumni often appreciate their education in direct proportion to the years that have passed since they experienced it.

The image is tempting: I emerged from the dark of the subway at 116th and Broadway to enter the light of a beautiful September day on the Columbia campus. But my pre-Columbian life had certainly not been dark—though shaded by large zones of ignorance—and my Columbia days were certainly not all bright.

College alumni often appreciate their education in direct proportion to the years that have passed since they experienced it, but I was an appreciative student almost from day one. Day one itself, however, was intimidating. There were choices to be made, meetings to attend, and forms to be filled out. I knew hardly any of my six hundred classmates, so when I saw Marty Rabinowitz, my friend from Bronx Science, I was overjoyed.

Marty had long since forgiven me for getting him into trouble during our senior year. Several of us were launching empty milk containers into the air of the lunch room. When Marty refused to participate, we taunted him mercilessly. Finally, he yielded and got off a beautifully parabolic shot that landed on top of the head of a fragile classmate who ran screaming to the teacher in charge of the lunch room. Marty's mother was summoned to school, but since he was an exemplary student, nothing more was made of it.

Marty and I would move almost in lockstep through both college and law school, and we remain close friends to this day. Our college experience differed, however, in one vital respect. He could afford to live in a dormitory, and I could not.

Columbia's extracurricular life was open to commuters, but traveling back and forth from the Bronx obviously limited the possibilities for me. That didn't stop me from running for freshman class president. I finished thirteenth in a field of sixteen. The winner, remarkable for 1949, was one of the few black men in our class.

Marty and I joined the Debate Council and debated as a team. But this is not a story of medals won and brilliant futures presaged. We were fairly casual about our debates, performing creditably at Princeton and Yale but running into a surprise at Brooklyn Polytechnic Institute (now part of NYU). College debating is not usually a spectator sport. The typical event is attended by a handful of people, including the judges. Marty and I were stunned to find that we were meeting our adversaries in a sizeable Brooklyn Polytech auditorium filled almost to capacity. They were far better prepared, and we lost.

Every student at Columbia College was entitled to a free ticket to football games. Since we could always get another ticket from someone who wasn't going, Saturday afternoons at Baker Field were great cheap dates. And on occasional Saturday nights we could, for five dollars a couple, attend dances with a live band and a headlining vocalist. I still remember a thrilling performance by Edith Piaf. The fact that I was a clumsy dancer didn't stop me from having a good time.

It did, however, keep me from meeting anyone from Barnard. From time to time Barnard and Columbia would host "mixers," where all I had to do was ask a girl to dance. But I couldn't bring myself to do it. When I tell people today that I was once shy, they refuse to believe me, but in that context I was in fact hopelessly so. I needed to meet girls in a more natural environment, like class, but there were no girls in our classes. One year I went so far as to enroll in a Barnard course, but it was cancelled.

It is no accident that I became the Columbia president who admitted women to the College and assured every student the opportunity to live on campus.

Almost everyone I knew was planning to go on to professional school. My mother had hoped I would become a doctor, and my father's illness had engendered fantasies about my discovering a cure for cancer. But I wasn't motivated enough to endure the long slog to become a physician. I enrolled as a prelaw student. Then, as now, that entails no course requirements. Nor did Columbia have a system of majors. To ensure that we did not spend four years taking introductory courses, what Columbia did have was a requirement that we earn sixty maturity credits attached only to advanced courses. We called them puberty credits.

Believing that there is a certain irreducible minimum of history, philosophy, literature, science, and the arts that one must be familiar with to be an educated citizen, the Columbia faculty insisted that its students meet a rigorous set of requirements. A critiqued essay each week during our freshman year offered some hope that we could write respectably. Two years of a foreign language in small sections brought us close to proficiency. Two years of science sought to open the window on that vital sphere of learning.

For my two years of science I chose calculus and psychology. The psychology course included four hours a week in a lab learning about conditioning. We did this by feeding rats in a glass Skinner box, which had a levered bar and a small opening to receive food pellets. The beginning exercise called for us to give the rat a pellet every time it pushed the bar. We were not exactly surprised to find that this caused the rat to push the bar a lot. In fact, as boredom took hold and my mind wandered, I conceived of a cartoon with two rats in a Skinner box, one saying to the other: "Have I got this kid conditioned; every time I hit the bar, he gives me a pellet!" I shared this idea with my friend Richie, who found someone to draw it for *Jester*, the College's humor magazine.

Many years later my daughter Julie called from college to tell me it was in her psychology textbook.

The jewels in Columbia's crown were her Humanities and Contemporary Civilization courses, required offerings once widely emulated in America's colleges and universities. In Literature Humanities, or Lit Hum, as students call it, we read a book a week for an academic year. Over the three-quarters of a century since the course's founding, the selections have changed from time to time. When I looked recently, I found that only four works had been on the reading list every year: Homer's *Iliad*, Aeschylus's *Oresteia*, Sophocles' *Oedipus Rex*, and Dante's *Inferno*. Like the other books in the course, we were asked to read them in the expectation that they would move us and enlighten us about the human condition. We were not to treat them as gospel but as stimulus to reflect, to explore, to discuss intelligently. As I consider these works now, I am struck by how large a role the dysfunctional family plays in classical literature. No wonder the greatest American playwrights of the last century—O'Neill, Miller, and Williams—were similarly obsessed with it. Perhaps the very phrase "dysfunctional family" is redundant.

Music Humanities was a semester's exposure to great works from Bach to Copland along with a sampling of music theory. The instructor of my small section was Jack Beeson, who would become one of America's leading opera composers. I had known nothing of serious music before the course. It became one of the joys of my life. The Humanities semester of art history was not quite so dramatic for me. I had known something of painting and sculpture, but the course broadened and deepened my appreciation, the beginning of a life-long process.

Contemporary Civilization should really be called Foundations of Contemporary Civilization. The year-long course invited us to explore with the great thinkers of the past issues and ideas that continue to concern humankind, including freedom, autonomy, justice, equality, and democracy. The writers and works ranged from the Bible, Plato, and Aristotle to Adam Smith, Alexis de Tocqueville, the Federalist Papers, and on to Darwin, Marx, Nietzsche, and Freud.

All of these courses were taught in small sections—twenty students or so—enabling us to participate fully in discussions.

In the later decades of the twentieth century many universities dropped the mandatory reading of classical works. Others were attacked for forcing the writings of dead, white, Western males on their students. The education I prized was seen by some as an inflexible, irrelevant, masculine, Eurocentric syllabus.

And it is true the traditional offerings do not take account of the interdependence of cultures in the modern world, they miss insights to be gained from comparative study, and they fail to make the most of the interests of many college students, a far more diverse group, I am delighted to say, than in my day.

The answer to these shortcomings is obvious: add to the core curriculum, don't slash it. A first-class program in Western civilization is a thing of beauty. Columbia has complemented it, extending the core to other civilizations and to contemporary issues and contemporary thinkers. That is not a new idea. Columbia has long had a program in Asian Humanities and Asian Civilizations.

A classical education holds dear the idea of a healthy mind in a healthy body, and so the requirements included a course in hygiene and two years of physical education. These were not painful. The physical education program required us to engage in an individual sport, a team sport, and a combat sport. I bowled, played tennis, volleyball, and basketball, and learned how to fence. The alternatives to fencing in the combat-sport category were boxing and wrestling, which made fencing a very popular choice.

Before embarking on the physical education program, we had to pass a swimming test—one hundred yards using any stroke you wished. Not a strong swimmer, I started slowly, was swamped by my classmates' backwash, and flunked. That meant a swimming class for me until I was allowed to retake the test about two weeks later. With the whole pool to myself I was fine.

I was not the only one to flunk swimming. The philosopher and public intellectual Mortimer Adler's failure to pass the test back in the 1920s cost him his bachelor's degree. The Columbia College faculty was finally moved to waive the requirement for him retroactively. More than five decades after earning his Ph.D., Mortimer Adler stood at Commencement with the Columbia College Class of 1983 and at long last received his baccalaureate. Believing that a university's actions should be principled, I searched for a principle to govern what on its face appeared an arbitrary dispensation and ultimately decided that if a Columbia graduate can survive more than half a century without drowning, we should waive the swimming test.

A committee of the College faculty later recommended the complete abolition of the swimming requirement. We don't require courses in driving safety or other life survival skills, the argument went, and since swimming does nothing for the life of the mind, the test should go. To everyone's surprise, the gathering of intellectuals that is the College faculty voted to keep the requirement. And so it is that Columbia College alumni need not confine themselves to dry land.

During my sophomore year I took a basic political science course with an inspiring young teacher named Julian Franklin. That led me to take a seminar with him; my term paper was on President Roosevelt's failed attempts to defeat three congressional opponents in the election of 1938. I did much of my research in newspapers of the period, which were part of a collection dating from the nineteenth century. Housed in the basement of Butler Library, these were not on microfilm or facsimiles; they were the real thing.

With no custodian in sight I was free to browse as the spirit moved me. I read contemporary accounts of Lincoln's assassination and the Spanish American War and then came upon the Daily News of December 9, 1941. The front page held only two words: War Declared. I decided to borrow that edition, and during that evening's rush hour sat on the subway pretending to read the opened paper with the front page visible to all. Nobody paid the slightest attention.

That reminded me of an E. B. White piece in the *New Yorker*'s "Talk of the Town," in which he reported seeing eight elephants walking down Fifth Avenue. "Nobody that we could see paid much attention to them,"

White observed, "People just seemed to say, 'Hmmm, elephants,' and let it go at that. . . . We guess we were the only man in New York surprised to see eight elephants walking down Fifth Avenue."[1]

I hasten to add that I returned that *Daily News* the day after my experiment.

Midway through my junior year I married. Richie and his girlfriend, Myra, had introduced me to Leonore (Lenni) Goodman the previous year. She was a gifted musician, a graduate of the High School of Music and Art, who was studying at Hunter College when we met. If there was a piano at a party, she could be prevailed upon to play Rodgers and Hart, Cole Porter, and other standards of the day while we gathered around the piano and joined her in song. She had a terrific figure and beautiful eyes, and I found her very attractive. The one occasion on which I had persuaded her to go to bed with me (this was the fifties, after all) had resulted in a pregnancy, or so the obstetrician thought. Though I don't think either of us was in love, we cared about each other and decided to marry. (Neither we nor our mothers ever mentioned abortion in the long-ago before *Roe v. Wade*.) Under New York law women were free to marry at eighteen, men at twenty-one. Lenni was nineteen; I was twenty. We enjoyed the idea that I needed my mother's permission, which, despite her misgivings, she gave.

After we wed, it turned out that what Lenni was carrying was not a fetus but ovarian cysts. It seemed to me that to abandon her at that point would be despicable, so we continued to live in the two-bedroom apartment in the east Bronx where I had taken up residence with Lenni, her mother, and her younger brother. Lenni had the recommended surgery, which entailed the removal of one of her ovaries and half of the other. She made a quick recovery and resumed her education at Hunter College.

I spent the summers before and after my junior year as a busboy at the Raleigh Hotel in South Fallsburg, New York, the buckle of the "Borscht Belt," a cluster of resort hotels in the Catskill Mountains where New York Jews would spend all or part of their summers. The work was hard, roughly nine hours a day, seven days a week for ten weeks, but I was able to earn about five hundred dollars for the summer and save almost all of it. I managed to win a like amount in the Sunday night poker games when we were all flush with the week's tips. But Lenni and I still needed subsidies from our mothers (Lenni's father had also died) until she graduated and began teaching school.

In those days, in a program called "professional option," Columbia permitted a College student admitted to one of the university's professional schools to elect to have his first year in that school count as his senior year in the College. College and law school together would then take six years instead of seven. Saving a year's expense and beginning to earn a living a year earlier was irresistible. At that age a year seems a very long time, and a number of my classmates joined me in choosing the professional option.

12

COLUMBIA LAW SCHOOL

Education should be moral as well as intellectual.

Unlike my first day at the College, where I was awash in a sea of strangers, day one at law school was a happy reunion. Not only was I in the company of college classmates, but a number of friends from high school also turned up.

Today, when I tell my students that anyone with a B average at a respectable college could walk into law school back then, I put my credibility at risk. But it was true: the intense competition that attends law school admission today was unheard of in the fifties.

That had two relevant consequences. First, some of my classmates were essentially career shopping. Not having to struggle to get in, they felt free to leave if the work was not to their liking, and a number did. An apocryphal story had an unidentified classmate leaving in frustration over the many differences among states' laws, saying, "I'm going to medical school; cancer is cancer in all fifty jurisdictions."

The other consequence was that some of my classmates were not terribly bright. Some would flunk out: by the time we graduated our entering class of 240 had shrunk to 190. But some of the lesser lights managed to make it and were ultimately turned loose on an unsuspecting public. In fairness, though, a middling intelligence is sufficient for much lawyering, particularly for those who master a narrow specialty and stick to it.

We took all of our classes together in a windowless auditorium in the basement of Butler Library. The seats were equipped with a desklike arm that we would raise to support our books and fold down when it was time to rise. We managed to learn despite the depressing environment.

To prevent us from working after school and encourage us to use the library, the law faculty dictated a class schedule spaced throughout the day: our first class met at ten, the second at one, and the last at four. (We also had classes from ten to twelve on Saturday.) The effect on Marty Rabinowitz and me was enormously wasteful. While we occasionally did some serious work between classes, we spent a lot of those gaps playing cards in his room.

I did my best work at home, despite the presence of Lenni and her mother and brother. I would edit and type the notes I had taken that day and type my briefs of the cases for the next day's classes. On the morning subway ride I would review the work I had prepared for the day. On one occasion a fellow passenger, seeing my Property casebook, asked if I could help her with a problem she had with her landlord. I explained that I wasn't ready for that yet, but that if the case ever got to the Supreme Court of the United States, I'd be glad to help.

Law professors employed a style since made familiar by movies and television. Each of us was called on in turn, asked a question, and then subjected to a probing follow-up about what we had said. We were all supposed to participate "subvocally," as though we were the student being interrogated, and most of us did, particularly since the teacher might call on one of us next. Some professors questioned us gently, even supportively; others were brutal, truly frightening. I doubted the value of intimidation as a pedagogical tool, a doubt confirmed by my later experience as a teacher. I am happy to say that it has largely gone out of style. But the knowledge that one may be called upon in class is a powerful incentive to careful preparation. And I firmly believe in the value of the questioning process, the so-called Socratic dialogue.

Until the end of the first semester the only time we received feedback from our professors was when we were called upon. Our first and only written examinations came at semester's end, and the grades we received would be important determinants of our future.

We had a two-week break at Christmas, then classes resumed for two more weeks, and then we sat for each of our five examinations every other day. I thought it would be a good idea to use that Christmas recess to prepare for the last two weeks of class so that I could free up those two weeks for review and exam preparation. Marty likes to tell how I ruined the later part of his Christmas vacation when I told him I had just about finished my course work.

I was well prepared and fairly confident as I tackled my exams. Though we had been warned that first-year law students were poor judges of their performance, I thought I did well in Contracts, Torts, Civil Procedure, and Legal Method. But portions of the exam in the Development of Legal Institutions were baffling. The course was regarded as Columbia Law School's boot camp, taught by a brilliant scholar whose coursebook was ill suited to first-year law students and whose teaching style was bullying. A typical day in his class began with a handful of students being directed to empty seats in the first row. They would be asked to rise in turn, face their two hundred or so classmates and submit to interrogation about legal principles dating to pre-Tudor times. When the spirit moved him, he would hold "Ladies' Day," and ask only women to take those dreaded seats in the front row.

We were instructed to insert a self-addressed postcard in each of our exam books. As each teacher finished grading, he would have our grades entered on the postcards and mailed to us.

Thank heavens the card from Development of Legal Institutions came first. I was relieved to learn I had earned an A–. Little did I dream it would turn out to be my lowest grade.

As the other postcards dribbled in over the next few weeks, my classmates were abuzz over who was doing well, a buzz fed largely by rumor since there was no public disclosure of grades. People were especially curious about students who had volunteered a lot in class, at least a few of whom sounded impressive. I rarely spoke unless called upon, so my performance was not much noticed. But when all the results were in, my three A+'s, one A, and one A− placed me first in the class, having edged past my most outspoken classmates. I did nothing to keep my performance a secret.

In the middle of that first semester, I had to beg Marty's forgiveness again. When he fell asleep in our Civil Procedure class, I elbowed him and mischievously whispered, "He called on you." Marty sat straight up and said, "Excuse me, Professor. Would you repeat the question?" Our teacher looked baffled since he hadn't asked a question. Marty forgave me: he got a good story out of it. And his grades for the semester were close behind mine.

The second semester yielded five more A's and A+'s, winning me several prizes and assuring my place as first in the class and selection as a Kent Scholar, an honor reserved for the top five students. Marty, not far behind me, was also made a Kent Scholar. Named for James Kent, a distinguished jurist and scholar who delivered the first lectures in law at Columbia, the honor was unfortunately unsullied by a stipend.

Columbia Law School had awarded me a scholarship when I was admitted—$600 a year, which precisely matched the cost of tuition. Since my first year in law school was also my fourth year in college, I had another $350 from my New York State scholarship.

The law school raised tuition to $800 for my second year, but my scholarship stayed at $600. When Harriet Sturtevant Shapiro, a good friend from California, told me she was getting $1,000 a year, I went to see the faculty chairman of the Scholarship Committee. I knew that the school paid a premium to attract students from other parts of the country, but I thought my performance had earned me parity, particularly since my need was at least as great as hers. I was cordially received, but I learned to my surprise that the school was struggling financially. The scholarship budget for the entire student body was only $10,000, and it had all been committed. I was struck by the thought that Harriet and I were getting 16 percent of it.

The university's Placement Office had found me a summer job at the American Laundry Machinery Company, which sold and serviced laundry machines to hospitals, hotels, and other institutions with large-scale laundry requirements. I helped schedule service calls and did some bookkeeping as directed by congenial supervisors. We were within walking distance of the Morgan Library, and I spent many a lunch hour reading there.

My first-year record entitled me to an invitation to serve on the *Columbia Law Review*. Law reviews, the principal scholarly journals in the legal world, are run by students. Each issue contains articles from established scholars, judges, and lawyers alongside work done by the students themselves. Membership is a giant step in a legal career.

My cadre—twenty-three in all—was to start work on July 15. Since I was loathe to give up my summer income, I kept my job and worked nights and weekends on the *Law Review*. It was a tough schedule, but it was made a little easier by Lenni's and my move to an apartment less than a mile from campus. The street was dangerous, so the rent was manageable on my pay during the summer and Lenni's in the fall when she started teaching school. We moved to a slightly better place for my senior year.

The *Law Review* was an excellent learning experience for most of us. We would begin with a casenote, an analysis of a recent decision picked by a third-year editor. We would ultimately produce a note, a substantial work of scholarship covering a significant topic. In each instance we would do the research, write it up, and then submit to an intense one-on-one editing process conducted by third-year students. My note was on the definition of the market in antitrust law, which is a lot more interesting than it sounds. The concept is central to determining whether, for example, a monopoly exists or whether a merger may proceed.

While *Law Review* membership was terrific for those lucky enough to enjoy it, it was not an unalloyed blessing for the school. There was resentment by some who didn't make it, a problem exacerbated by the natural cliquishness that attends exclusive organizations. More importantly, during my years the *Law Review* editors conducted their affairs in such a way as to subvert the school's basic approach to learning.

The Socratic dialogue depends on active student involvement, and most *Law Review* members skipped classes wholesale and rarely participated when they went. To give an example from my own experience, I received an A+ in each of my two semesters in Commercial Transactions even though I attended only a handful of classes during the entire year.

How was that possible? Every course had a team of up to four *Law Review* editors assigned to it. Their job was to attend the classes, distill the class discussion, integrate it with summaries from the coursebook, and distribute it to *Law Review* students signed up for that course. The end product was, in essence, a textbook that could run to several hundred pages. We called them "purples" because they were duplicated on a machine that used purple ink.

Some professors didn't change their offerings much from year to year, and then the purple team was responsible only for whatever updating might be in order. In those classes the purples were particularly insidious because, using the purples from earlier years, the students had answers to the questions the teacher would ask. It is no wonder the faculty outlawed purples only two years later. The only question is why it took them so long.

I acquired a wonderful mentor during my second year. Elliott Evans Cheatham was a gentle, caring teacher close to retirement when I took his Conflict of Laws course. Though not required, its basic themes—the legal implications when transactions and parties are not limited to a single state—were seen as so central to the law that just about everyone took it, usually in the third year. I elected it in my second year and, because I was one of the purple-writing team, attended religiously and prepared thoroughly. (I taught the course a few years later and found our purple immensely helpful.)

After earning an A+ I was invited to visit Professor Cheatham. He told me I had written the best exam of the more than two hundred and that he was mildly surprised that a second-year student could do that. Emboldened, I told him that some day I would like to be a law professor. It was fortuitous that he was the faculty member most active in maintaining relationships with other schools that might be interested in hiring Columbians. The conversation would bear fruit much sooner than I anticipated.

On another visit to Professor Cheatham I was struck by his profound sense of moral responsibility. A college classmate of mine, Jack Molinas, had just been arrested for fixing basketball games. Jack was an extraordinarily gifted athlete who starred first for Columbia and then for the National Basketball Association's Pistons. He was expelled from the NBA for betting on his own team. The fixing charge came next. Years after he finished serving his prison sentence, he was gunned down in front of his home.

The conversation I am remembering took place the day the news of Molinas's arrest broke. The moment remains vivid. Professor Cheatham was standing in front of the window of his office, a chiaroscuro figure in shadow and sunlight, when he said, sadly: "We failed that boy." He believed without reservation that education should be moral as well as intellectual and that Columbia's teachers had let Molinas down. That didn't mean Molinas was to be excused, only that his teachers had also failed in their responsibilities.

That Elliott Cheatham was the most honorable of men did not protect him from student jokes about his name. Not, of course, to his face, but among ourselves the consensus was that he really should find a law partner named Ketcham so that they could form a firm called Ketcham & Cheatham. We heard that Professor Louis Loss of Harvard was the subject of similar conversations: his partner would be named Proffitt.

Professor Cheatham's reaction to Molinas's crime was the most dramatic demonstration of my teachers' ethical sensibilities. Some would address our ethical responsibilities explicitly, others by their examples of public service and other pro bono activities. They reached me: I have no doubt I left law school a better man than the one who entered.

The contrast with my friend Richie's experience in medical school was striking. To my horror, he was taught not to intervene in an accident lest he be sued. Later I came upon a sociological study that found that over the course of their education law students become less cynical and more idealistic while medical students move in the opposite direction.

Though my performance in Conflict of Laws also impressed the seniors on the *Law Review*, they still decided to pass over me when it came time to select my class's editor-in-chief, preferring my friend Harriet and electing me articles editor. They were under no obligation to explain their decision, and no one ever did.

I had two mildly intimidating experiences as articles editor. The first followed upon the death of Justice Robert Jackson. I was rash enough to resist Justice Felix Frankfurter's suggestion that we publish a memorial issue in honor of Jackson. We published only eight issues a year, and I had a considerable backlog of authors seeking space. (Half of each issue was devoted to student work.) I wrote Justice Frankfurter: "As much as we would like to devote to Mr. Justice Jackson the large amount of space he obviously deserves, commitments to important authors make it impossible for us to provide the sort of coverage you suggest. . . . I hope, then, that you will reconsider your reluctance to go it alone, and that you will do Mr. Justice Jackson and ourselves the honor of writing a few words."[1]

Justice Frankfurter was not to be persuaded by a brash student. He replied: "No doubt authors whose contributions have been accepted are 'impatient,' but presumably they are mature and reasonable men and, therefore, would understand that editors are not automata, that planning about intellectual matters is not a mechanical process, and that an event in the history of law like the death of a significant member of the Supreme Court is not to be disregarded because it has not been scheduled."

Ken Jones, who was clerking at the Supreme Court at the time, called to underscore Justice Frankfurter's displeasure. I beat a hasty retreat, munching crow all the way:

Dear Mr. Justice:

Mr. Kenneth Jones was kind enough to call us yesterday to reiterate your dissatisfaction with our stand on the issue of Mr. Justice Jackson. Perhaps we have overestimated our obligation to those authors to whom we have already committed ourselves, and I hope you will forgive our mistaken sense of proportion. . . .

In the end I was forgiven for my "mistaken sense of proportion." Not only did the justice agree to write a foreword for the issue, but I was treated to the following letter:

February 3, 1955

My dear Mr. Sovern:

"It won't write" is an old phrase down here to describe the recalcitrancy of an opinion to get itself on paper. I do not think I ever attempted a piece of writing that was so stubbornly resistant as my attempt to say something briefly about Mr. Justice Jackson. There are two reasons for this. One is the discretion under which I labor as a member of the Court; the other, my deep feeling about the late Justice. My trouble is not want of things to say but freedom in saying them. Writing under wraps is not conducive to writing.

I am troubling you with my difficulties in order to explain what may seem to you an absurd delay in sending you the promised little piece. While I could talk by the hour about Mr. Justice Jackson I find myself constrained as I do in writing something that may take only a few minutes to read. The point of this letter is to tell you that you ought not to hold up the pagination of your leading articles to await my small Foreword. What I shall finally send you will, I know, absorb three pages. This assurance will I hope enable you to go ahead without further delay and at the same time enable me to stew some more in my own difficulty.

Cordially yours,
Justice Felix Frankfurter

Note the closing: no longer was the Justice only "Sincerely" mine. And the issue turned out to be one of the best for which I was responsible.[2]

Jackson was a great subject—a small-town lawyer (Jamestown, New York) who rose to be attorney general of the United States and then a justice of the Supreme Court. He was also the chief prosecutor at the Nuremberg war crimes trials, an assignment he managed by taking an almost unprecedented leave of absence from the Supreme Court. He also could be funny: when an advocate before the court discovered to his great joy that Jackson as attorney general had issued an opinion taking precisely the position the advocate was urging, he made a point of invoking it; Jackson replied: "I am amazed that a man of my intelligence should have been guilty of giving such an opinion."[3] And he could craft phrases with the best of them. In *Michelson v. United States*, responding to an argument that one aspect of a much criticized rule should be reformed, he wrote: "To pull one misshapen stone out of the grotesque structure is more likely . . . to upset its present balance . . . than to establish a rational edifice."[4] All of this made it relatively easy to recruit first-rate people to write about him. Years later, one of them—Telford Taylor, who was also a Nuremberg prosecutor and who wrote the portion of the issue about that aspect of Jackson's career—would become my colleague, friend, and tennis partner.

My other brush with authority came when I brought a heavy editor's pen to an article by Professor Walter Gellhorn. Gellhorn was one of Columbia's giants. Much honored for his scholarly shaping of the unruly field of administrative law, he also wrote about the Swedish ombudsman and was responsible for bringing that institution to America.

After Cheatham retired, it was Gellhorn who placed Columbians in teaching positions all over America. This was a natural evolution: he was already serving as a one-man placement office for his students. One of his notable placements was a response to Thurgood Marshall's search for an assistant when he was head of the NAACP Legal Defense Fund. Gellhorn offered Jack Greenberg, a young Navy veteran and recent graduate, who would ultimately succeed Marshall and argue dozens of cases before the Supreme Court.

We were delighted to publish a piece by Gellhorn. My working it over was not a mark of disrespect. It may seem presumptuous for a third-year student to be editing a giant, but that was the nature of the *Law Review*. After receiving his edited article, Gellhorn telephoned me: "Mr. Sovern, I'd like to talk to you about *your* article." Clearly, only one of us thought I had improved his work. But he didn't pull rank and club me into submission. He deputized a young collaborator of his to go over the article with me section by section. Some of my changes actually survived.

Professor Arthur Nussbaum, a great scholar, who came to Columbia as a refugee from Nazi Germany, found the American law review tradition seriously defective. He complained that it was not "pleasant for a mature scholar to be subjected to the supreme and irrevocable judgment of incompletely trained students."[5] When, as a twenty-three-year-old assistant professor, I submitted a piece to the *Columbia Law Review* and an editor from the class following mine changed a few words, I drew upon Professor Nussbaum, lamenting that an "incompletely trained student" was presuming to edit the work of a "mature scholar."

When editing an article, I often worked at home, not appearing at the *Law Review* office for several days. One day I arrived at the office to find a message from Professor Cheatham: he had arranged for me to meet the dean of the Minnesota Law School. To my great embarrassment the appointment was for the previous day. I called Cheatham at once and apologized profusely. He kindly told me not to worry about it: Dean Maynard Pirsig would be passing through New York again in several days and he would arrange a fresh appointment.

When I had told Professor Cheatham about my ambition to be a law professor, I was thinking several years into the future. I had hoped that on graduation I would receive a Supreme Court clerkship, spend two or three years with a law firm, and then make my move. My breakfast with Dean Pirsig was the beginning of the end of that plan. He invited me to meet the rest of the faculty when they came to New York in December for the Association of American Law Schools convention. Then, early in the new year, I received an offer of an assistant professorship at the grand salary of $5,000 per year. (Wall Street was paying $4,000 to $4,200.)

I asked whether they would wait a year if I received a Supreme Court clerkship. I had already been interviewed by Justice Clark, for whom my friend Ken Jones was clerking, and was scheduled for interviews with two other justices. No, I was told, they needed someone right away. I agonized. A Supreme Court clerkship was a superb educational and professional experience. I was not at risk of unemployment if it failed to materialize. I had a dream offer from the Paul Weiss law firm to litigate with the superstar Simon Rifkind and work with the dean of the theatrical bar, John Wharton, and they were willing to await the outcome of my Supreme Court quest.

So I called Ken Jones. Any chance of an early decision from Justice Clark? No, he still had a number of applicants to see. I went to see Professor Cheatham. He shared three thoughts with me. One, the Minnesota Law School was a very good place. Two, these offers do not come along every day. And three, do not accept it in the expectation that it would necessarily lead to an invitation to return to Columbia. Lots of good men, he said, never get that call.

That was close to the heart of the matter. What I really wanted to know was which decision was more likely to lead back to Columbia. And no one, including me, could answer that question. I accepted Minnesota's offer.

It's a rare student who finds the final semester of law school exciting. I was not that rarity, though I held my first place in the class to the end, winning the John Ordronaux Prize for that accomplishment. When Professor Robert Anthoine saw me looking at the bulletin board that declared me the winner, he said, "You know, you almost didn't win that prize. When I first read your exam I thought it was a B." "And then," I replied, "you read it again and saw its true merit?" "No," he said, "I read the other papers."

The Ordronaux Prize was named for an early member of the faculty who was more eccentric than most. According to *A History of the School of Law*, "He would sometimes sleep with his head in a bandbox, to outwit the bats that might get into his hair." I was glad to get the prize anyway, particularly since it included a modest cash award.

The most memorable feature of Commencement was the chance to introduce my mother to Professor Cheatham. He was, as always, gracious and she was thrilled.

The bar exam was scheduled for the last two days in June, and the cram course had already begun when we were graduated early that month. Audiotapes were available for the missed sessions, and the rest of the month was nonstop review via lectures and texts.

The night before the first day of the exam I resolved to go to bed at eleven and get a good night's sleep. My brain refused to shut down: the last time I looked at the clock before falling asleep, it was four-thirty a.m. I slept through the alarm.

I awoke thirty minutes before the exam was to begin, hopped into my clothes, and was out of our apartment on 110th Street in five minutes. I explained my plight to a sympathetic taxi driver: if I was not downtown at Vesey Street within twenty-five minutes I was doomed. No one would be admitted to the exam once it began. With moves worthy of the Indianapolis 500, he got me there on time.

The application form for the bar exam included a space for employment. In a flush of pride over my new job, I filled in: "Assistant Professor, University of Minnesota Law School." When I reached Minnesota, I found a letter from the bar examiners awaiting me. How had I fulfilled the residence requirement for the New York State bar examination while working in Minnesota? I returned the affidavit they requested, swearing under oath that I had been a New York resident, and that straightened the matter out.

13

MINNESOTA

Over the years the thought that it's hard for others to
tell when I don't know what I'm talking about has been
a great source of comfort.

Three days after the bar exam Lenni and I left for Minnesota
with everything we owned packed into a 1949 Chevrolet sedan
purchased for $350. Earlier that year I had learned to drive again: this
time my instructor was my sister Denise, and I passed the road test
without any illicit help.

With a six-year old car, membership in the AAA with its excellent
road service was a must. When I visited AAA headquarters in Manhattan to transfer my membership from New York to Minneapolis, I
was told at first that they weren't sure the Minneapolis branch accepted
Jews. This was 1955; Hitler had been dead for ten years. I knew Minneapolis had a bad history, but I thought Hubert Humphrey had shaped
the place up when he was mayor. I was right. The initial reaction to my
transfer request turned out to be a false alarm.

We spent the summer house-sitting for a colleague in a beautiful
modern home overlooking one of Minnesota's ten thousand lakes. One
evening, upon returning from dinner at a neighbor's, we found a ladder propped up against a second-story window. Rushing back to the
neighbors, we called the police. They responded within what seemed

two minutes. With guns drawn, they went to confront the intruder, who turned out to be our landlord's son. He had returned early from his summer holiday without his keys. Fortunately, our rescuers were not trigger happy, and no harm was done.

I had three courses to prepare for the coming academic year. As junior man I was assigned the classes no one else wanted to teach— Agency, Forms of Action, and Creditors' Remedies. As a student I had taken only one of them. I was also to serve as faculty advisor to the *Law Review*.

The *Columbia Law Review* hadn't had a faculty advisor, so I wasn't quite sure what the role entailed. It turned out to be a delight. The student editors were, of course, my contemporaries. Some, in fact, were older than I. They assumed, with perhaps a modicum of justice, that a Columbia education was superior to theirs and that I would have something to teach them. My memories of my faculty advisor days, however, are less of wisdom imparted than of friendships formed. One of those friendships was with a senior law student named Walter F. Mondale. Decades later I would accept his invitation to help him prepare for his presidential campaign debates against Ronald Reagan.

Creditors' Remedies, the one course I had taken as a student, also proved to be the only one that interested me. Forms of Action was an antiquarian relic: after teaching it once, I recommended its abolition, and my colleagues concurred. The subject of Agency was too easy to warrant a whole course, and many law schools have since dropped it as well. At the time I hadn't yet acquired the perspective to make that judgment.

I spent the summer of 1955 preparing for my fall classes. My confidence was buttressed by an experience I had two years before. Professor Robert K. Webb had invited me to serve as reader in his Columbia College class in British constitutional history. The post entailed grading papers and giving an occasional lecture. I asked if I might share the responsibilities with Marty Rabinowitz, and Professor Webb agreed. In due course I gave my first lecture, and Marty volunteered the following appraisal: "I know you don't know much about the subject; you know that too—but that was very impressive." Over the years the thought that it's hard for others to tell when I don't know what I'm talking about has been a great source of comfort.

A few days before classes were to begin at Minnesota, I managed to shake my confidence. I took a look at the classroom in which I was scheduled to teach. It was an intimidating sight, a large room with about two hundred seats rising in raked rows to what seemed a great height. My place would be in the well, looking up at 180 first-year students.

Happily, the anxiety that sight induced passed as I began to teach them. I still had a long way to go to become the teacher I wanted to be, but my students and colleagues gave my performance high marks. In that first year I taught my students 100 percent of what I knew; as the years went by and my knowledge grew, that percentage would fall lower and lower.

I have always subscribed to the Socratic style of teaching, and while I am happy to call on students who volunteer, I believe it is vitally important to call on students who do not volunteer. The practice motivates careful preparation and tends to keep everyone awake. And I've discovered, particularly with first-year classes, that once called upon, many a student who was originally too shy to volunteer becomes an eager participant.

Today I use a seating chart with names and pictures, which helps me get to know at least some of my students. In 1955, at Minnesota I was lucky to get a class list by the end of the first week. A colleague advised, "just call on Olsen, Anderson, and Johnson; you'll have enough of those to get you through the first week." And I did.

A good law faculty is wonderfully collegial. Though I was a lowly assistant professor and all of my colleagues were full professors, I was welcomed as an equal participant in the affairs of the school. This was most striking in our search for a new dean. (Maynard Pirsig was forced out after losing the confidence of the faculty.) I joined in the interviewing of decanal candidates, distinguished scholars and deans of other schools. Whatever they may have thought on encountering a twenty-three-year-old novice playing a role in the search process, they kept it to themselves.

I also found myself a member of the university's Faculty Senate. Each of the university's constituent schools and faculties was entitled to elect one senator for every ten associate and full professors and one for every forty assistant professors or fraction thereof. As the law school's only assistant professor, I was the "fraction thereof." And even if I had been humble enough to vote for somebody else, there was nobody else.

The regular exposure to my elders offered a painless education. In fact, I felt like a favorite nephew of my law school colleagues, the youngest of whom was thirty-five. I lunched regularly with several of them at the faculty club and about once a month went off campus for a really good lunch with two men who became my close friends—Monrad Paulsen and Kenneth Davis.

Ken, a highly disciplined scholar in his late forties, was working on a multivolume treatise on administrative law that would become a leading work in the field. Monrad and I would never dream of trying to tempt him into a long lunch during the week, but on Saturdays we thought he was fair game. Yielding to our entreaties to join us, he would threaten to include us in the credits for his treatise along these lines: "To Monrad Paulsen and Mike Sovern, without whom I would have finished this work a year earlier." Years later, after the treatise had become enormously influential, Ken paid me the supreme compliment of inviting me to be the author of succeeding editions. By then my scholarship had taken a different direction. I declined with warm thanks.

Distance is a great eroder of friendships. After I moved back to Columbia, Ken and I stayed in touch, and I visited with him after he moved to the University of Chicago, but the years and the miles separating us proved too much, and we stopped writing. My friendship with Monrad was more enduring. In the middle of my first year in Minnesota, he was considered for a possible invitation to the Columbia faculty and I for the University of Pennsylvania faculty. We sweated out the post-interview interval together and then counseled with each other after the offers arrived. Before accepting Columbia's offer, he asked them to increase it by $500, which they did. He explained to me that, at thirty-five, he could reasonably expect to teach another thirty years and that the extra $500 in his base might well be worth $15,000.

Monrad, a memorable figure, was about six-foot-five and 240 pounds when he was in reasonably good shape, crowned with a full head of hair as yellow as the corn from his native Iowa. Later, Columbia's students came up with the perfect nickname: they called him the Great White Whale.

Before the Pennsylvania faculty asked me to meet with them, they had, of course, asked my Minnesota colleagues what they thought of me. With that notice of Pennsylvania's interest, the Minnesota faculty decided upon a preemptive strike. Not long after my twenty-fourth birthday, I was informed that I was to be promoted to associate professor with tenure and that my salary would be increased by 50 percent to $7,500 per year. Minnesota's extraordinary expression of confidence, buttressed by Monrad's assurance that he would work toward a Columbia invitation for me, led me to decline the Pennsylvania offer. I did it as gracefully as I could, and it must have been graceful enough because they invited me again the following year.

While we were still at Minnesota, Monrad and I collaborated on a *Columbia Law Review* article that proved to be an important work— "'Public Policy' in the Conflict of Laws."[1] And I managed to succeed him in teaching the Conflict of Laws course, an offering he used to characterize as the queen of the curriculum. I didn't have to go that far to be delighted to substitute it for Forms of Action and Agency.

During my Minnesota years I wrote two other pieces. One was a technical article in the creditors' remedies field that is memorable for me only because, in the course of researching it, I came upon my paternal grandfather's bankruptcy. Though my father also went broke, I thought it unlikely that I had a genetic predisposition for financial overextension. My other work was a book review of Telford Taylor's *Grand Inquest*, a superb study of congressional investigations. Happily, I could give it a highly favorable review.[2]

I have written only one book review since—an elegant but nasty piece of work in the administrative law field that appeared in the *Columbia Law Review* in 1959.[3] Years later I would read it and wince at its heartless cruelty. I have never thought of myself as arrogant, or for that matter have I been accused of arrogance, but that review was an arrogant piece of work. I regret it. But that isn't why I have never returned to the genre. First-rate book reviews are serious scholarly efforts, but they tend to get lost in the legal literature. In that world a scholar's time is better devoted to books and articles.

My Minnesota years were especially significant for the birth of our first child—my son Jeffrey. Since we wanted children but Lenni had only half an ovary left after her surgery, we decided we had better get on with it. Lenni went into labor during Christmas dinner at Ken Davis's home, and Jeff emerged the following day.

During my first year at Minnesota we had two salaries—Lenni taught second grade in a St. Paul school—plus an additional stipend I received for teaching a summer class. For the 1955–1956 academic year we earned just about $10,000. That was all we had, having exhausted our slender savings by the time we received our first paychecks. But we managed to attend movies, an occasional concert, and a little live theater (the Guthrie hadn't been founded yet), dine out from time to time, and add a piano and television set to our furnished apartment. Our 1949 Chevrolet occasionally failed to start during the long Minnesota winter, but we lived only half a mile from campus and, properly bundled up, I could easily walk back and forth. I even managed the walk the day the temperature dropped to seventeen below zero. Lenni, lacking a driver's license, took the bus.

Minnesota was the third state in which I took a driving test, and, though I had driven from New York without incident, I flunked. Since the grace period on my New York license hadn't expired, I could keep driving until I passed on my second try. (I always got a 100 on the written test.)

During our second academic year we had to make do without Lenni's salary, but fortunately my raise closed most of the gap, and our only capital expenditure was the purchase of a crib. In the middle of the year, Bill Warren, the dean of the Columbia Law School, called to offer a one-year appointment as a visiting assistant professor at the same salary I was already earning—$7,500 a year. Following Monrad's example, I asked for and got an additional $500, but there was nothing to be done about the less than exalted rank I was being offered. I was, after all, only twenty-four years old and a year and a half out of law school. I may have been prodigious, but not that prodigious.

My Minnesota colleagues graciously granted me a leave of absence so that I could return if I wished, and I accepted Columbia's invitation. Everyone, including me, assumed Columbia would ultimately invite me to stay, but my time at Minnesota was so satisfying that none of us ruled out the possibility that I might choose to return. My remaining months at Minnesota, therefore, continued as a time of warm collegiality uncontaminated by a feeling that I had rejected my friends.

14

COMING HOME

I received a dramatic lesson in professional ethics.

In August Columbia arranged a two-bedroom apartment for us on 120th Street and Amsterdam Avenue, a four-block walk to the law school. We shipped our piano and television set, Lenni and our eight-month-old son Jeff flew home, and I set forth, accompanied by our remaining belongings, in our aging Chevrolet.

Most of the Columbia faculty were old enough to be my father, some old enough to be my grandfather, but collegiality, here as in Minnesota, was the order of the day. We were all on a first-name basis, strained as that sometimes felt when I was addressing a former teacher.

I was to teach Administrative Law and two sections of Evidence. Administrative Law was all new for me—I had skipped it as a student—but Walter Gellhorn, who had written the book for the course, had also written a superb teacher's manual that got me through. Though I would never teach the course again, I was glad to fill a significant gap in my education. As one of the authors of the Evidence purple, I was better prepared for that assignment.

It was good to be reunited with Monrad, who helped ease the transition into my new world. We were not the only ex-Minnesotans on the Columbia faculty—Charlie Meyers had been a visiting professor two years before me. He and Monrad were very close, and Monrad was delighted when Charlie and I hit it off, since people one chooses for friends don't necessarily choose to be friends with one another. Charlie was from Texas, and when I introduced him to a Jewish delicatessen on the Upper West Side, his Texas accent applied to the ordering of hot pastrami gave the waiters special pleasure.

No one could have predicted that all three of us would become law school deans—Charlie at Stanford (by then he was known by the more dignified Charles); Monrad at Virginia, from which he would go on to found Yeshiva's law school; and I at Columbia.

My visiting status at Columbia meant that the faculty would have to decide by the middle of the year whether to tender me a regular appointment. In due course they did—an associate professorship without tenure at a salary of $8,500. For its time the salary was not bad, but I already had tenure at Minnesota, and it seemed to me that Columbia should have matched that. To complicate matters, Minnesota countered with an offer of a full professorship at $10,000. Not bad for a twenty-six-year-old and, with a second child—my daughter Beth—on the way, that $1,500 mattered.

Monrad and Charlie assured me that an award of tenure was only a matter of time, a few years at most, and that, as a member of the Columbia faculty, I would have ample opportunities to supplement my income with all sorts of moonlighting assignments. Monrad made good on that prediction almost at once, inviting me to share in a project he and Walter Gellhorn were working on for the New York State legislature. The topic was the inadequacy of state regulation of private investigators. My enduring memory of that study was how little resemblance the typical private eye bore to the heroes of film noir. A dull, marginal subsistence was the best most could manage.

My friends' assurances about tenure would have been more comforting had they not also admitted that there were a couple of older faculty who were concerned about the faculty becoming "too Jewish." The world had improved enough so that no one would dare say that in an open faculty meeting, but the old boys could still say it privately to one another. Monrad and Charlie were emphatic that the anti-Semitism was a vestigial remnant that would have no effect on my future.

My friends at Minnesota insisted that we come for a short visit to talk about possibilities, and so Lenni and I returned for what proved to be a two-day love fest. In addition to its superior offer, Minnesota had arranged an invitation for a summer job at an excellent Minneapolis law firm so that I could begin to have some first-hand experience practicing law. On my return to New York I received a movingly affectionate letter from my friend Ken Davis, in which he emphasized how important I was to Minnesota and how, as good as I was, I could never matter as much to Columbia. I treasure that bit of failed prophecy.

As tempting as it was to return to the warmth of Minnesota (metaphorically speaking), Columbia was clearly the right choice for me. The University of Minnesota and its law school were excellent institutions, but Columbia was far stronger, the twin cities were not remotely comparable to New York and, of course, my family and countless friends would be nearby. In fact, had Columbia included tenure in its offer, there would have been no issue.

When I told Dean Warren that Minnesota had arranged for me to spend the summer at a local law firm, he responded by calling Milton Handler, a Columbia colleague who was also a senior partner at Kaye, Scholer, Fierman, Hays and Handler. Milton was happy to have his firm take me on for the summer.

There remained only the question of what I would teach now that I was to be a regular member of the faculty. The law school had recently begun offering more than one section of large courses, a practice that opened up a number of possibilities for a new boy. I enjoyed teaching Evidence, so I wanted to keep a section of that. I had taken the Labor Law course with Paul Hays, who had made it seem fascinating. Besides, I could follow his example and supplement income by arbitrating labor disputes. Beyond those two courses, the school needed me to teach half a section of Torts and share a seminar for foreign students. I gave up the Torts course when I received two irresistible invitations—one from Paul

Hays to share his collective bargaining seminar, an opportunity to learn from a master; the other from Walter Gellhorn to share his seminar in legal education, a chance to explore the nature of teaching and learning with one of our greats.

The summer gave me an idea of what the big firm practice of law was like. As, in a sense, Milton Handler's guest, I was treated with special consideration. The firm's labor law partners spent more time with me than they would have with an ordinary associate, and I was exposed to a broader range of problems than a summer associate would usually encounter. My work with the labor law group ended when I was tapped to join Milton Handler's antitrust team, an experience that also advanced my education.

One memory stands out. I was sitting in the office of Stanley Robinson, a young partner, when he took a call from a client seeking his advice. Stanley told him that what he was planning was a clear violation of law. The client apparently indicated that he was going to do it anyway. At that point Stanley told him that if he did that, he would cease to be his lawyer. I don't know what the client ultimately did, but I do know that I had just received a dramatic lesson in professional ethics.

The summer of 1958 also saw the birth of my daughter Beth. It was time to start looking for a larger apartment.

I didn't get much writing done during my first two years at Columbia. Preparing all those new courses was nearly a full-time job, and Paul Hays was introducing me to the labor law world. I couldn't have asked for a more thoughtful mentor. His life was busy enough without looking after me. He used to joke that the *New York Times* thought he was three people. Its index listed Paul R. Hays, the academic; Paul R. Hays, the head of the Liberal Party, then a mildly left-of-center third party in New York State; and Paul R. Hays, the labor arbitrator. But he found the time to get me appointed to the City Bar Association's Labor Law Committee, to arrange a committee co-chairmanship in the American Bar Association's Labor Law Section, and to persuade the New Jersey Board of Mediation to place me on its list of arbitrators. Later he would help me get on the arbitrator lists of the Federal Mediation Service and the American Arbitration Association. Having my name on all those lists did not necessarily mean that anyone would pick me to hear their disputes, but the bar association activity would introduce me to a lot of the people who did the picking.

We would have almost five years as colleagues, and he was generous to me throughout. Sharing his collective bargaining seminar, I learned almost as much from him as our students did. The students' final assignment was a term paper that they were instructed to leave in Paul's mailbox. Collegiality at Columbia extended to elders' sharing the workload with their junior colleagues, so it didn't surprise me that Paul didn't dump all those papers in my lap, but he gave me only six of the thirteen submissions. I protested that I should take the seventh paper. Paul replied that he had tossed a coin to decide who should have to grade it and he had lost.

By the end of my second year I had my new courses under control, my arbitration practice was still in its infancy, and my summer was free. I accepted the invitation of Maurice Rosenberg, a senior colleague, to join him on a research project designed to learn more about "Delay and the Dynamics of Personal Injury Litigation," the title of the resulting article we would publish in the *Columbia Law Review*.[1] The experience taught me a little about judicial administration and a lot about empirical research, but it left me with no appetite to go further with either.

During my third year back at Columbia, the faculty decided I was worthy and granted me tenure. They combined it with a pleasant surprise, promoting me to full professor. On July 1, 1960, at the age of twenty-eight, I became the youngest full professor in Columbia's modern history.

In 1965, the *New York Times* mistakenly conferred that honor on my worthier friend, the Nobel laureate T. D. Lee. Monrad Paulsen wrote to correct the record:

You recently reported [July 15] Columbia University's promotion of Dr. Harry B. Gray, 29 years and eight months, to the rank of full professor, and noted he was probably the second-youngest full professor in the university's modern history.

Your story gives first place in the beardless youth division of Columbia's professoriat to Dr. Tsung-Dao Lee, the Nobel Prize–winning physicist, who received his full professorship at the age of 29 years two months. I write to correct and amplify your archives on Columbia's professorial toddlers.

First, the laurel for precocity properly belongs to neither Dr. Lee nor Dr. Gray but, probably to my colleague, Michael I. Sovern, whose appointment as full professor became effective when he was 28 years seven months and four hours old.

Second, your story neglected to mention Professor Gray's address, which was also Professor Lee's address until he vacated the apartment into which Professor Sovern moved about the time of his promotion. A close examination of the elevator in the old building has shown it capable of providing adequate service, but nothing to account for the rapid ascent of three of the tenants.[2]

15

PUBLISHING AND MOONLIGHTING

Walter Gellhorn said, "Mike, you have to understand, power cor-rupts but the absence of power corrupts absolutely."

T he years following my promotion were productive, yielding ar-ticles on the tension between the jurisdiction of the National Labor Relations Board and the courts to enforce collective bargaining agreements (*Harvard Law Review*), on labor and the antitrust laws (*Labor Law Journal*), and on the National Labor Relations Act and racial discrimination (*Columbia Law Review*).[1]

Monrad was helpful yet again. He and his wife, Elsa, had become friends with Adolf and Beatrice Berle. Beatrice was a fascinating and accomplished woman, and Adolf was a brilliant scholar and statesman. He wrote the classic work on the modern corporation with Gardiner Means,[2] served as assistant secretary of state under FDR, and had also been ambassador to Brazil.

In the 1960s Adolf was practicing law and serving as chairman of the Twentieth Century Fund. I had taken the Corporations course with him, but the enrollment was well over a hundred students, and he and I had never met. He was important to my work now because I thought the Twentieth Century Fund might support a project I was considering. Monrad arranged an introduction, and Adolf seemed receptive: he advised me to submit a proposal for staff consideration and set up an appointment for me with August Heckscher, the president of the foundation.

My proposal was ultimately approved, and I received a $25,000 grant to write a book with the working title *Legal Restraints on Racial Discrimination in Employment.* In the end neither I nor anyone at the foundation managed to think of a better name, so that lumpy formulation became the actual title of my first book.

The foundation grant provided me with a summer stipend and research support. Walter Gellhorn, knowing I was shopping for a research assistant, suggested I hire Jack Greenberg, Thurgood Marshall's number two at the NAACP Legal Defense Fund. The fund couldn't afford to pay very well, so Jack was allowed to supplement his income by moonlighting. Jack became and still is a close friend.

Jack Greenberg was a highly regarded civil rights lawyer, part of the team that argued the school segregation cases that became known simply as *Brown v. Board of Education.* He was very helpful to me, but only for a little while. Not long after taking office, President Kennedy appointed Thurgood Marshall to the Court of Appeals for the Second Circuit, and Jack was soon selected to succeed him as head of the Legal Defense Fund, a job that left him no time for my project.

President Kennedy had other things on his mind than my book project, but he did hit me with a one-two punch. He accompanied the Marshall appointment with the appointment of Paul Hays to the same court. On top of losing my research assistant, I now had to teach Paul's section of Labor Law in addition to my own.

To make matters worse, I had underestimated the difficulty of my project and took on yet another assignment. Walter Gellhorn, again looking out for a younger colleague, introduced me to Anthony Savarese, who had just been named the Republican chairman of New York State's Joint Legislative Committee on Industrial and Labor Conditions. This was a new and important assignment for Tony, and he wasn't content to rely on his politically appointed staff: he wanted to retain a labor law expert as special counsel. The job was a great chance to experience the legislative process up close, and the money would come in handy. I accepted Tony's offer. The committee over which he presided was unusual, almost unique: it was truly bipartisan, consisting of equal numbers of Democrats and Republicans and members of both the State Senate and Assembly.

My first assignment was to make recommendations to address the problem of labor unrest in New York City's nonprofit hospitals. For several years strikes and threats of strikes that could put patients at risk had caused widespread public concern. Hospital workers were an anomalous group, one covered by neither the federal nor the state labor relations act. They depended on their organizational strength to extract concessions from employers.

Minnesota had embarked on a promising experiment. That state's labor relations law included hospital workers but added a special wrinkle: strikes by hospital workers were barred; either the union or the employer could invoke compulsory arbitration to resolve a dispute. I arranged a series of interviews with union, management, and government officials in Minnesota, and Tony and I flew there to take a closer look.

While we were en route President Kennedy announced the presence of Soviet missiles in Cuba and his decision to quarantine the island. Since there wasn't much we could do about that, Tony and I went about our business and ultimately concluded that we would recommend the Minnesota approach for New York. We issued our report as 1962 was drawing to a close, and the following year the New York State Legislature enacted a law similar to Minnesota's.

My second assignment concerned collective bargaining for government workers, a much thornier subject. The law at the time penalized government workers for striking, but the sanctions were rarely imposed. No one was disposed to grant the right to strike, but the question of what to do about illegal strikes was highly divisive.

I remember one committee meeting that seemed interminable because members would frequently ask that we pause while they sought instructions from their political leaders. When I told Walter Gellhorn of my frustration at this, he said, "Mike, you have to understand, power corrupts, but the absence of power corrupts absolutely."

In the end the committee's work turned out to be irrelevant. Governor Rockefeller sought the advice of George Taylor, a leading labor mediator, and proposed a tough new law with serious financial penalties for both the strikers and their union. When enacted, it was called the Taylor Law because, it was said, the governor certainly didn't want it called the Rockefeller Law.

My hope that I would learn a great deal from the committee assignment was vindicated. In addition to learning something about my labor law specialty, I developed a new skill—legislative drafting. But most important was the chance to see the legislative process from the inside. I found ample evidence to support a cynical view—no-show jobs for the politically faithful, legislators who knew little or nothing about what they were voting for—but I also met decent people seeking to do a responsible job. Tony Savarese was such a man. We had a simple working relationship: I would tell him what I believed was the best thing to do, and he would tell me what he thought was politically feasible. A liberal Republican, he was ultimately defeated for reelection to the State Assembly by a candidate who managed to secure the endorsements of the Democratic and Conservative parties.

My family life was, to say the least, not uneventful during this period. My son Douglas was born in 1961, and Lenni and I came to a parting of ways in 1963. She soon remarried, and so did I—to Eleanor Leen, who would enroll in law school and become my student.

The book project was suffering, but by working most weekends I was able to move it along. I was learning that writing a book is exponentially more difficult than writing an article, particularly when one is exploring multiple sources of law. When I began work on the book, there was no federal statute barring discrimination in employment. There was a presidential order and possibilities in the National Labor Relations Act that could be mined. (This last would yield an article for the *Columbia Law Review* as well as a chapter in the book.) But most of the relevant material was to be found in different state laws.

In 1964, as I was finishing, it began to appear that Congress might actually pass a law barring discrimination in employment. The good news was that I had the opportunity to publish the first book analyzing the new statute. The bad news was that my book would be delayed yet again. I would come to regard the question, "How's your book coming?" as hostile. But finish I did, to highly favorable reviews in the *Harvard* and *Columbia Law Reviews*.[3] The *University of Chicago Law Review* dedicated a lengthy article to the book, which the author judged inadequate because, among other reasons, he had "grave doubts about the wisdom of fair employment programs generally."[4] Several friends urged me to write a reply, but I had lived long enough with that work. It was time to move on.

Along the way I had, however, invented the least imitated innovation in publishing. My manuscript was copiously footnoted. As a reader of similarly documented works, I had always found footnotes a frustrating experience. On the bottom of the page they could be a distraction; in the rear of the chapter or the book they were difficult to access. My solution was to place them in a separate pamphlet nestled in a pocket in the inside cover of the book. The interested reader could simply place it alongside the book and refer to it as desired; the reader uninterested in sources and digressions could read on without distraction. In the more than forty years since, I have never seen my invention copied.

Though I had no interest in replying to a critic of the book, I was happy to share my analysis of Title VII, the employment section of the Civil Rights Act of 1964, with the cooperating attorneys of the NAACP Legal Defense Fund. Jack Greenberg, now the head of the fund, would, from time to time, gather virtually all the civil rights attorneys in America for a long weekend of education. I was the member of his pickup faculty who specialized in employment discrimination. We would meet at Airlie Lodge, a conference center in Warrenton, Virginia, about an hour's drive from Washington. My fellow faculty were outstanding professors and practitioners who would share insights on desegregating education, equalizing public services, federal procedure, criminal law, housing discrimination, and more.

I obviously learned a great deal sitting in on these presentations, but getting to know the civil rights lawyers was an even more enriching experience. Almost all were African American and most were from the South, some living in communities where there was an ever-present risk that violence would be directed at those who dared challenge the racial status quo. Their quiet courage was complemented by an ability to live with outrage without exploding. One lawyer told me, for example, how uncomfortable it was to drive to our meeting when there was no "colored" bathroom anywhere on his route through the South. But the anger I assumed he must have felt did not show in the telling.

These were old-style lawyers in the sense that they would deal with any problem brought to them. Even those who were the only black lawyer in town weren't about to get rich from their practices.

The conferences were organized by my friend and Columbia colleague Marvin Frankel. When he was appointed to the bench in 1965, Marvin suggested that I assume responsibility for future gatherings, and Jack Greenberg happily concurred. For the next ten years or so I put together the ad hoc faculty that taught the cooperating attorneys and presided at their get-togethers. We soon added attorneys from the new War on Poverty program of the Johnson administration and held sessions as often as six times a year. We also varied the venue, adding Fort Lauderdale and Lake Tahoe to our meeting places. (I said that our motto should be: "Doing good works in nice places.") Jack assigned a young attorney to serve as my part-time assistant and paid me an honorarium of $6,500 a year.

On one occasion we were visited by Dick Gregory, a civil rights activist and for a time a popular comic. Gregory came to Airlie for a consultation with his lawyers, but when I offered him the microphone he accepted with alacrity. The targets of his humor that day included J. Edgar Hoover and his own attorneys, whom he berated for always telling him he shouldn't do what he was planning. "If the Mafia had lawyers like you," he complained, "there'd be no dope sold in America."

During the years I began meeting with black lawyers, I was encountering almost no black law students. The entire student body at Columbia Law School would typically include only one black student. (My own class had none.) This was generally true of all the elite law schools. This meant, of course, that the elite bar, from which many leaders of our society are drawn, was and would continue to be lily white.

Many of us, including our dean, Bill Warren, found this insupportable. Bill proposed increasing the size of the class from three hundred to 305, reserving the additional spaces for black applicants. The proposal was delusively attractive: white students, it might be argued, could not complain of their exclusion from those five places because the spaces would not exist but for the affirmative action program. I preferred to face the reality that once those spaces were created, whites would normally be entitled to compete for them, but the benefits of affirmative action outweighed their interest. We were not alone in beginning an affirmative action program. Many other schools were or soon would be acting.

I would continue to support affirmative action as dean, provost, and president. The benefits to our society, in my judgment, have been incalculable. I do understand that white students have, in fact, been discriminated against, and I do not minimize the unfairness to them. But I believe now, as I believed more than forty years ago, that the damage to them—having to attend an institution that they regard as less desirable—is relatively modest, particularly when compared to the benefits of opening access to the upper echelons of our society to the more than 10 percent of our nation who previously had little hope of ever getting there.

The Supreme Court has justified affirmative action on a different ground. In a series of cases culminating recently in *Fisher v. University of Texas*, a divided court has said that universities my take race into account in their admissions process in order to achieve the educational benefits of a diverse student body. But, the *Fisher* case emphasized, the university must demonstrate "that no race-neutral alternatives would produce the educational benefits of diversity.[5]

Much more might be and has been said about affirmative action, but this is not the place to rehearse all those arguments. I believe that in the end a candid assessment requires a judgment about whether affirmative action still confers significant benefits on society and whether these benefits outweigh the harm done.

Marvin Frankel recommended me for another choice assignment when he became a judge. I succeeded him as legal advisor to *Time*, meeting with its editors every week to consult on what they might write about and reading what they wrote for accuracy. I kept that assignment for fourteen years, working with a series of gifted writers and editors in a role that required me to stay in touch with a broad range of legal developments. The American Bar Association has a gavel award for outstanding media coverage of the law, and we won it three times. I was proud of the fact that in all those years no one ever wrote a letter to *Time* saying we got a legal story wrong.

We did have a set-to with the chief justice of the United States. While America was awaiting the result in *Roe v. Wade*, Dave Beckwith, *Time*'s Supreme Court correspondent, managed to crack the court's normally ironclad secrecy and report to us that Roe would prevail. Henry Grunewald, *Time*'s managing editor, asked my advice on how to handle this information. I pointed out that the court had one more conference day before the decision would be announced and it was possible, though not likely, that positions would change. To put the question of whether to publish in full context, I said that I could see no harm from the result in this case appearing prematurely, but in many cases—for example, a case of corporate liability—fortunes could be made with early information.

In the end, Henry, I suspect in consultation with his corporate superiors, decided to publish, prompting an immediate reaction from Chief Justice Warren Burger. He summoned Henry and Hedley Donovan, his boss, to the court.

Henry and Hedley asked me what I thought of an offer that they proposed to put to the chief justice. They would promise not to reveal the court's decisions in advance if the chief would agree to have the court give twenty-four hours' notice when it was about to hand down a decision, so the press could prepare to cover it adequately. I pointed out that *Time* was under no legal obligation to forbear, and the proposal seemed to me to be a fair, public-spirited one.

They never got to make the proposal. The chief chewed them out relentlessly, without seeming even to pause for breath. I guess he didn't see the irony: the head of the institution charged with protecting freedom of the press, and doing a pretty good job of it, haranguing two leading journalists for doing what they had every right to do. The issue never arose again during my time at *Time*.

In 1967, I took on another media assignment: I agreed to do a television series for WNBC on due process in criminal cases. The format was essentially a version of what I do in class. Instead of having a student state a case for discussion, I had actors perform it and then two guests discuss it with me. My budget allowed for only two actors; when I needed three, I joined the actors myself.

The station manager explained to me that under their union contract I would have to join AFTRA, the American Federation of Television and Radio Artists. He didn't realize he was dealing with a professor of labor law. We were going to do ten programs, taping at the rate of two a week, spanning a period of twenty-nine days. Under the National Labor Relations Act, an employee cannot be compelled to join a union in less than thirty days. When I pointed this out, the station manager's discomfort was visible. I never found out what sort of labor difficulties he envisioned if this maverick went to work at his station. Since the union dues were not exorbitant, I relented and joined AFTRA. I may yet be entitled to a pension of a dollar and change per month.

My favorite program in the series presented the classic right to counsel case—*Gideon v. Wainwright*.[6] The presentation began with an actor portraying Gideon cross-examining an actor playing the chief witness against him. Gideon botched the job and was found guilty. (The dramatization used the actual record in the case.) When *Gideon v. Wainwright* reached the U.S. Supreme Court, in a decision of monumental importance the court held that the constitutional right to due process includes the right to counsel in felony prosecutions. Gideon's case was remanded for a new trial.

Having informed our audience about that decision, I performed the role of Gideon's counsel at his new trial. This time the cross-examination was devastating, and Gideon was acquitted. While I allowed myself the hero's role, I hasten to add that the cross-examination was again based on the actual record. A more powerful demonstration of the importance of counsel in a criminal case would be hard to imagine.

In another program I was wired to a lie detector and interrogated by a leading practitioner of that art. He was perfect, detecting my lies and recognizing the truth. Critics have maintained that people can be trained to fool the machine and that pathological liars are immune to it. And it is clear that not all those who hold themselves out as competent to administer the test are good enough. But I left persuaded that an ordinary mortal is not likely to fool a master of the craft.

Other programs dealt with such topics as juvenile justice, searches and seizures, the tension between a press free to comment on criminal prosecutions and the right to a fair trial—one of my guests was F. Lee Bailey, who had just won a reversal of the conviction of Sam Shepard because of press coverage.

We didn't generate great ratings, but the American Bar Association did confer a gavel on us, possibly making me the only person fortunate enough to have received gavel awards in two different media.

For an overdue sabbatical semester, Ellie and I decided on a trip to Europe—first Rome, Florence, and Pisa, and then Paris, where Ellie had spent much of her childhood. Our new daughter, Julie, was nine months old, and since she would be traveling with us, it would be helpful to have a nanny. I had lectured in the Netherlands the previous summer, and friends we had made there found us an art history graduate student who was fluent in English and Italian. Finally, we added my mother, who had never been abroad, to our little group.

To Italian men, who yield to no one in their appreciation of women, I was a prodigious figure. Accompanied wherever I went by my attractive wife, my handsome mother, and our nanny, who turned out to be a strikingly good-looking blonde, we drew whistles. Our sampling of antiquities, art, and, of course, food left me with what proved to be an insatiable appetite for Rome and Paris.

When we returned, my teaching continued to go well. While staying current in labor law was time consuming, I had taught both Evidence and Labor Law about ten times, so they didn't require much preparation. I was ready for a big scholarly project. Labor law, unlike many fields of law, lacked a magisterial treatise, an analytical compendium of the subject. I entered into a contract with a publisher to produce a multivolume version. But events were to intervene.

The spring of 1968 had arrived, and I was about to embark on a course that would lead to Columbia's presidency.

16

CLIMBING OUT OF A HOLE

*All of the stocks and bonds in the unrestricted endowment
had been sold to cover the deficits the university ran
from 1968 to 1978.*

When I accepted the presidency, I had a pretty good idea of
what I was getting into, but the state of the university's finances was daunting. The accumulated deferred maintenance looked as
though it would cost close to a billion dollars to fix. Columbia's total endowment was only $360 million, but that number had little to
do with reality. Columbia included in its endowment the real estate it
owned near campus—a treasure trove of approximately six thousand
apartments. But those apartments were needed to house faculty, staff,
and students at below-market rates. While the asset was invaluable, it
yielded nothing.

Columbia had another valuable piece of real estate. It owned the
land on which Rockefeller Center sits. That, too, sounded better than
it was. The land was subject to a long-term lease, terminating in 2069,
that had been entered into in 1929 between John D. Rockefeller Jr. and
Columbia's president, Nicholas Murray Butler. The lease would reopen
periodically, allowing the parties to renegotiate the rent: if they couldn't
agree, a tripartite panel would value the land and award Columbia an
annual rent of 6 percent of that value.

The rent had last been set in 1973 after a difficult negotiation. (The Rockefellers were extraordinarily generous as philanthropists, but not when they were conducting business.) Columbia was to receive $9,000,000 a year, increasing by $200,000 per annum for the next twenty-one years. Our balance sheet listed the land at $33.6 million, but a note to the financial statements said it was really worth $200 million. That was a heartening upgrade, but it only served to underscore the fact that for more than the next decade the land's yield would increase by only one-tenth of 1 percent of that value per year. Moreover, the commercial real estate market is notoriously cyclical: if it was in the dumps when the lease reopened in 1994, Columbia might get no increase at all for the next twenty-one years. If we could get the right price for the land, it made sense to sell it.

So that was our entire unrestricted endowment as it existed in 1980—no-yield apartments and an illiquid asset with little growth in income for the foreseeable future. All of the stocks and bonds had been sold to cover the deficits the university ran from 1968 to 1978. The stated endowment figure of $336 million consisted mostly of securities earmarked by their donors for specific purposes; these were restricted funds that could not be tapped for general university purposes.

Strengthening the university's financial base had to be my first priority, though there were other pressing concerns. We moved on three fronts. Terry Holcombe helped with the fundraising, and, when Peter Buchanan arrived, our planning for a capital campaign took off. We got lucky with respect to intellectual property, about which more shortly. And we focused on selling the Rockefeller Center land.

Early in the nineteenth century the New York State Legislature had given the land to Columbia after our trustees complained that Columbia had been left out of a recent group of grants to New York colleges. At the time the future Rockefeller Center was a rundown herb garden and lovers' lane just north of the city. The state had acquired it as a bequest from Dr. David Hosack, who grew medicinal plants there and hoped the state would carry on his work. It didn't. (Dr. Hosack was the physician who attended Alexander Hamilton at his duel with Aaron

Burr.) The land had little value until the city grew to the north and Columbia began leasing it. By 1980 it had become the invaluable jewel of Rockefeller Center, a mecca for millions of tourists and the home of NBC, the Associated Press, and dozens of major firms.

Bill McGill and Arthur Krim had opened negotiations for the sale of the land with J. Richardson Dilworth and Alton Marshall representing the Rockefellers, but the talks hadn't gone anywhere. Arthur and I decided to reopen them. We met for lunch in the dining room of a private apartment on top of Radio City Music Hall. We chatted amiably for a while and got down to business around dessert. I said we would sell for $500,000,000 but clearly signaled that we would settle for $400,000,000. Dilworth and Marshall were noncommittal, but they didn't say no, at least not yet. A few days later I received a surprising call from Dilworth to tell me that Arthur Krim was persona non grata and that the talks would go nowhere if he remained a part of our negotiating team.

That seemed a high-handed position to take with respect to the chairman of our trustees, but it didn't leave us much choice if we wanted to continue. Apparently the earlier round of rent negotiations had left an especially bad taste, and Arthur's involvement had contaminated him. Arthur and I agreed that I would continue without him but keep him fully informed.

As it turned out, Arthur didn't miss much. Further conversations culminated in a visit to Cape Cod, where I was vacationing, by the Rockefellers' investment banker, a Columbia graduate named Harvey Krueger, who brought their final offer of $200,000,000. By this time U.S. Treasury bonds were paying around 15 percent, so Harvey argued that $200,000,000 was a very generous price: it would yield $30,000,000 a year, almost three times what we were receiving in rent. I suspected that the offer was influenced by the Rockefellers' awareness of our poor financial circumstances and the hope that we might be feeling desperate. I gave Harvey a good lobster lunch, thanked him for coming, and regretted that he had wasted his time. Our price was $400,000,000.

We hired Goldman Sachs to serve as our investment banker but insisted on halving the fee because we would be doing much of the work ourselves. Then we shopped the property to the handful of real-estate investors who might be able to meet our price. Tony Knerr, our CFO, even traveled to Switzerland to meet with a representative of the sultan of Brunei. There were no takers.

Within the university only a few people were privy to our efforts. I kept the Executive Committee of the trustees informed, and I worked with a small team that included only Tony Knerr; Mason Harding, the university's general counsel; and my old friend Marty Rabinowitz, who was both a lawyer and an investment banker.

The Rockefellers got wind of our efforts and were concerned that we might sell the land to someone who could prove to be a more troublesome landlord than Columbia. Moreover, if they did not buy us out, they had no way of predicting what they would have to pay us in rent when the lease reopened in the early nineties. That would make setting the rents they would seek from their own tenants extremely difficult.

After we had sat on our hands for well over a year, the Rockefellers came back to the table. Their team had changed. It was led by Dick Voell, the CEO of Rockefeller Center, and though he probed a bit, he had gotten our message. We quickly agreed on the $400,000,000 price after I made one concession: though we made the deal in early February, they would not have to pay until the end of the month. That may seem trivial, but with the high interest rates at the time, that concession was probably worth about $4 million.

We were ecstatic. The agreement was subject to approval by the Columbia trustees, but I knew they would love it too. Dick Voell and I concluded our negotiations on a Sunday. The trustees regularly met in the afternoon of the first Monday of the month, which happened to be the following day. David Rockefeller called me that Monday morning to ask for my assurance that I wasn't planning to use our agreement to try to get a higher price from someone else. I was happy to give him that assurance. I didn't bother to mention that there was nobody else. But the call did prompt the sort of second thought that sometimes afflicts negotiators: was I too quick to concede that $4 million? I suspect I was.

As I knew they would, the trustees approved the deal, adding their warm congratulations. The *New York Times* said ours was the highest price ever paid for a piece of land in New York,[1] and, for all I know, it still is. A few days later Dick Voell called: he pointed out that ours was the sort of historic agreement that would normally be marked by a photograph showing him handing me a check, but with modern funds transfers there never would be an actual paper check; instead, would I come down for a photo in Rockefeller Center's beautiful Channel Gardens? As we walked to the photo shoot, Dick told me that, since the *Times* story appeared, he had been deluged with offers to buy the property. I said, "Well, why don't you decide what it's worth, double it and make that your asking price"? He replied, smiling, "Yes. I learned that from you."

We invested the proceeds in U.S. Treasuries at the then going rate of about 11 percent, converting an income stream of $11 million into one of $44 million. Not only was the yield phenomenal, but I wanted to build a cushion before we risked our inheritance in the stock market. About a year later we moved the fund into the stock market and rode the bull market up.

The Rockefeller Center transaction supported Columbia's restoration during my presidency and remains the cornerstone of our $8 billion endowment. It was the single most important financial event of my term, perhaps of any Columbia president's term.

We had earlier tapped into a new income stream, a way to exploit our intellectual property. Congress passed the Bayh-Dole Act, a statute that permitted universities to patent discoveries even though federal grants had paid for their development. During the summer of 1981, we adopted a new policy conferring patent ownership on Columbia and providing for the sharing of any resulting revenues among the inventor, the inventor's department and school, and the central university, with the university taking the lion's share. Since its adoption the policy has generated well over a billion dollars.

The University Senate was not pleased that we had adopted the policy without consulting them. I apologized, explaining that we wanted to move as quickly as possible and that the Senate didn't really function during the summer. I agreed to consider any changes the Senate suggested. They did offer a few constructive suggestions, and we adopted them.

Patent revenues were responsible for one of my favorite faculty encounters. Richard Axel, a brilliant young scientist and later a Nobel Prize winner, came to see me about his discovery of a method to transfer genes from one animal cell to another. The patent was sure to generate substantial revenue. (It would ultimately yield almost eight hundred million dollars.) Richard wanted to be sure that some of the profit would be used to support the humanities. In this and in many other ways, Richard was far from the typical scientific researcher. A man of extraordinary range and a delightful sense of humor, Richard is the sort of person one can imagine winning yet another Nobel.

Richard tells the story of his encounter with Lew Alcindor (later Kareem Jabbar), one of the greatest basketball players of all time. Alcindor was then the center on the Power Memorial High School team, and Richard, who was the center on the Stuyvesant High School team, was obliged to play against him. As Richard tells it, Alcindor scored at will and guarded Richard so well that his teammates couldn't get the ball to him. Finally a pass got through, but Alcindor singlehandedly surrounded Richard, looked down at him, and asked: "All right, Einstein, what are you going to do now?"

The third path we took to improve our finances was a capital campaign. Everyone uses that phrase, but in most instances it is a misnomer. The funds raised are used for current expenses as well as for capital purposes. I don't mean to suggest misrepresentation by anyone; campaign literature typically spells out all the campaign's subgoals, which usually include some current expenditures. It is simply more efficient to embrace all of a university's hopes under a single umbrella rather than run annual funds in competition with a capital campaign.

Preparing for a capital campaign in an institution as complex as Columbia is no easy task. Requests for information cascade down through the university. What, for example, are the Health Sciences' hopes and dreams? That question is retransmitted down through the individual schools to the individual departments. How much for financial aid? For faculty chairs? For physical facilities? And so it went for all sixteen of the university's schools.

The numbers that come back inevitably add up to far more than the university can possibly raise, and so the hard part begins. In consultation with the provost, the vice president for development, and the deans, I must ultimately decide on what we will seek and how the goals will be apportioned. That decision rests in part on practical considerations like how much can a particular school raise from its traditional donors and how much money do we think we can raise overall; in part on our view of the university's needs—for example, do we need a new science building—and in part on our assessment of the relative quality of the university's constituent parts.

The ritual calls for a special campaign brochure to be prepared by a firm that specializes in such work, and since I didn't know any better, I agreed. We received a fancy product that didn't seem to me at all to capture what Columbia is about. Jacques Barzun, one of Columbia's greatest scholars and most elegant writers, agreed to rewrite it for me, and he produced a characteristically elegant document, which we proceeded to give to major donors. Despite his wonderful work, I felt that the brochure made absolutely no difference, and I refused to be bothered with one when we launched a second capital campaign some years later.

We hadn't even begun our first campaign when I think I frightened Peter Buchanan, who was working very hard to get us started. "After we finish this campaign," I told him, "we'll take a breather and then begin a second one."

It was clear to me even at that early stage that capital campaigns were efficient fundraising engines and that private universities would have to continue to increase the support they received from alumni and others if they were to maintain their quality. I did not foresee that public universities would one day be forced to a similar strategy.

Capital campaigns begin with a so-called silent phase, a period in which the institution raises perhaps a quarter of its ultimate goal both to test the waters and to give the campaign a running start when it is announced. It was during our silent phase that Arthur Krim introduced me to John Kluge, a man who would become my good friend and the most generous donor in Columbia's history.

John had come to America from Germany as a child and graduated from Columbia College in 1937. Happily for Columbia, he had attended on a scholarship, for which he continued to be grateful. I asked him to head the major-gifts segment of the campaign and to contribute a million dollars. He agreed to do both but wanted to wait on announcing the gift because he was in the middle of a difficult divorce and didn't want to call extra attention to his wealth.

John was a man of many talents. He had taught ballroom dancing, served as an officer in Army Intelligence during World War II, was an excellent pool player and a collector of aboriginal art, but most of all he was a brilliant businessman. His main company, called Metromedia, owned, among other assets, the Ice Capades, the Harlem Globetrotters, the largest billboard company in the country, and a group of television stations. John offered to buy his public shareholders out. They accepted. He then proceeded to sell the company off piecemeal, netting billions. The television stations were bought by Rupert Murdoch, which is the origin of the Fox network. The deal helped elevate John from the merely rich to one of the richest men in the world.

By the time John made good on his promise to contribute to the campaign it was 1987, and his gift had grown to $25 million, the largest gift in Columbia's history. That was just the beginning. He would add $25 million more several years later, and the best was still to come.

We had come out of the quiet phase with an announcement that we were seeking $400,000,000. Though that was the largest campaign in Columbia's history, we were confident we could make it. In fact, we decided to err on the conservative side: the remainder of the campaign was scheduled to last five years. But we did so well we increased the goal to $500,000,000. In the end we raised $605,000,000.

All this activity was just the means to the end of addressing our critical needs—enhancing faculty quality, increasing student support, and fixing and enlarging our physical plant.

For example, we wanted to make it possible for every Columbia College student to live on campus for all four years. But we lacked both the residence halls and the financial aid to do that. We had made a start on residence hall expansion during Bill McGill's last year, and the new East Campus residence hall, with over five hundred beds, came on line during my first year. We were also able to renovate Hartley and Livingston Halls, two virtually identical dormitories. Bill had made a deal with Ira Wallach, a very generous alumnus of the College and law school, to change the name of Hartley to Wallach Hall in return for a $2 million contribution towards the $5 million cost of renovation. When Bill told me about this, I immediately called Jerry Greene and said: "Have I got a deal for you. For $2 million, we'll change the name of Livingston to Greene Hall." Jerry loved the idea.

But when the time came to change the names, a number of students and alumni protested vociferously against renaming these venerable halls. Ira's reaction was that in a few years they would forget, or at least no longer care, that Wallach Hall was not its original name. Jerry decided to settle for a plaque acknowledging his generous gift, and the episode damaged neither our friendship nor his warm feeling for Columbia.

We were still short of the space we needed, even with the allotment of some of our apartments to undergraduates. In fact, we did not reach our goal entirely until we dedicated Morris A. Shapiro Hall in 1988.

For every visible step we took toward improving the physical plant, there were countless invisible ones. We replaced roofs, enlarged cooling systems, and invested in our power plant so that it could run on either oil or gas, whichever was cheaper at the time. My favorite project of this kind was the replacement of the foundation for the steps leading up to Low Library. Unless remedial action was taken, this glorious esplanade would soon slide down onto the walk below. One by one, the steps were removed, the undergirding restored and the steps returned. The project cost a million dollars, and when it was finished, not even the most practiced eye could tell that anything had been done.

John Kluge's gift made it possible for us to adhere to our need-blind financial aid policy for Columbia College. A small number of American colleges and universities—twenty or so—admit students without regard to whether they will need financial aid and commit to provide whatever aid they will need to get through. Columbia is one of those colleges. But the cost of maintaining that policy rose year by year as tuition increased and as we sought to enable every student to live on campus. I believed in raising tuition more than we otherwise would in order to pump more money into scholarships, but that still left a gap we had to fill with gifts and endowment income. John's gift enabled us to continue to make a Columbia education available to students who couldn't afford to pay for it.

Financial aid was by no means a free ride. A rigorous review of a family's financial circumstances would yield a need to be filled with a package consisting of a scholarship, a loan, and a job. This is the very same package Columbia offered to recruited athletes, whom we believed should be treated the same as other students. Most universities outside the Ivy League treat athletes far more generously, so we tend to lose the best athletes in the big-money sports—basketball and football. But the Ivies share the conviction that we exist to educate, not to entertain. Our athletes do much of their best work in the classroom.

Rebuilding the faculty was a tougher challenge, but with more money available we were able to hold on to our stars and attract a large number of outstanding faculty from other top universities, even as we promoted the best from our own junior ranks.

By the end of my first ten years in office, our progress was thoroughly documented. Each year the National Science Foundation seeks the best young scientist in America to receive the Waterman Award: Columbia professors had won it three times. Other young faculty won twenty-four National Science Foundation Presidential Young Investigator Awards and joined their senior colleagues in winning eighty-eight Guggenheim Fellowships, fourteen MacArthur Foundation "genius" fellowships, and thirty-two fellowships from the Alfred P. Sloan Foundation.

Fortunately, we were blessed with a strong foundation on which to do our rebuilding, as evidenced by the sixteen Nobel Prizes won by Columbia alumni and faculty during those same ten years.

17

CEREMONIES

As Bishop Tutu drove us to lunch in Soweto, Joan remembered
reading that whites needed a permit to visit a black township.
Desmond said, "Yes, but surely the government cannot complain
when friends wish to break bread together. Of course," he added
with a smile, "it is you who are committing the crime."

A university president's life sometimes seems an unending series of ceremonial events. They can be unique—for example, introducing the Dalai Lama or Boris Yeltsin to a university audience. Or they can be traditional—the induction into Phi Beta Kappa of the handful of students who made it on the basis of three years of work, a ceremony I never missed in happy memory of my own induction; Commencement, which at Columbia is a colorful, multifaceted pageant; the annual Commemoration gathering, at which we remembered each of the students, faculty, and staff who had died during the year; the Alexander Hamilton Dinner; and many, many more.

The Hamilton Dinner celebrates an outstanding alumnus of Columbia College. We take great pride in Hamilton, one of the most influential shapers of the republic, though he never graduated. A brilliant student, he left to join George Washington's staff and rose to the rank of colonel during the Revolution. Before leaving college, he is remembered as having addressed a mob seeking to tar and feather the president of King's College, as we were named then. President Myles Cooper was a Tory, and there is some dispute as to whether Hamilton was urging the mob on or counseling restraint. Columbia's current president (and my former student), Lee Bollinger, maintains that Hamilton's intervention allowed Cooper to escape. "Hamilton," he says, "thus earned a special place in the heart of every Columbia president—including me—for bravely standing up for the principle that one's sworn political opponents shouldn't be tarred and feathered for their views."[1]

President Cooper fled to a British ship in the harbor only to meet an unhappier fate. With no Heimlich maneuver to save him, he choked to death back in Britain when a piece of food stuck in his throat.

Hamilton's death at the hand of Aaron Burr gives us a claim to the oldest intercollegiate rivalry in America, for Burr was the son of the president of Princeton.

On occasion we hold special convocations to award honorary degrees. One such was for Sandro Pertini, the president of Italy and a hero of the anti-Mussolini resistance. Because the Red Guards were a serious threat in Italy, security was very tight. Before President Pertini arrived in my office, the Secret Service brought a bomb dog. As he approached my wastebasket, his handler threw something into it; the dog sniffed and began barking loudly. Giving the dog a reward, the agent explained, "We have to let him find something every now and then, or he will lose his conditioning."

Not long thereafter I was the recipient of an unusual honorary degree. Instead of the LL.D that American universities typically confer, Tel Aviv University awarded me an honorary Ph.D., which my colleagues are quick to point out is not the same as earning one. But even law school graduates receive a doctorate these days—the Juris Doctor degree. I am a proud holder of the LL.B., the Bachelor of Laws, which was the degree awarded by most law schools when I graduated. During the 1970s, when I was dean, law schools generally switched to the Juris Doctor. We offered, for a small fee, to allow past graduates to trade in their bachelor's degrees for doctorates. The response was overwhelming, but, in a surge of reverse snobbism, I chose to keep my LL.B. My only regret about that is that had I elected to swap, as dean, I could have signed my own diploma. And since there are two signatures on Columbia diplomas, the dean's and the president's, when I became president I could have conferred the Juris Doctor on myself and signed both lines.

Perhaps the most eventful of Columbia's honorary degree ceremonies was the one for Bishop Desmond Tutu, an inspiring opponent of apartheid. The South African government had confiscated his passport and refused to allow him to travel to our Commencement. I spoke of him nonetheless in my address, and our row of honorary degree recipients held an empty chair to emphasize his forced absence.

Arthur Krim suggested that since Desmond Tutu couldn't come to us, we go to him to confer the degree, and he further offered to finance the trip. I thought it was a brilliant idea, and so did Desmond. He later told me that attention like ours was vital to his being able to stay free. We decided on a small delegation of Arthur; my wife, Joan (Ellie and I had parted some years before), and me; Sam Higginbottom, who was succeeding Arthur as chairman of the trustees, and his wife, Fair; and Moran Weston, Columbia's first African American trustee, and his wife, Miriam. Unfortunately, shortly before we were to go, Moran broke his leg in an accident and was unable to travel. That made our delegation all white, but at that late date there was nothing to do about it.

I didn't want the South African government to be able to claim that we were there on false pretenses. Where the visa application asked for the purpose of my visit, I wrote: "To confer an honorary degree on Bishop Tutu." And where it asked for length of stay, I entered dates that would just cover the time we would be spending with Desmond. I was still expecting Moran Weston to be with us, and I knew our integrated group wouldn't get very far as tourists. Joan, Arthur, and I planned to go on to Kenya for a brief safari. The South Africans kept our group waiting until almost the last minute before they granted the visas.

With a friend's help, we were able to use the University of Witswatersrand for a traditional academic procession and honorary degree ceremony, and so this all-white university was treated to an unforgettable ceremony that mixed marching professors, black dignitaries, and dancing and singing Africans. Desmond and I spoke, and he was, as always, funny and moving, all delivered in his wonderfully lilting English.

The next day Desmond picked us up at our hotel to take us to lunch at his home in the black township of Soweto. As he was driving us, Joan remembered reading somewhere that whites needed a permit to visit a black township. She asked Desmond if that was so. Desmond replied: "Yes, but surely the government cannot complain when friends wish to break bread together." Then, pausing to smile, he continued, "Of course, it is you who are committing the crime." Desmond expressed his confidence that South Africa would find a peaceful transition from apartheid to a just state. Only my great respect for him kept me from saying: "Are you crazy?" His prediction seemed the stuff of fantasy, but, of course, he proved right.

We couldn't go on to Kenya as planned because the Kenyan Air Force had rebelled, and our State Department advised against traveling there. A South African game preserve adjoining Krueger National Park seemed the next best thing, but Joan's and my visas were about to expire. To my pleasant surprise the South Africans courteously extended our visas, and we were ultimately granted certificates of our own by the game preserve attesting that we had seen the big five—lion, elephant, black rhino, cheetah, and leopard.

Back in New York, we were about to celebrate an American statesman and his generosity. Harvard, Yale, and Columbia had all been competing for a gift from Averell Harriman, the former governor of New York, ambassador to the Soviet Union, President Roosevelt's special envoy to Great Britain, cabinet member, and presidential candidate. We prevailed because my colleague Marshall Shulman, a preeminent specialist in the Soviet Union and a long-time advisor to Harriman, persuaded him and his wife, Pamela, that America's relations with the Soviet Union were vital to our future and that the best use of his gift would be for Soviet studies.

I was a supporting actor to Marshall's leading role in this drama, but that didn't keep me from enjoying my part. The Harrimans were fascinating people. Their Georgetown home, which contained a superb collection of paintings, was an old-fashioned salon where leading Democratic politicians were frequent dinner guests. Walking into the living room of their Westchester home, I noticed a picture of Winston Churchill with a small boy and remembered that Pamela's first husband was Winston Churchill's son. The picture I had noticed was just her son with his grandpa.

It didn't take long for Pamela and me to call each other by our first names, but Averell was old enough to be my father, even my grandfather. I continued to call him governor until one day I decided we knew each other well enough and called him Averell. When he continued to call me "Mr. President," I feared I had overreached.

But that didn't stop him from giving us $10 million for the W. Averell Harriman Institute for the Advanced Study of the Soviet Union. John Kluge had not yet made his gift, so this was the largest gift in Columbia's history and the largest gift to any university made that year. It was well publicized and may have been an icebreaker: gifts to universities soon moved up from the standard million- and occasional five-million-dollar mark.

We celebrated Averell's generosity before an invited audience that filled the spacious Low Library rotunda. The speakers were Averell, Marshall, former Secretary of State Cyrus Vance, and I. Before the ceremony, we gathered in my office, where Averell and Pamela, accompanied by Kitty Carlisle Hart, my neighbor and one of Pamela's closest friends, arrived first. When Cy Vance and his wife, Gay, arrived, I greeted him with a "Hello, Cy," and he replied with a "Hi, Mike." At that point Averell relieved my misgivings over his continuing to call me Mr. President. He took me aside and asked: "He calls you Mike; may I?"

That same month Larry Wien, one of the most generous College and law school alumni, was about to turn seventy-five. His daughters and sons-in-law—the Malkins and the Morses—wanted to make an appropriate gift to the university in his honor. Some years earlier Larry had embarked on a campaign to persuade corporations to increase their charitable giving. He would buy shares in a company with a poor record of giving and call upon the chief executive to urge improvement, gently warning that in the absence of improvement he would make the case at the company's annual meeting of shareholders. Larry's own record of giving and his stature in the business community were such that he could bring this off. A number of companies did in fact increase their annual giving.

That history pointed the way for the Malkins and Morses. They created the Lawrence A. Wien Prize in Corporate Social Responsibility. The recipient would be recognized by Columbia at a public ceremony, and five students in the law and business schools would receive one-year scholarships bearing the winning company's name. Characteristically, when Larry learned of this, he added to the prize fund.

Recipients of the award included Ben and Jerry's ice cream and Paul Newman's food company. Not surprisingly, Newman's acceptance of the Wien Prize drew a very large crowd. After a dozen years or so, the purpose of the prize was changed to recognize individuals for their efforts on behalf of the public good. Many years later, long after I had left the presidency, it was awarded to me. It was a sweet moment.

The first time I talked with Larry Wien other than in a large group was when, as a brand-new dean, I called to suggest lunch. He invited me to meet him in his office in one of the buildings he and his partners owned. (Another was the Empire State Building.) He was excellent company, a great storyteller, and lunch passed quickly. Over dessert he asked what he could do for me. Larry's gifts were already responsible for, among other things, the law school's largest scholarship program, so I replied: "Larry, I just thought it would be nice if every now and then someone just came to you and said, 'Thank you.'" He paused a moment and asked, "Will $50,000 be enough?"

Larry had helped found Brandeis University and build Lincoln Center. He gave Columbia about a million dollars a year for most of my presidency. On one occasion I watched as he tried to persuade two other alumni to join him in giving a million dollars each to help fund a new football stadium at Columbia's venerable Baker Field. When they declined, he put up the three million himself, and that is how our football stadium came to be called Lawrence A. Wien Stadium.

When our soccer team played Indiana for the national championship, Larry went to Tampa to see the game. Seated with Al Paul, our

1. The author as the newly elected co-chairman
of the Executive Committee of the Faculty.

Source: Photograph by Manny Warman, courtesy of Columbia University.

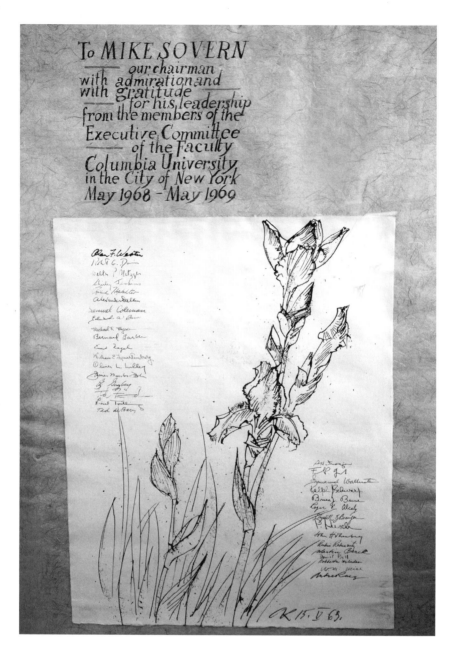

2. An expression of appreciation by the Executive Committee.

Source: Photograph by Eileen Barroso.

3. Portrait of the author as dean.

Source: Courtesy of the artist, John Hardy.

4. Dawn and Jerome Greene.

Source: Author's collection.

5. The author with Justice William O. Douglas and other Columbians.

Source: Courtesy of University Archives, Columbia University in the City of New York.

6. The author with his predecessor, President William J. McGill.

Source: Photograph by Joe Pineiro, courtesy of Columbia University.

7. Awarding an honorary degree to Joe DiMaggio.

Source: Photograph by Joe Pineiro, courtesy of Columbia University

8. The author with his mother.

Source: Author's collection.

9. Growing up in the Bronx.

Source: Author's collection.

10. The author in Minnesota.

Source: Author's collection.

11. The author with John Kluge and a group of Kluge scholars.

Source: Photograph by Joe Pineiro, courtesy of Columbia University.

12. The author with Pamela and Averell Harriman.

Source: Photograph by Manny Warman, courtesy of Columbia University.

13. At Baker Field with Larry Wien, at right, and the athletic director Al Paul.

Source: Photograph by Joe Pineiro, courtesy of Columbia University.

14. The picture speaks for itself.

Source: Photograph by Joe Pineiro, courtesy of Columbia University.

15. Vice President Mondale on a visit to Columbia.

Source: Photograph by Manny Warman, courtesy of Columbia University.

16. The author at his inauguration as president of Columbia University.

Source: Photograph by Joe Pineiro, courtesy of Columbia University.

17. The 1986 honorary degree class: Justice Brennan is second from the right in the first row, George F. Kennan is first on the left in the second row, Benny Goodman is second from the right in the second row. Another well-known honorand in the photo is Fred Friendly, in the middle of the second row.

Source: Photograph by Joe Pineiro, courtesy of Columbia University.

18. Awarding an honorary degree to Bob Hope.

Source: Photograph by Joe Pineiro, courtesy of Columbia University.

19. The author with Vaclav Havel and Milos Foreman.

Source: Photograph by Joe Pineiro, courtesy of University Archives, Columbia University in the City of New York.

20. Salman Rushdie surrounded by guards.

Source: Photograph by Mark Lennihan/Associated Press.

21. The author standing next to his current successor, Lee Bollinger, and accompanied by other Columbians.

Source: Author's collection.

22. The author with his wife Patricia in Kyoto, Japan.

Source: Author's collection.

23. A visit to Yue Minjun's studio in China.

Source: Author's collection.

24. The author with a few of his students.

Source: Photograph by Jon Roemer.

athletic director, Larry was so excited he promised that if we won, he would pay for a new soccer stadium. We lost in double overtime, but I knew that Larry would build the stadium anyway. And he did.

The Harriman commitment and the Wien Prize gift were not-so-silent contributions to our capital campaign's silent phase, which was about to end. (Larry's stadium gifts came later.) I had asked my friend Schuyler Chapin, dean of our School of the Arts and former general manager of the Metropolitan Opera, for any thoughts he might have about how best to launch the public phase of the Campaign for Columbia. He in turn asked what I would like to accomplish with the kickoff. I told him that I hoped about four hundred of our most promising prospects would accept my invitation to dinner and that we would not bore them to death but, rather, give them an evening they would not soon forget.

Schuyler proposed a musical comedy written around Columbia themes lasting perhaps an hour. And so a brilliant team of writers, composers, and actors delivered a delightful performance. I was struck, not for the first time, by how much underemployed theater talent we have in New York. Our guests loved the show and went home talking about it and, I hoped, about the campaign.

18

DOING THE
RIGHT THING

Coeducation, Charter Revision, and Columbia Football

Columbia's leader has an obligation to insure
that the university behave ethically.

The year 1983 was a big one for Columbia College: it was the year we admitted women. In one respect it was an easy decision. Admitting only males was hurting the College badly. Not only did it deny access to half of the brightest high-school seniors; in addition, many young men were not interested in a school without women. At this time the College was not seeing the surfeit of applicants it would later come to enjoy. In fact, it was admitting close to half of those who applied, a worrisome state of affairs. I suggested jokingly that the following year we should reject all the applicants, making us fashionable as the toughest school in America to get into.

Beyond the practical, I didn't like the whole idea of gender discrimination. The challenge was to manage the admission of women to the College in such a way that we protected Barnard, one of the world's finest women's colleges, from becoming collateral damage. It wasn't just that I didn't want to go down in history as the "Butcher of Barnard"; Barnard had been founded because Columbia's trustees had refused to admit women, and for Columbia now to cause her great distress was unacceptable to me.

I believed that Columbia's leader has an obligation to insure that the university behave ethically. Our strong stances on freedom of expression, apartheid, and other thorny issues exemplified my view that a university's own actions are powerful lessons and that it is the president's responsibility to see that the university lives up to its ideals. Students have a keen eye for hypocrisy.

We couldn't sacrifice Barnard to solve our problems. Fortunately, Barnard's president was Ellen Futter, an able young lawyer and former student of mine. Over a series of meetings, she and I worked out a plan that, among other things, assured prospective Barnard applicants that they would still have access to Columbia's courses and libraries. We also made sure that Barnard faculty would not be adversely affected by the move. We announced the new era together in a joint statement reaffirming Columbia's continuing commitment to Barnard.

We were immeasurably strengthened—Columbia College received almost 29,000 applicants in 2011, up from fewer than 3,500 in 1983—and Barnard has continued to flourish.

Ethical behavior includes accepting the responsibilities of good citizenship. When Mayor Koch called on me to chair a commission to revise New York City's Charter, I felt I couldn't refuse. I asked Frank Grad, who had done such a good job for the Columbia Executive Committee back in 1968, to serve as staff director. He prepared a number of studies to educate the commission about the Charter and possible improvements. We held hearings on our proposals in each of the city's five boroughs. The commission's creation was prompted in large part by doubts about the constitutionality of the powerful New York City Board of Estimate's composition. But since the litigation that would resolve that issue was still pending when we concluded our work, we thought it best to leave the question of how to reconstitute or replace the board to a later commission. Our most significant proposal called for the establishment of a districting commission with governing guidelines to assure that the periodic redistricting of City Council districts would be done fairly. Our recommendations were submitted to a referendum at the next election and passed with comfortable majorities.

In the spring my wife, Joan, and I delighted the College's students when we oversaw the installation of two Henry Moore sculptures on the lawn in front of Butler Library. Moore loved to see his sculptures in unspoiled outdoor settings. While the lawn outside Butler hardly qualified, our Arden House campus did. That property—a former Harriman home set amidst hundreds of forested acres—had been given to Columbia by Averell Harriman when Dwight Eisenhower led the university. On a visit to Henry Moore, Joan and I convinced him that his work would look beautiful there. He gave his permission for a long-term loan of three of his sculptures. He preferred a loan to a gift, he explained, because it assured we could never sell the works.

Since the three pieces would have to come via New York, I assumed he would have no objection if two of them—*Seated Woman* and *Reclining Woman*—rested a short while on our main campus. They were a big hit with the students, before resuming their journey to Arden House.

Would that we had given our students as much to cheer about on the football field. Columbia is not exactly known as an athletic powerhouse, though we regularly have national champions in fencing and do well in tennis, swimming, soccer, and baseball. Yet our twenty-four trustees recently included the owners of two professional football teams—Bob Kraft, the owner of the New England Patriots, and Al Lerner, who bought the Cleveland Browns—and the commissioner of the National Basketball Association, Dave Stern, who became chairman of the trustees.

In September 1984, we dedicated the football stadium Larry Wien had helped pay for. But our team continued to struggle. We frequently played a pretty good first half but lacked the depth to sustain the effort. I facetiously proposed to the presidents of the Ivy League that we cut football games to thirty minutes.

We had known better times. On an alumni trip to Chicago I met one of football's greats—Columbia quarterback Sid Luckman, who went on to lead the Chicago Bears to a record-breaking 73–0 defeat of the Washington Redskins in the 1940 National Football League Championship game.

In 1986 we honored a great era in Columbia football (yes, we had one—in fact, two). We looked back to 1947 when Army's team was dominating the sport. They hadn't lost a game in three years when they came to Baker Field to play us. At half-time, they led 20 to 7. The final score was Columbia 21–20. It wasn't a fluke. For several years after World War II, we beat almost every team we played.

Gene Rossides, later a successful attorney and assistant secretary of the Treasury, quarterbacked those teams. He told me why they were so successful. With the G.I. bill paying tuition and expenses for returning veterans, the best football players didn't have to accept football scholarships to attend college. They could afford to go where they thought they could get the best education. Columbia was a major beneficiary.

Those scholar-athletes all returned to be honored at a halftime ceremony. Every member of that team save one who had died was there, and his widow attended in his place. In the current era of three-hundred-pound linemen and larger-than-life quarterbacks, I was struck by the human scale of our heroes. With forty years to put on extra weight, I didn't see anyone who looked as though he weighed as much as two hundred pounds. Amid jokes about how they should suit up, Columbia lost that day.

In fact, our current football team was experiencing the agony of defeat. We had recently hired Jim Garrett as head coach. It was a calculated risk. He had spent much of his career in professional football, most recently with the Giants, the Saints, and the Browns. In his interviews he certainly sounded as though he could adapt to the strictly amateur Ivy League. But it turned out he couldn't, and we had to fire him after a single season.

Turnover in the coaching staff is unsettling enough to a sports program, but Garrett had three sons on the team. One was a wide receiver already at Columbia when his father was hired, but the other two—a star running back and a potentially great quarterback—chose Columbia after their father signed with us. They were the planned nucleus of a wonderful future for Columbia football.

We knew that firing Coach Garrett would destroy that future, but it was the right thing to do. He proved unable to ratchet down to Ivy football from the demands a coach can make on players in a major football program. As we expected, his sons exhibited the appropriate filial piety and applied to transfer to Princeton. The NCAA, the governing body of intercollegiate sports, requires transferring athletes to sit out a year of play. We joined Princeton in a petition to the NCAA to waive the rule for the Garrett sons since this was not a case of one school poaching from another or of athletes shopping around, but the petition was denied. Two of the three ultimately did play for Princeton, and they played well. Jason Garrett made it as a quarterback with the pros and is currently the coach of the Dallas Cowboys. His brothers are the Dallas tight ends' coach and the director of scouting.

That is the story behind Columbia going winless for forty-four football games in a row. I felt particular sympathy for the cohort of players who went all four years without tasting victory even once. Finally, in 1988, against a Princeton football team led by the Garrett brothers, we triumphed 16–13.

I was always sorry to lose, but as long as Columbia's Nobel Prizes won exceeded its football games lost, we would be all right. The year we broke the streak and beat Princeton, we also won three more Nobel Prizes in physics, as my classmate at Bronx Science and Columbia, Mel Schwartz, and two other Columbians received their invitations to Stockholm.

We lost a very special Nobel laureate when I. I. Rabi died that year. Even measured against Columbia's best, Rabi, as most called him, stood out. A Brooklyn boy who would go on to win the Nobel Prize in physics—the MRI is based on his work—Rabi helped build the best physics department in the world. As chairman he recruited people of such promise and laid such a solid foundation that Columbia physicists would win another eleven Nobel Prizes. Rabi was respected by statesmen as well as scientists, having organized the first International Conference on the Peaceful Uses of Atomic Energy, bringing together delegates from the West and the Soviet Union.

Though he had a healthy appreciation of his own abilities and achievements, Rabi was not puffed up by them. "Great scientists," he once said, "usually show up when and where in the history of science they are needed. I know perfectly well that there are people living now who could have created quantum mechanics, but they were born too late." On another occasion, he observed: "Science tells you how much smarter the world is than you are."

19

THE PULITZER PRIZES

---

*I was amazed to discover that a Pulitzer
Prize winner received his prize in the mail.*

One of my favorite annual events was the meeting of the Pulitzer Prize Board. The prizes were created by a gift to Columbia from Joseph Pulitzer in 1917 and have been awarded by Columbia ever since.

Until the 1970s, the Columbia trustees actually voted on the awards, but their discomfort over effectively rubber-stamping the Pulitzer Prize Board's choices whether they agreed with them or not finally led them to give up this role and make the board's vote final. Columbia's president continued to be a voting member of the board, and the dean of the journalism school served as a nonvoting member.

In every category the entries are vetted by a jury, which is instructed to send on three nominees, unranked. An occasional rebellious jury may send four, and more than one jury has insisted on ranking its selections. I remember one jury that gave us only one choice. We gave no prize in that category that year.

The board gives great weight to the juries' recommendations but will occasionally award a prize to an entry the jury passed over. That inevitably stirs a public fuss as the snubbed jurors express their outrage. For the most part, though, our meetings focused sharply on the three nominees presented to us.

All the journalism nominees' entries were contained in a single giant volume called the "White Book." As nearly as I could tell, everyone read it all. (It was a lot of reading. I remember the pleasure and relief I felt when I came to the editorial cartoon and photography entries.) Some decisions would be easy; others would provoke extended discussion and occasional close votes. Except for me and the dean, all the board members were elected by the board itself. The process had produced a very high quality group of people, most of them, but not all, journalists.

Before I joined, the board had chosen President Hannah Gray of the University of Chicago to be its first female member. The choice infuriated women journalists, who saw the selection as implying that none of them was worthy. She was a great choice, but the board could have been more diplomatic and admitted a working journalist to the old boys' club first.

The strength of the group made for fascinating debates when we differed. Arguments might arise over the quality of a reporter's writing, the value of a series when the public service prize was under discussion, or journalistic ethics in the case of a reporter who had gotten a great story by deception. These were the sorts of discussions in which I felt comfortable behaving as a full participant. My colleagues must not have objected: they elected me chairman pro tem for a year. (The regular chairmanship was reserved for a journalist.)

The letters awards categories entailed even more reading. Three books in each of six categories were more than some of us could handle, so we divided into subcommittees—one for fiction, one for biography, etc. I was excused from service on a subcommittee but would read a few books that seemed to me likely to be worth reading based on what the jurors had said, reviews I had read, or the recommendation of a reliable friend. If a subcommittee's members were in serious disagreement, they usually let us know in advance to give us an opportunity to judge for ourselves.

During Professor Helen Vendler's time on the board, she chaired the poetry subcommittee. She was so respected and her recommendations so compellingly rendered that we always voted for her choices. Something similar happened when Russell Baker chaired the fiction subcommittee. His orally rendered mini-essays on each of the nominees were so gracefully and eloquently framed that he almost always carried the day.

We had a separate subcommittee on special prizes awarded outside of the regular categories. I chaired that subcommittee, and we were very parsimonious. Over the years only a handful of special Pulitzers were awarded. The first one I voted for was Dr. Seuss, né Theodor Seuss Geisel. Several were posthumous. The music prize did not begin until 1943, so it seemed appropriate to make special awards to Scott Joplin and George Gershwin. Duke Ellington was voted a special award later.

When I joined the board I was amazed to discover that a Pulitzer Prize winner received his prize certificate and check in the mail. Columbia offered no occasion for the winners to come together, receive their prizes, and celebrate. At that time the board was chaired by Joseph Pulitzer Jr., the grandson of the original Joseph Pulitzer. I set about persuading him that the winner of a Pulitzer Prize deserved better. He feared the prizes would deteriorate into the Academy Awards, but I finally convinced him that we could manage an awards ceremony with appropriate dignity.

We agreed that we would not try for a suspenseful event to which all the nominees would be invited, with two out of three going home disappointed. We would continue to announce the prizes in April, as we always had, following with a luncheon in May, at which I would present the prizes to the winners. The first Pulitzer Prize luncheon was held on May 21, 1984.

I presided at ten such luncheons, and in all that time only one living prize winner failed to attend—Dr. Seuss was too ill to come. The winners obviously enjoyed meeting one another almost as much as they savored their moment in the sun. And so did I, with such luncheon partners as Toni Morrison, David McCullough, August Wilson, and Tom Friedman.

The recipients were firmly instructed that a simple thank you was all that was desired of them; neither mother nor agent was to be saluted on this day. Only once did I grant an exemption. The Spot Photography Prize had been won by a picture of a "firefighter giving mouth-to-mouth resuscitation to a child pulled from a burning building." We happily allowed the winning photographer to introduce the firefighter.

The luncheons were such a hit that it wasn't hard to persuade the board that we should celebrate the seventy-fifth anniversary of the prizes in 1992. We invited all the living prize winners to Columbia for a simple ceremony consisting of talks by Michael Pulitzer, Russell Baker, and me, followed by a luncheon, at which once again the major attraction was the guests themselves.

I suspect that everyone there that day still remembers Russell's opening: "It's a macabre experience to look out over this large assembly and realize that I already know how the obituaries of at least half of you will begin. They will start with a descriptive three-word phrase beloved by all obituary writers. The phrase of course is 'Pulitzer-Prize winning . . .'" Russell's wit and elegance made him a natural choice for the occasion. Besides, he was one of only two people ever to have won a Pulitzer in both journalism and letters, the first for his columns, the second for his memoir, *Growing Up.* (The other was Anthony Lukas.)

That we were the home of the Pulitzer Prize probably helped us succeed in persuading the Gannet Foundation to establish its newly conceived Media Studies Center at Columbia rather than at any of the universities with which we were competing. Housed in the journalism school in quarters Gannet refurbished to the envy of the journalism faculty, the center's fellowship program brought interesting people to Columbia who often participated in university programs.

We would later add the George T. Delacorte Center for Magazine Journalism. George was ninety-one at the time but still going strong. He had made his fortune as the founder of Dell Publishing and was having a delightful time giving it away. He decorated Central Park with several of its most loved features—the Alice-in-Wonderland statue, the Delacorte Fountain, and the Delacorte Clock adorned with the now-famous dancing bear, an elephant playing a concertina, and other animals performing to the music of a glockenspiel every half-hour. And the Delacorte Theater is the home of Shakespeare in the Park.

A member of the Class of 1913 and a steadfast Columbia supporter, George was on my must-see list when I became president. Apparently sensitive to the possibility that I might think Valerie, his younger, former movie actress wife, had married him for his money, he told me her story almost as soon as we met. But first he showed me an album of photographs from her performing days. She was stunningly beautiful, in a class with Hedy Lamarr.

Valerie's first husband was Gabriel Pascal, the producer-director who had persuaded George Bernard Shaw to allow him to turn Shaw's plays into movies. (*Major Barbara* and *Pygmalion* can still occasionally be seen on late-night television.) Because Pascal owned the film rights, the movie of *My Fair Lady*, the musical version of *Pygmalion*, entitled him to substantial royalties. He died right in the middle of divorce proceedings that never became final. That left Valerie as his widow and a major beneficiary of those royalties. Thus Valerie did not need George's money.

George was easy to like, and we developed a special bond when he thought I had saved his life. We were attending a party in Shubert Alley, the pedestrian way linking Forty-fourth and Forty-fifth Streets next to the Shubert and Booth Theatres, when George collapsed. I caught him and helped carry him to a nearby restaurant, where we laid him out on a table and called for help. Police and paramedics arrived promptly. George came to, was thoroughly examined, and pronounced fit.

The police offered him a ride home, and I kept him company in the squad car as we raced through Central Park, free of traffic at that time of night. I left him seeming fine, apparently the victim of a fainting spell with no serious cause. When George later referred to the episode as the night I saved his life, I thought he was joking, but it turned out he meant it. None of my protestations could persuade him otherwise.

George had given and would continue to give generously to Columbia, paying for, among other things, beautiful gates, a humanities professorship, and the Delacorte Center for Magazine Journalism. George died six years later at the age of ninety-seven.

20

REAGAN VERSUS MONDALE

My job was to make Reagan's arguments and mount his attacks.

In 1984, Walter F. Mondale (Fritz, as he was widely known) was challenging President Ronald Reagan in his bid for reelection. As in every election since 1960, the candidates were scheduled to debate each other before a mammoth television audience. This year there would be two debates, one devoted to domestic issues, the other to foreign policy and defense.

The consensus was that the best way to prepare was to engage in simulated debates with someone performing the role of your opponent. I was to be that someone for Fritz Mondale. I never asked Fritz why he picked me, but I assumed he wanted to be sure that his pseudo-Reagan didn't go easy on him and, as his former professor at the University of Minnesota Law School, I was less likely to be intimidated when I opposed him.

When asked to take on the assignment, I barely hesitated on the question whether there was any tension between my position as

---

An adaptation of this chapter appeared in Michael I. Sovern, "What I Learned from Playing the Gipper," *New York Times*, September 30, 2012, shortly before the Obama-Romney debates.

Columbia's president and a partisan political role. Dwight Eisenhower had run for president when he was still nominally Columbia's president, and Nicholas Murray Butler had accepted the vice presidential nomination on the Republican ticket in 1912 when the original nominee died. A university president must be sure he does not seem to be committing his institution to a political party. That does not mean he must be a political eunuch himself.

I liked and respected Fritz. He had served America well as senator and vice president, and I thought he was well qualified—by experience, character, temperament, and intelligence—to be president. I could manage the two weeks away from the university since I would have a few hours available each day for whatever I might need to do on the telephone. And I thought the experience would be fascinating. I accepted with enthusiasm.

I was not asked to be a mimic. I could sound like Kermit the Frog for all that mattered. My job was to make Reagan's arguments and mount his attacks. To prepare, I read all of Reagan's major speeches and watched videos of his previous debates. Fritz's staff prepared a briefing book for me that organized Reagan's statements by subject matter so that to the extent possible I could speak in his actual words.

The debate rules barred the use of notes, and, to simulate the conditions under which he would have to perform, Fritz used no notes during our rehearsals. But there was no reason I shouldn't use them. During our preparations for the defense and foreign policy debate, I got carried away. To buttress Reagan's claim that Fritz was weak on defense, I reeled off a long list of defense appropriation bills Fritz had voted against. Fritz interrupted: "Reagan could never do that." He was right, of course. Without my notes, I probably couldn't have either.

In each of the preparation weeks, we met each day, from Monday to Friday, at the Mondale home in Washington, and debated. Using the family dining room and adjoining living room, we stood at lecterns a few feet apart, with another Mondale friend questioning us in the format the actual debate would follow. A video camera was fixed on Fritz—we didn't care what I looked like—and recorded the entire session. We would then perform a postmortem, assessing his answers and how he looked both when he was speaking and when I was speaking. Fritz is a highly intelligent man and an experienced politician, and he was very good at this, but there is always room for improvement, and the process enabled us to help him be even better.

Interruptions during these sessions were rare, but occasionally a campaign aide would need a quick answer, and we would take a brief break. It was a very homey atmosphere. Joan, Fritz's wife, could be seen passing to and from the kitchen. On one occasion I overheard Fritz's son tell his mother, "I'm so proud of him."

Fritz' staff were not happy with one bit of business he was doing on the campaign trail, but they couldn't talk him out of it. They asked me to see what I could do to get him to stop, for they were sure he would do it during our debates. And he did. Waxing eloquent about Medicare, he said something like this: "My father was a minister, not a wealthy man, and, when he died, all he left my mother, apart from our home, was a small insurance policy. When she became ill and exhausted the proceeds of that policy, if it hadn't been for Medicare, she would have been forced to go on welfare."

My turn: "That was a very moving story, but I like to think that in those difficult circumstances Mrs. Mondale's son would have helped out." Fritz turned to me and shouted: "You son of a bitch!" He came to enjoy my response, telling others about it, but I don't think he used that story again.

We didn't want to overdo it, so Saturday was a day off from debating. Instead we relaxed for a couple of hours and tried to think of snappy one-liners. On Sunday we didn't work together at all, though Fritz presumably did a little reviewing. We made our way to Louisville, Kentucky, for the first debate and to Kansas City, Missouri, for the second. At the appointed hour Fritz and his family, some aides, and I bundled into cars and vans to follow our police escort to the auditorium where the debate would take place. For the first debate I sat in the auditorium; for the second I sat backstage in a television viewing room so that I could see what the television audience was actually seeing.

Immediately after the debates campaign staffers deployed to the press room to explain why their candidate had the better of the match. In the judgment of most of the press, Fritz won the first debate handily, a judgment in which I naturally concurred. The second debate was generally regarded as a standoff.

The outcomes confirmed two theories of mine based on my viewing of all the available presidential debate videos. First, a candidate challenging an incumbent president has the advantage. The president of the United States is an awesome figure. Merely to share the platform with him on equal terms is to gain in stature: a good performance will be judged even better. Second, the order in which the candidates answer the first question matters when the format has them answering the same questions. The one who goes second will have time to think about his answer, a luxury his adversary will not have. Not only does that give him a chance to do well on that question; it also helps him to settle in comfortably for the evening.

One other observation about this particular art form. Each of the participants has a major objective and a minor one, in addition, of course, to appearing presidential. The major one is to get his messages across even if the questions don't ask for them. The minor one is to avoid seeming unresponsive. That is why you will see practiced debaters answer some of the questions at lightning speed, leaving time for what the candidate actually wants to talk about.

After the first debate, Fritz's poll numbers improved markedly, but they tailed off from there. In the end he carried only one state—Minnesota. In fairness to my old friend, I don't think anyone could have beaten Reagan that year. Fritz did at least give America its first female vice presidential candidate in Geraldine Ferraro.

21

DISAPPOINTING MY PEERS

Divestiture and Earmarks

We were the first university with a significant
endowment to resolve to divest its investments in
companies doing business in apartheid South Africa.

A s the events of 1968 so dramatically demonstrated, university
campuses are far from immune to controversies agitating the
larger world. The point was driven home again in the 1980s when the
abomination of apartheid in South Africa prompted protests at countless colleges and universities. The cry: Divest!

It was not that universities had themselves invested in South Africa; it was, rather, that they invested in companies that did business in
South Africa. University trustees resisted the divestiture movement on
two grounds.

Those who were candid would admit that they were moved in part
by finances. Many successful corporations were doing business in South
Africa; to exclude them from an endowment's universe of possible investments could risk hurting the endowment's performance, an outcome
that trustees typically regarded as a breach of their fiduciary duty. The
second ground engaged directly with the divestiture movement's moral
fervor. The objective of divestiture was to persuade affected corporations
to leave South Africa, inflicting such enormous pain on the country that
the government would have no choice but to abandon apartheid. But

much of that economic pain would fall on South Africa's black citizens. It would be better, the counterargument went, for the companies to stay, to ameliorate the condition of its black majority through a variety of programs, and to use their influence to press the South African government to abolish apartheid.

Columbia had made its opposition to apartheid clear. Our award of an honorary degree to Desmond Tutu was the best evidence of that. The trustees had also voted not to hold any investment in companies doing business in South Africa that failed to subscribe to the Sullivan Principles. Among other things, the Sullivan Principles committed a company to support universal rights, promote equal opportunity for its employees, seek to provide training and opportunity for workers from disadvantaged backgrounds, and promote the application of those principles by those with whom it does business.

For some, this was not enough. I had taken another step. In 1984, with the consent of Columbia's trustees, I agreed with the University Senate that the university would cap its holdings of companies doing business in South Africa at the current level of $39 million. The move was essentially symbolic. Our endowment was still very modest. A $39-million cap would probably give our investment managers adequate flexibility and so do no harm. Yet the move did underscore our opposition to apartheid.

None of this protected us from protests. On March 25, 1985, seven Columbia students began a hunger strike, which generated some attention and support. On Friday, April 5, a group of students chained the front doors of Hamilton Hall and declared they would not leave until the trustees agreed to "issue a written public statement of their intention to divest." Several hundred students joined them. Later I learned that they couldn't understand why I didn't call the police to remove them. Ahistorical as students commonly are, they obviously knew nothing about the lessons of 1968.

I could not count on being able to remove hundreds of students from the relatively confined space in front of Hamilton without injury. In addition to the protestors themselves, many more students and faculty onlookers would be at risk in the ensuing confusion. While most Columbians disapproved of the blockade, there was widespread agreement with its objectives. It would be a serious blunder for me to turn the offenders into victims.

Instead we obtained a court order calling for the protestors to end their blockade. That tactic had occasionally worked in the past. It didn't this time. We could afford to wait because there was another way in and out of Hamilton, but I didn't want to leave the protesters unanswered. On Sunday, I wrote a letter to the Columbia community emphasizing that "the offenders do not, they could not, claim that any of the countless avenues of free speech were closed to them," noting that they had "spoken in the University Senate, where their position was overwhelmingly rejected by a vote of 43 to 13." I observed that they were "twice offered the opportunity to meet with the trustees' special committee on investment policy" and reminded readers of my letter that many ardent foes of racism opposed divestiture.

I hadn't paid much attention to the hunger strikers, not knowing whether to believe they really were starving themselves and unwilling to submit to a form of blackmail. But several colleagues I respected expressed their serious concern to me. I agreed to a meeting subject to several conditions. First, it would be private, not an occasion for publicity; second, I would hear them out but promise nothing; and finally, in return for my meeting with them, they would end their hunger strike. My terms were accepted, we had an entirely civil meeting, and that particular protest was over.

There remained the Hamilton Hall demonstrations. Though they attracted considerable attention—Desmond Tutu endorsed their efforts; Jesse Jackson led a rally on campus—the university went about its business without interruption. Perhaps the most striking symbol of the university's ability to function in the face of protests was seen the evening that twenty-five hundred protestors marched as hundreds of alumni in black tie entered Low Library to attend the annual John Jay Dinner.

I felt strongly that conceding anything to a group that blockaded a building, however ineffectually, was not an option. So we waited and endured. Final exams were approaching, attention spans were limited, and so, after three weeks, the protestors departed. The demonstration was over. Fifteen students were ultimately denied degrees for their role in the blockade.

The quiet of summer gave me a chance to think afresh about our position. An important new factor had intruded. After taking what had seemed a sensible step—agreeing with the University Senate to cap Columbia's investments in companies doing business in South Africa at $39 million—we had sold the land under Rockefeller Center. We now had $400 million more to invest. My promise to the Senate precluded us from investing any of that money in companies doing business in South Africa. Did it make sense to refuse to divest when such companies were already barred from more than 90 percent of our endowment?

The answer to the moral choice—divestiture or the Sullivan Principles—was not obvious, but the fact that Desmond Tutu and other black South African leaders favored divestiture was a powerful argument. For Columbia the financial consequences bordered on the trivial: whether we could invest substantially less than 10 percent of the endowment in companies doing business in South Africa hardly mattered.

While we could endure the repeated disruptions that were sure to attend continued unwillingness to divest, the side effects would be divisive and damaging. Both faculty and students were virtually unanimous in their condemnation of South Africa, but there was no such unanimity favoring pro-divestiture demonstrations. Columbia could become an unpleasant place to be, one unattractive to potential students and faculty. Our community relations with neighboring Harlem would suffer. So would our relations with the dozen unions representing Columbia workers, which generally supported divestiture. Principle and pragmatism were coming together. I concluded it was time to divest.

I was not alone in rethinking our policy. Quite independently, several of the trustees' leaders were coming to the same conclusion I had reached. Chuck Luce, head of Consolidated Edison, vice chairman of the trustees, and chairman of the Finance Committee, thought we should get out. G. G. Michelson, a senior executive at Macy's and a member of the board of General Electric, who would later become the first woman to chair the trustees, was of like mind. Sam Higginbottom, the chairman of the trustees, was the head of Rolls Royce America, and his parent company had facilities in South Africa. When Sam told the parent company that the trustees he led were about to vote to divest, they were not happy with him. He told them they were free to fire him, but we were going ahead. He kept his job.

Not all of the trustees agreed. Joe Williams, the head of Warner Lambert, believed that his company's activities in South Africa were immensely beneficial to the black population there, and he made a powerful case. Two other trustees thought we were making a mistake. But nobody voted against the resolution to divest. The tally was twenty-one in favor, with three abstentions. For Columbia, it was the right decision.

We were the first university with a significant endowment to resolve to divest. A number of colleges had adopted similar resolutions, but, lacking serious money, their votes were largely symbolic.

I had to do some damage control. I met with the head of Mobil Oil, whose stock we would be shunning. He came to lunch with Herb Schmertz, an important Mobil vice president and a classmate of mine. The conversation was not easy. I emphasized that we were not presuming to judge his company; we were simply doing what we believed was right for Columbia. At the end, testing my moral fiber, he asked, "Well, would you still accept gifts from us?" I said, "You bet we will!" I didn't think Mobil was evil; we just differed about how to respond to the evil in South Africa. I had a rougher session with the head of Citibank, who really didn't like what we were doing. But I'm happy to say there didn't seem to be much disposition in corporate America to punish us.

A number of my colleagues leading other universities were upset by our decision: it increased the pressure on them. But my job was to do what was right for Columbia.

I angered my presidential colleagues on another front as well. With the help of a lobbying firm, Senators Moynihan and D'Amato, and Representative Rangel, we obtained money for new construction directly from Congress—so-called earmarks. The funds provided by the federal government enabled us to expand our chemistry facilities. We repeated the process at our medical center.

Colleagues around the country were upset by our actions because they believed it would subvert the system of peer-reviewed federal research grants. In general, federal support for research is dispensed by agencies—like the National Institutes of Health and the National Science Foundation—that submit applications for grants to review by other scientists, the "peers" of the applicants. They then award the grants to those receiving the highest ratings by the peers. My response to my colleagues was that we fully supported peer review for research grants and that we would support such a system for facilities construction as well, but no construction program existed. When it came to construction, the choice was not between peer review and politics but between doing without and politics. We were taking the only path open to us.

And our needs were greater than most. Many of the top state universities had relatively new facilities built for them by open-handed legislatures. A low-interest federal loan program had enabled both public and private universities to expand their facilities at manageable cost. Columbia had foolishly failed to take advantage of that opportunity, and it had expired.

My peers elsewhere may not have been happy with me, but Columbia was thriving. As 1985 was drawing to a close, the committee conducting Columbia's periodic reaccreditation reported:

> Hope and confidence have been restored. Urgent problems have been effectively addressed and in some areas already resolved. Prolonged depression has been succeeded by optimism. President Sovern's leadership has earned a consensus of full confidence and deserves enormous credit for this transformation. He is rightly perceived both as its principal agent and personal symbol.

22

CITY CORRUPTION AND COLUMBIA UNREST

A society that asks its public officials to behave honorably sends a conflicting message when its electoral process is awash in money.

I was awaiting Senator Moynihan in his Washington office when Governor Mario Cuomo reached me. He and Mayor Koch would appreciate it if I would head a commission on corruption in government. The request was prompted by a bribery scandal that generated banner headlines when it led to the suicide of the Queens borough president.

After I learned what the governor and mayor had in mind, I asked for an adequate budget, a say in the choice of the commission members, and a deadline allowing enough time to do the job right. I also suggested that we call our new body the Commission on Integrity in Government, which we did.

My fellow commissioners and I, aided by the ever helpful Frank Grad, defined our task as identifying "the elements that corrupt the ethical environment in which government employees live and work [and] to shape recommendations" for the elimination of those elements.[1] Over the next nine months we issued six reports.

We observed that "A society that asks its public officials to behave honorably sends a conflicting message when its electoral process is awash in money, much of it provided by those seeking something from government." We began by proposing limits on campaign financing coupled with public funding of election campaigns.

I had not been a believer in public funding until obliged to address the corrupting effects of money on elections. Once convinced, I brought the passion of the convert to the idea, going so far as to propose that when a candidate opted out of public funding, thereby gaining freedom to spend without limit, his opponent's public funding should be increased. That idea, which I believe originated with us, was enacted in a variety of versions in New York City and elsewhere.[2]

We followed our opening initiative with recommendations on conflicts of interest, protection for whistleblowers, city procurement and contracting practices, and merit selection for judges. In our final report, expressing our beliefs that "honest government need not be an oxymoron" but that "Like liberty, honest government requires constant vigilance," we recommended the creation of a successor commission with the power "to probe deeply, wherever abuse is to be found in our City and State, and report fully." That commission was created and ably led by John Feerick, the dean of Fordham Law School, but it only lasted until 1990. It has had to be recreated from time to time.

In October 1985, we endured the first strike of my administration. We were not seriously inconvenienced, but I was sorry to see about one thousand of our technical and clerical workers, represented by District 65 of the United Auto Workers, lose five days' pay. I was pretty sure we would have reached the same agreement without the strike, but unions are political institutions, and their leaders, like other political figures, are ever mindful of what their constituents think of them. There is nothing like a short strike to rally the troops. (District 65 would strike again for two days in 1991, and that time I had no doubt that the resulting agreement was unaffected by the work stoppage.)

During my time as president, we negotiated more than forty contracts with ten different unions. District 65 was the only one that ever walked.

Labor disputes are largely predictable. Not so student unrest. On a warm Sunday in March 1987, Joan and I were enjoying a relaxed breakfast at home when a phone call brought news of a racial brawl on campus. My reaction was: "There goes the spring."

Later that day some 150 students gathered to protest what they claimed was the beating of a group of black students and two black security guards by a mob of twenty white students. Four white students named as assailants maintained that the black students had started the fight, but that did not deter the black students from filing charges with the police. A newly formed group called Concerned Black Students at Columbia (CBSC) claimed that "white students have declared 'open season' on people of African descent" and demanded expulsion of the white students involved.

By Thursday, CBSC's charges, augmented by allegations that the attackers had threatened to "kill all of you fucking niggers," brought more than a thousand people to an angry rally. CBSC plastered the campus with posters containing the names and pictures of the four white students, characterizing them as a lynch mob.

I invited a CBSC delegation to meet with me. I did not have high hopes for that get-together. But my personal commitment to due process would not allow me to take any action against the accused white students unless a fair inquiry found them guilty. The black students were refusing to cooperate with our internal investigation of the incident. CBSC had also rejected a police request for interviews.

The CBSC's "Wanted" posters struck me as a dangerous incitement to violence, and I felt obliged to tell them that. I did promise to request the Manhattan district attorney's office to accelerate its inquiry, but that did not satisfy the group. They went away unhappy.

Then a freshman decided to display a Confederate flag from his window. Sixty students entered the dorm and demanded he take it down. He did, and that particular flame never grew into a conflagration.

Thirty days after the fight that started it all, twenty protestors chained the doors of Hamilton Hall. About one hundred more gathered around them. A thousand sympathizers rallied in front of Low, some asserting that I had interfered with the police department's investigation in order to protect the accused white students. I took the trouble to deny that outrageous claim.

This blockade of Hamilton Hall was very different from its predecessor two years earlier. In 1985, the campus was united in opposition to apartheid even if it was divided on the means of opposing it. I had decided to wait the protestors out rather than risk a major confrontation between students and the police. This time the protestors might well be sparking a dangerous racial confrontation. I had to get them out of there and reopen Hamilton. By the end of the following day, the police had arrested over ninety Hamilton Hall occupiers without incident, and free access to the building was fully restored.

That same day the two College deans who had been investigating the initial episode made their report. Though the complaining black students had refused to cooperate with the inquiry, the deans had managed to interview twenty-four witnesses. They determined that a white student made a racially offensive remark to a black student earlier in the evening. When he later emerged from the campus social center with four or five white students, a half dozen black students were waiting for them.

The report was agnostic on who started the ensuing clash but did find that the first undeniable assault occurred when another white student who happened on the scene was, without provocation, hit by an unidentified black man. The fight grew from there. In the course of it, one white student screamed racial epithets. The black security guards believed that the punches that struck them were not aimed at them but landed when they stepped in front of the brawlers. The guards felt harassed not by the white students but by a black woman who called them "Uncle Toms." The entire episode lasted less than five minutes.

Now the show was over, but not because of the report. The best campus pacifier was imminent: final exams.

The regular life of the university went on, of course. We dedicated the Donald Keene Center for Japanese Culture. I do not exaggerate when I say that Donald is the foremost scholar of Japanese literature in the Western world. In fact, since he has been honored with the Yomiuri Literary Prize for the best book of literary criticism written in Japanese, perhaps I should strike "Western." In any case, we are proud of him, and the creation of the Donald Keene Center was an expression of that pride.

We announced John Kluge's first twenty-five-million-dollar gift, creating the John Kluge Presidential Scholars Program, which coupled financial assistance to minority students in need with supplementary opportunities for intellectual growth such as summer research assistantships. John's own experience as a scholarship student and his commitment to equal opportunity made this program a perfect fit. Over the years, meeting the students and alumni who benefited from his generosity would give John enormous pleasure.

Large universities are in a constant state of renewal. Faculty retire or depart. New ones join us. So it is with a university's administration. The previous year we had lost a key colleague when Benno Schmidt, a brilliant scholar and very promising dean of the law school, left to become president of Yale. I went to New Haven to speak at a luncheon as part of Benno's presidential inauguration festivities

With Derek Bok at Harvard, Benno at Yale, and me at Columbia, three Ivy League universities were now headed by law deans. Jim Friedman's subsequent selection to head Dartmouth made four of us. I described this as a major sign of the decline of Western civilization. At he law faculty's suggestion, I appointed another brilliant scholar, Barbara Black, to succeed Benno. Barbara was my law school classmate, but the law faculty's enthusiastic support of her spared us from suggestions of cronyism.

This year we would lose another important leader. Patricia Battin, the head of libraries and vice president for information services, retired, a move that proved to be a step toward the end of my restructuring of the provost's job. In seeking a successor, we discovered that the best candidates didn't want to report to the executive vice president for academic affairs. They wanted to report to the provost, the officer with the highest status next to the president. I soon abolished the separate position of executive vice president for academic affairs.

23

A SABBATICAL LEAVE
AND A RETURN TO
CELEBRATIONS

*The unspoken fear of a chief executive who dares to take a leave is
that no one will even notice he's gone.*

In the fall of 1987, I took a sabbatical leave. The unspoken fear of a
chief executive who dares to take a leave is that no one will even
notice he's gone. I claimed that I had the place running so smoothly
that it could run without me for four months but not a moment longer. I knew that I wouldn't get a full sabbatical—I didn't even leave the
Northeast—but I would get relief from countless meetings and ceremonial occasions and wind up with about half time off. The biggest benefit
of that sabbatical was my summer break: instead of having to crank up
in August for all that had to be done at the start of the semester, we
spent most of the summer at Cape Cod.

When we returned to the city, there were, as I knew there would be,
some tasks that only a president could handle, though Bob Goldberger
was performing creditably as acting president. For example, I had to
recruit Herb Pardes to be dean of the medical school and vice president
for health sciences. He was then chairman of our psychiatry department
and head of the psychiatric institute and had an offer to run one of New
York City's big hospitals at a salary that was more than twice what we

were planning to pay. There was no way the president of the university should or could delegate that courtship.

I did pass on receiving the crown prince and princess of Japan, now the emperor and empress, but we would meet on other occasions. I didn't go to meetings of the University Senate, didn't preside at all the faculty meetings I usually attended, and gave very few speeches. I returned to the job refreshed, and there were plenty of gatherings to attend and speeches to give.

We dedicated Morris A. Schapiro Hall, which finally enabled Columbia College to become fully residential. Morris and his brother Meyer, one of the greatest art historians of the twentieth century, were both Columbia graduates, commuters from Brooklyn. Morris had originally gone into mining but soon turned to investment banking, where he proved to be immensely successful and very generous to Alma Mater.

Fred Knubel, our unfailingly reliable director of public information, was overseeing the press coverage of our new residence hall when a *New York Times* photographer asked for a picture of me and the building. Not for him the conventional photo of the proud president in front of his newest addition. He had lined up a shot in which I would lean way out over the parapet of a tall building across the street, with Schapiro Hall in the background. It looked dangerous. Fred Knubel offered to hold on to me from behind, out of view. I had never used the cliché that expresses complete faith in another human being—"I would trust him with my life"—but on that occasion that is precisely what I did with Fred.

Several years later this exemplary human being was killed in a freak accident. Fred was riding his bike in East Hampton when a car traveling in the opposite direction struck a deer that flew through the air and fatally injured Fred. I still miss him.

Columbia was not alone in seizing opportunities to celebrate. Before the year was out, I spoke at the centennials of Barnard, Teachers College and the University of Minnesota Law School. It was fun to go back to Minnesota and see old friends, but it was also a shock. I hadn't seen them in over thirty years: in my memory they were in their twenties, and here they were well into their fifties. Fritz Mondale introduced me; we had a private talk later, at which he asked my advice as to whether he should allow himself to be considered for the presidency of the University of Minnesota, which had recently become vacant. I thought it a bad idea despite the fact that Fritz would have made an excellent university president. The leadership pool for America's universities is very shallow, yet their faculties are mistrustful of any potential president who isn't an academic. I warned Fritz that when something went wrong at the university, and something always goes wrong sooner or later, there would be a serious risk that the faculty would turn on him. I don't know how seriously he took my advice, but he passed on the job.

A few weeks after we dedicated Schapiro Hall, we opened the Kathryn Bache Miller Theater. Before its rebuilding, it had been a decrepit academic theater, a very large lecture hall with a balcony that was ill suited for instruction. It was, in fact, the same McMillan Theatre where in 1968 I had spoken against a faculty strike. As the reborn Miller Theater, it became a much praised venue for music.

I gave the first of three parties at the President's House for our fencing team. I had done the same for the soccer team when they played for the national championship and promised at that time that I would throw a party for any Columbia team that finished first or second in the country. The fencing team qualified three times, and each time they brought me a present. As a result, I am the proud possessor of a sword, a lovely print depicting a fencing match, and a sweatshirt bearing the inscription: "Columbia F———ing Team." Even our best scholar-athletes don't take themselves too seriously.

I enjoyed celebrating the achievements of our athletes. A few years later, one of those celebrations led to a special treat for me. Gene Larkin, a Columbia alumnus who broke all the records Lou Gehrig had set when he played for Columbia, went on to play for the Minnesota Twins. He drove in the winning run in the tenth inning of the seventh game of the 1991 World Series.

That seemed to us to warrant recognition by his alma mater, so we arranged for me to present Gene with an alumni award at Yankee Stadium the following spring when the Twins were visiting the Yankees. I was asked whether I would like to throw out the first ball before the game. Easiest question I was ever asked.

President Bush had been ridiculed earlier that year when, throwing out the first ball to start the season, he bounced it in to the catcher. (I was told he had been wearing a bulletproof vest, not usually recommended pitching attire.) Though I would be unencumbered, I decided to throw a few practice pitches at Baker Field, drafting Joe, my driver, to serve as catcher.

When the afternoon of my major league debut arrived, I was escorted to the Yankee dugout, where I sat with the team until the public address announcer introduced me. Then I trotted out to the mound, whipped a respectable throw in to the catcher, who gave me the ball as a souvenir, and returned to the dugout. The Yankee photographer, who had been complaining to me about the umpires in the American League, said of my throw: "With the officiating in this league, that was a strike."

My favorite days of the academic year were its bookends, the beginning and the end. I began at the College's freshman orientation, joining the dean of the College and its director of admissions in greeting the new arrivals, and I closed at Commencement, sending out those who had arrived four years earlier and the thousands of seniors graduating from our other schools.

Unlike many of our annual events, delivering the welcoming talk always guaranteed a new audience of about a thousand fresh arrivals, so I didn't require a new text. As much as I respected what I had to say, I felt compelled to observe that "Several decades ago I sat where you sit, listening to our then President, Dwight Eisenhower, and I cannot remember a single word that estimable gentleman said."

We had a second empty-chair Commencement after we attempted to award an honorary degree to Bronislaw Geremek, a distinguished scholar and one of the leaders of Poland's Solidarity movement. The

Communist government, still in power, would not let him come. As we had with Desmond Tutu, we kept an empty chair for him. Happily, the following year he was able to fill it. Solidarity had succeeded in taking over the government, and Geremek was now a leader of the legislature. It was a special thrill to welcome him to Columbia.

For me Commencement Day was Parents' Day, the occasion on which families saw their dreams for their sons and daughters come true. (I always thought of my mother on that day.) But, of course, Commencement really belonged to those sons and daughters, a shared celebration of what they had accomplished and what they hoped still lay ahead. To enhance the day, I always insisted that the complement of worthies to whom we awarded honorary degrees include a recipient who would make the graduates say "Wow!" During my administration, we made honorary Columbians of, among many others, Katherine Hepburn, Mikhail Baryshnikov, Lauren Bacall, Dizzy Gillespie, and, of course, Joe DiMaggio.

At Columbia, honorary degree recipients do not speak at Commencement, but that didn't keep Harry Belafonte from providing a dramatic moment. As I handed him his degree, he asked, "Can I sing 'Day-O'?" Absolutely. And I doubt that any of those in attendance will ever forget the sight and sound of Harry Belafonte singing responsively with 35,000 people.

The Alumni Association would traditionally invite one of the honorary degree recipients to address its Commencement Day luncheon. One year I thought they would have a difficult time choosing between the brilliant diplomat George Kennan and the equally brilliant Justice William Brennan. Instead they chose the great clarinetist Benny Goodman. Since good manners would keep us from asking him to play, I thought they had a made a foolish choice. That didn't keep me from enjoying Benny Goodman as my luncheon companion and, after making brief self-deprecatory remarks, in which he said that his music spoke for him, he took out his clarinet and proceeded to play, beautifully, "Body and Soul."

One other honorary degree recipient's response was memorable. When our Eye Institute sought help in its pursuit of Bob Hope for a major gift after he had been a patient there, we agreed to hold a special convocation at which he would be awarded an honorary degree. Before the ceremony, I told him that we had set aside five minutes for him to respond. After I presented him with his degree, he moved to the lectern and announced: "President Sovern has told me I have five minutes. I usually take that long to respond to the applause."

It rained only once on Commencement during my thirteen years as president. Our rain contingency program instructed students and their families to go to the gym instead of Low Plaza, College Walk, and South Field, the great outdoor space where we normally gathered. The problem was that the gym couldn't possibly hold all the people we were directing there. We could have had a terrible tragedy. Fortunately, I took a look at the Commencement packet in advance, and the rain program part was dropped. Our rain program had become: Get Wet.

On our one rainy Commencement, I considered the possibility of erecting a temporary canopy over our honorary degree recipients and the podium, but I didn't like the idea of our staying dry while everyone else was rained upon. I did accept a very tall student's offer to hold two umbrellas over me, but he never got the rhythm of the proceedings. Every time I turned to welcome an honorand, he shifted the umbrellas, and a load of water poured over me.

I offered to cut the ceremony short, but thousands of voices answered me as one: "No!" Wet or dry, the graduates wanted their day. I then announced that I would dispense with my Commencement Address. *That* was met with a great cheer.

Nineteen eighty-eight was the year that Moody's raised the rating on Columbia's bonds to triple A. We had come a long way.

Marking the twentieth anniversary of the 1968 uprising, the *New York Times Magazine* ran a cover story entitled "Columbia Recovered," displaying the statue of Alma Mater and students relaxing on the steps of Low. "Columbia is in the midst of a dramatic resurgence. . . . If any one person is responsible for Columbia's recovery, it is surely Michael Sovern."[1] Of course no one person was responsible. I had a lot of help from very talented people.

24

REMEMBERING MALCOLM X
AND WORKING WITH THE
COMMUNITY

*Assessments of leaders devote too little attention to what
didn't happen on their watch.*

As densely populated as it is, the island of Manhattan still contained at least one five-acre tract on which nobody lived and
where little of commercial value was going on. It happened to be across
the street from our medical center. Eager to expand our own space and
believing the location was a natural for biomedical startup companies,
we thought the City of New York, the owner of the land, might let us
have it on favorable terms. Though the negotiations with the city were
lengthy and complex—we started in the administration of Mayor Koch,
and I concluded the deal in 1990 with Mayor Dinkins—they were the
least of the challenges we faced.

The site contained the Audubon Ballroom, an abandoned relic, on a
street where addicts would come to resupply. Preservationists loved its
façade and, though they had paid no attention to it until our plans became known and wouldn't dream of going there, they rallied to protect
it. We had anticipated what could have been a more serious problem.
Malcolm X had been assassinated in the Audubon Ballroom. No one
had paid much attention to this fact either, but we knew that our plans
would stimulate interest in its preservation.

Assessments of leaders devote too little attention to what didn't happen on their watch. And we didn't have any Malcolm X problems because we worked hard to be sure we wouldn't have any Malcolm X problems. We informed Betty Shabazz, Malcolm's widow, of our plans, seeking her permission to create Malcolm X Scholarships in the Medical School and to create a Malcolm X memorial in the first building to be erected on the site. I don't think it had anything to do with her support for our project, but at that year's Harlem Hospital Gala, I even had the privilege of dancing with her.

With only one exception, we received the support of every elected official representing a district that included our main campus or medical center. That meant our congressman, members of the State Senate and Assembly and City Council, and, of course, the mayor. (Half of them were African American.)

The one exception was Ruth Messinger, Manhattan's borough president. She initially objected to the project in support of the preservationists, not because of Malcolm X. But she clearly felt lonely opposing a project that would generate both jobs and scientific discoveries and that was supported by every other elected official. She solved her problem by offering to pay for the preservation of the façade with funds from the Borough president's capital budget. And so the façade of the Audubon Ballroom became the façade of the first building we erected on the Audubon site.

We were still confronted by some nuts. One group picketed my home, claiming that the Audubon project was genocidal and would decimate Harlem's population. I was never clear as to whether they thought we intended this or that it would be caused by careless medical experimentation. After a few days of chanting, they went away. Another group seemed more dangerous. They came after me in Low and punched a security chief when he blocked their way, but they were quickly repulsed and never reappeared.

Larry Dais, our assistant vice president for community relations, Greg Fusco, and I had years of effort invested in bringing us to the point where we could count on sympathetic reactions to productive projects from local politicians.

A community engagement we were particularly proud of was our provision of medical services to Harlem Hospital. The hospital belonged to the city but it contracted with Columbia to provide the doctors who then enjoyed Columbia appointments. Everything else was directly paid for by the city. Our negotiations could be difficult, and we usually lost money on these contracts, but, like the other hospitals with which we were affiliated, Harlem Hospital provided educational opportunities for our medical students. Most importantly, our doctors provided high-quality medical care to Harlem's residents.

I remember one of my visits with special pleasure. We were dedicating the hospital's new Neonatal Intensive Care Unit, a triumph for Dr. Margaret Haggerty, the hospital's superb chief of pediatrics. After the ICU dedication, Dr. Haggerty showed me around the rest of her pediatric empire. The nursery was full of unwanted infants born to AIDS-infected mothers. No one wanted to adopt even the uninfected infants because of their mothers' histories, and the hospital lacked the staff to spend time with them. When I returned to campus, I arranged for student volunteers to visit the hospital and cuddle the babies.

Columbia's community relations had fallen to a low point in the 1960s. The gym in Morningside Park, conceived as a mutually beneficial project to provide facilities for both Columbians and local residents, had instead become a symbol of segregation. As the surrounding neighborhood deteriorated, Columbia bought properties when it could. Several of these were single-room-occupancy hotels, occupied in part by prostitutes and addicts. While some of our neighbors were grateful when Columbia cleaned these out, others saw us as oppressors. Still others were fearful that our acquisition of apartment houses would lead to their eviction, though most were fully protected by New York's rent-control laws. It must be admitted that Columbia had acted with a heavy hand, with little concern for local reaction.

Andy Cordier began the process of making friends with our neighbors, and Bill McGill continued it, but building trust takes time, and there was still much to do. An important contaminant remained.

Columbia's roughly six thousand apartments contained three categories of tenants. A majority were Columbia students, faculty, and staff, all of whom had agreed to the affiliation clause, a promise that they would vacate their apartments when they ceased to be Columbians. Most of the rest had been living in their apartments when Columbia bought their buildings. They were protected in their occupancy by New York's rent-control and stabilization laws: the university could not assign their apartments to Columbians until these tenants left. The remainder—fewer than a hundred—were ex-Columbians. Though they too had promised to leave when their affiliation with Columbia ended, the combination of Columbia's relatively low rents and New York's housing shortage had induced them to stay on in violation of their promise.

We needed those apartments, so we embarked on a serious effort to enforce the affiliation agreement. I didn't have much sympathy for the occupants. They would not, after all, even be in those apartments if the people who had preceded them hadn't honored their promises and moved out. There was nothing sneaky about the affiliation agreement: everyone knew what they were getting into.

Not everyone was as hardhearted as I. Our local assemblyman, Ed Sullivan, was particularly sympathetic to the tenants' cause and allowed one of his aides, Kenneth Schaeffer, to serve as their lawyer. Tenants' complaints were generally grist for the mill of local politicians, so each had someone on the staff who would try to help.

Since there was no doubt that the tenants were legally obliged to leave, most did. But some fought hard. Though we could undoubtedly win all the cases in time, the controversy was poisoning our relations with our representatives. I invited them all to meet with me so that I could explain how critical our need for apartments was and how we could not afford to lose them by not enforcing the affiliation clause. My invitation was explicit: principals only, a condition that angered our local congressman, Ted Weiss. He came but angrily asked who I thought

I was to tell him who he should send to a meeting. I explained that if I hadn't done that, he would have sent his staffer who looks after tenants, and my message would at best have been watered down before it got to him. That calmed him down.

The meeting proved to be highly useful. Not long after, we gave a little. Since I had to acknowledge that, until we became aggressive, Columbia's enforcement of the affiliation clause had been casual, we conceded that families whose failure to move had been ignored for several years could stay on. Everyone else had to go. And that was the end of that.

25

INTERNATIONAL GUESTS, ANNIVERSARIES, DEDICATIONS, AND A NEW CAMPAIGN

We invited all of our living Nobel laureates back to campus.
Nineteen came.

B oris Yeltsin was not yet Russia's president when I introduced him to an overflow crowd in Low. When his microphone failed, he joked, "They do that to me at home too."

We conferred an honorary degree on President Cossiga of Italy, a leader I had come to know and respect as we worked toward the creation of the Italian Academy for Advanced Studies at Columbia.

On Washington's birthday, 1990, we awarded an honorary degree to Vaclav Havel, a man with extraordinary appeal for us. A revered intellectual and playwright, he had survived imprisonment by Czechoslovakia's Communist regime and had since been elected president of his country.

Havel's friend and countryman and member of our School of the Arts Faculty, the film director Milos Forman, wanted us to present the degree at the Cathedral of St. John the Divine, a few blocks away, where Milos was arranging a star-studded ceremony. I explained that Columbia had only awarded honorary degrees off campus three times in over two hundred years—to Abraham Lincoln in Washington, when he was too busy with the Civil War to come to us; to an incapacitated William O. Douglas; and to Desmond Tutu, when the South African government would not let him out of the country. There was no comparable reason why Havel couldn't come to campus.

Milos was not happy, but he finally agreed: early in the evening I would award the degree in Low, Havel would accept with brief remarks, and then we would proceed to St. John's, passing between rows of students holding lighted candles, which turned out to be quite beautiful. Milos was a terrific director—he had already won Academy Awards for *Amadeus* and *One Flew Over the Cuckoo's Nest*—and it showed that evening. The ceremony at St. John's, culminating in Havel's own speech, was deeply moving. And the kid from the South Bronx got to sit next to Gregory Peck.

Trips to Washington, D.C., and Aspen, Colorado, yielded notable experiences. I flew to Washington to speak at the inauguration of Father Leo O'Donovan as the new president of Georgetown University. I was nominally there to represent American higher education, but I assumed I was picked because his mother had been a maid at Columbia, and I was, ex officio, part of a great American success story.

The day was overcast and the marshal of the ceremony, after looking worriedly at the sky, decided we could proceed to the outdoor space set up for the event. It was a bad call. Not long after the procession stepped out, the heavens opened. We made it to a sheltered platform, but everyone else got very wet.

As the guests marched to their seats, I was striking whole paragraphs from my speech. I couldn't offer to scrap the whole thing, as I had at our rainy Commencement, but I could show some consideration by keeping it brief. All for naught. After a whispered consultation, Leo announced to the assembly that the rain had soaked the wiring of the public address system so thoroughly that any speaker would be risking electrocution. I was sorry Leo had to miss most of the special pleasure of his own inauguration.

The Aspen Institute's fortieth anniversary was quite a party, featuring Prime Minister Margaret Thatcher and the first President Bush, Bill Moyers, and Barbara Walters. President Bush had to leave early because

Iraq had just invaded Kuwait, but not before he delivered his remarks and I delivered mine from his traveling lectern, which was still in place when I spoke.

I was there because the Aspen Institute is a direct descendant of Columbia's Humanities course. When Mortimer Adler was a young member of the Columbia faculty, Robert M. Hutchins, the president of the University of Chicago, recruited him to bring the great books course to Chicago. The chairman of Chicago's trustees was so captivated by the offering that he invited him to present a condensed version for some friends at his vacation home in Aspen.

I gave a serious talk, remaining faithful to my view that an audience should not have to listen to me for more than twenty minutes. The reaction was enthusiastic, and I must still have been enjoying the glow of that warm reception because on the way home a flight attendant told me I was the sexiest man on the plane. (I know what you're thinking: that I was the only man on the plane.)

In October we celebrated the centennial of the birth of Columbia's thirteenth president and America's thirty-fourth, Dwight Eisenhower. With his granddaughters Susan and Anne in attendance, we named a project in which he had shown great interest the Eisenhower Center for the Conservation of Human Resources.

I believe the center and a portrait are the only indications on campus that President Eisenhower passed this way. He was nominally president of Columbia from 1948 to January 1953, when he moved out of the Columbia president's house into the White House, but for much of that time he was on leave as the founding head of NATO and then fully engaged in his presidential campaign. As a consequence, happy as I am to claim him as a predecessor, he had little impact on the university.

In November I led a celebration of great teaching, announcing the endowment of ten new professorships honoring the art of teaching and the funding of a challenge grant to help create twenty more such chairs. Jacques Barzun, one of Columbia's greatest humanists, had until this moment resolutely refused all formal honors, but I persuaded him to let us name one of the new professorships for him, and he traveled from his retirement in Texas to be with us for the occasion.

We created the Eilenberg Professorship. Sammy Eilenberg was an extraordinary man, one of the most respected mathematicians in the world who had also put together a coveted collection of art from the Indian subcontinent. The Eilenberg professorship was the result of a creative melding of these two aspects of Sammy's persona. Most of his collection went to the Metropolitan Museum of Art on condition that they arrange for the funding of a professorship in mathematics at Columbia.

We dedicated the Temple Hoyne Buell Center for the Study of American Architecture, funded by Mr. Buell. The new center was housed in freshly refurbished space in the only building on campus that predated Columbia's arrival on Morningside Heights. It had been the gate house for the Bloomingdale Insane Asylum, Columbia's predecessor on the site. Old-timers referred to Columbia students as the new inmates.

When we launched our new campaign, John Kluge came through once again, giving the campaign a running start with his second $25 million gift. This time the goal was $1.15 billion, the largest in the history of higher education. Its achievement was assured by the time I retired from the presidency three years later.

We had launched the first campaign with a tailor-made theatrical event. This time we invited all of our living Nobel laureates back to campus, conferred honorary degrees on those who had not yet received them from us, and gave specially created awards to all of them. Nineteen laureates returned for the festivities, underlining Columbia's outsized contribution to human understanding.

The big event at Columbia in the spring of 1991 was the dedication of the Italian Academy for Advanced Studies in America. This was the culmination of several years of sustained effort by Professor Maristella Lorch; Provost Jonathan Cole, who had succeeded Bob Goldberger; and me. We persuaded the Italian government to create the academy and house it in Columbia's Casa Italiana, a seven-story Renaissance-style palazzo immediately adjacent to the law school.

The academy was to be a center for advanced research in areas relating to Italian culture and society. It would also provide a place for collaborative projects between senior Italian and American scholars, particularly those open to interdisciplinary research. The Italian government gave us seven and a half million dollars to renovate the Casa and ten million for the academy's programs. And they helped us raise a few million more in endowment.

I enjoyed pointing out to our Italian benefactors that Columbia was the only major American university named for an Italian. Columbia does in fact have a long history of teaching and scholarship in Italian studies. The origins go all the way back to a chance meeting in a Broadway bookstore early in the nineteenth century. Clement Clarke Moore, a classical scholar, the author of the poem best known as "T'was the Night Before Christmas," and the son of Bishop Benjamin Moore, the fifth president of Columbia, struck up a conversation with a fellow browser. His new acquaintance turned out to be Lorenzo DaPonte, Mozart's librettist for *Don Giovanni* and other operas. Moore brought Signor DaPonte home to meet his father, who made his home available for DaPonte's first Italian classes in America. Thus was begun Columbia's first professorship in Italian.

President Cossiga, Prime Minister Andreotti, and a host of other dignitaries came for the dedication of the academy. When speaking to a group from another country, I always tried to say a few words in that country's language, and so I greeted our guests with "Signor Presidente; Primo Ministro Andreotti; illustri invitati e cari amici; loyal friends of Columbia and of the magnificent land of our namesake, Cristoforo Colombo: Benvenuti. Questo è un giorno particolare e lieto per noi." Later a young reporter from RAI, the Italian network, asked to interview me, saying, "Since you speak Italian, let's do the interview in Italian." I replied: "You have heard all my Italian."

To create the academy, we had to overcome two difficult technical obstacles. First, under Italian law, to obtain the funds for the renovation of the Casa, we had to sell the building to Italy. But we didn't want to give up a campus facility. The solution was to couple the sale with options extending far into the future allowing us to repurchase the building at the original price. But once we sold the building it was no longer entitled to Columbia's exemption from the real estate tax, and Italy's real estate tax exemption applied only to its diplomatic facilities.

Fortunately, the creation of the academy was so well received, especially by Italian Americans in the New York State Legislature, that we had relatively little difficulty persuading the legislature to enact a special law granting the academy a tax exemption. Our forays out of the ivory tower into the politics of Italy and of New York State turned out well.

26

CLOSING A SCHOOL

*Columbia's library school was founded by the most famous
librarian in America and perhaps the world.*

O nce, driving in India, I found myself fascinated by how many
other means of transport shared the street. I saw an elephant, a
horse, a bicycle, and a man carrying a bundle of sticks on his head. Even
after the advent of the automobile, beasts of burden, including man,
were still in use in India. I said, "It's just like a university. Things may be
added, but nothing is eliminated."

I turned out to be wrong in at least one instance. Even as we were
planning the creation of the Italian Academy, we were planning to close
Columbia's School of Library Service.

I knew that even hinting at such a step could rouse alumni as no
fundraising solicitation can. They in turn would generate protests from
other interested parties. While I was reflecting on the recommendation
of our provost and our chief financial officer that we close the library
school, a recommendation that had been signaled in a widely circulated
report from the provost, I heard not only from the librarians we had
trained but from many others maintaining that our future graduates
would be desperately needed.

What I hadn't had occasion to think about was that closing a school is relatively expensive, at least for a time. The tuition revenue dries up, but obligations to faculty and staff take time to run off.

When closing a school, universities have the right to dismiss even tenured faculty, but we pride ourselves on being humane institutions, loyal to those who have served us well for many years. Fortunately, the School of Library Service was our smallest, with only a handful of tenured professors. Two would find jobs elsewhere, two retired, and we found a position elsewhere in the university for the one who remained.

Why did we close the school? Why take the heat and the near-term financial penalty? I had to be prepared to explain our decision, especially since Columbia's was the oldest library school in the country and once arguably the best. It was founded by the most famous librarian in America, and perhaps the world, Melville Dewey, the creator of the Dewey Decimal System, once the library world's most widely used classification system.

The school was at a crossroads. It was no longer one of the best in the country. It had to improve, or it wasn't worth keeping. Since the school lacked the capacity to generate the additional funds needed for improvement, the university would have to make the school's needs a high priority if we were to save it.

In the end we found needs elsewhere in the university more compelling. We were not persuaded that the school's loss would damage the library world. Perhaps most telling was that no one else in the university came forward to say that the school's work was important to them. I contrasted this with my experience as dean of the law school when I proposed to let our course in Roman law die. I was called upon by a delegation from the classics, history, and political science departments to tell me how important the course was to them, persuading me that we should at least offer Roman law occasionally.

Under the circumstances I did not feel we could justify dedicating resources to the school, resources that were badly needed elsewhere. Closing it was the right choice.

27

SALMAN RUSHDIE AT RISK

To make sure my conscience would not go quietly, Caroline Kennedy was among the evening's speakers. Causing harm to any of the evening's participants would be unforgivable, but adding to her family's tragedies was unthinkable.

Joan Konner, the dean of the journalism school, called me with surprising news. Salman Rushdie was willing to come and speak at Columbia at a time when he was still living under armed guard to protect him from assassination. His novel *The Satanic Verses* had prompted Ayatollah Khomeini to issue a fatwa, condemning Rushdie to death and calling on all zealous Muslims to execute him.

The journalism school had the perfect occasion for Rushdie—a dinner celebrating the two hundredth anniversary of the First Amendment. But Dean Konner was quite properly consulting me to be sure the university had no objection to her pursuing the possibility. We both knew that a Rushdie translator in Japan had been murdered and that another in Italy had barely survived an attempt on his life. What implications would a Rushdie appearance have for the safety of Columbia's students and staff? Would we have to live in fear for an extended period? I told Dean Konner I needed to know more.

This chapter appeared in *Sesquicentennial Essays of the Faculty of Columbia Law School* (New York: Columbia Law School, 2008), 230– 232.

What I learned was that Rushdie had made a few limited appearances in the United Kingdom without any consequences for the places at which he appeared. And Columbia's security chief assured me that our relations with the New York Police Department were such that he was confident that, working with them, we could protect Rushdie. I told Dean Konner to take the next steps but to keep me informed.

Within a few days I received another surprising phone call. A mutual friend had been asked by Lawrence Eagleburger, then deputy secretary of state, to have me call him about the Rushdie matter. When I did, Eagleburger explained that negotiations to obtain the release of Terry Anderson and the other hostages being held by Hezbollah in Lebanon were close to success. An appearance by Rushdie in the United States would derail those negotiations. Moreover, Eagleburger wanted to be sure I understood that the people intent on killing Rushdie were very serious and that they wouldn't care about collateral damage.

I certainly did not want to be responsible for preventing the release of people who had already endured more than six years of harsh imprisonment. But there was a real possibility that the hostages would be released before we had to make a final decision about Rushdie. Eagleburger and I agreed to await events and stay in touch.

Happily, the hostages were released, and we proceeded with our plans for a Rushdie visit. But how to get him here? No commercial airline could carry him. The British had a weekly official flight to Washington. If they would take him, we could handle the rest. But they wouldn't do it without official permission from Washington. It was time for a call to my new friend Larry Eagleburger. He was mindful of my cooperation when he needed it, and he willingly signed off on Rushdie's traveling with the Brits. An American company agreed to lend us a corporate jet to fly Rushdie from Washington to New York. A combination of Columbia's security force, the New York City police, and absolute secrecy would presumably take care of the rest.

Still, I was worried about those attending the First Amendment celebration. We were exposing them to risk of harm if an attempt were made on Rushdie's life, and we were doing so without giving them any choice in the matter. To make sure my conscience would not go quietly, Caroline Kennedy was among the evening's speakers. Causing harm to any of the evening's participants would be unforgivable, but adding to her family's tragedies was unthinkable.

To help me work the problem through, I called Punch Sulzberger, then the publisher of the *New York Times*, a co-chairman of the evening, and one of the few who knew Rushdie was coming. We agreed that I would notify each of the evening's program participants twenty-four hours in advance and offer them an opportunity to withdraw. (None did.) And we reassured ourselves that the quality of the security to be provided was as good as it gets. On earlier occasions we had helped protect a number of heads of state and government whose lives were at risk, including Rajiv Gandhi, whose own security, sadly enough, later failed.

I needed reassurance on one other score. Our guests included several hundred journalists. What would save us from several hundred cell phones spreading the word of Rushdie's whereabouts as soon as he appeared? I tested Low Library's rotunda myself. No cell phone signal could penetrate its thick walls. When we gathered there for dinner, no one outside would know what was happening inside.

The evening arrived. A number of those in attendance asked me why they had to pass through metal detectors. I smiled and told them the safety of our guests was very important to us. No one pressed the question. While our guests were enjoying cocktails and dinner, an armor-plated, bomb-proof car was bringing Rushdie from his hotel to Columbia. A curtain parted, and, flanked by six armed plainclothesmen, Rushdie stepped to the podium.

It was the first time I had ever heard several hundred people gasp in unison. He spoke feelingly and eloquently, telling us of his times of hope and despair. He shared the pain of isolation. And he tried for the long view:

Sometimes I think that one day, Muslims will be ashamed of what Muslims did in these times, will find the "Rushdie affair" as improbable as the West now finds martyr-burning. One day they may agree that—

as the European Enlightenment demonstrated—freedom of thought is precisely freedom from religious control, freedom from accusations of blasphemy. Maybe they'll agree, too, that the row over *The Satanic Verses* was at bottom an argument about who should have power over the grand narrative, the Story of Islam, and that that power must belong equally to everyone. That even if my novel were incompetent, its attempt to retell the story would still be important. That if I've failed, others must succeed, because those who do not have power over the story that dominates their lives, power to retell it, re-think it, deconstruct it, joke about it, and change it as times change, truly are powerless, because they cannot think new thoughts.

One day. Maybe. But not today.

And then we spirited him away. The First Amendment had a fitting send-off for the beginning of its third century.

28

HAIL AND FAREWELL

Though the presidency is indeed a bully pulpit, it is a pulpit without intimacy, without the sustained dialogue of the mutually nourishing teacher–pupil relationship.

B ill McGill had retired after ten years as Columbia's president and had advised me to do the same, but I was still going strong at the ten-year mark and ignored his advice.

Our balanced budget had grown an average of more than 10 percent a year for ten years, fueling a strengthening of financial aid and a doubling of faculty salaries even as we increased the size of the faculty. And that doesn't count the hundreds of millions we were pouring into the restoration and expansion of our physical plant. At the same time we increased the value of our endowment by a billion dollars. Columbia's growing strength renewed my confidence during years ten and eleven.

But year twelve would prove to be a difficult one. When I accepted the presidency, I had said something like this to my wife, Joan: "The law school was a wonderfully comfortable community, manageable, almost intimate, in its scale. This is going to be different. With over ten thousand employees, on any given day someone I don't even know can make me look like an idiot." And someone did.

I got my first inkling of the problem late on a Friday afternoon. A *New York Times* reporter called to ask what I had to say about Columbia's destruction of records backing up research costs for which we had billed the federal government. I said I would have to get back to him. I had no idea what he was talking about, but, with the Memorial Day weekend about to begin, I assumed I had time to find out.

I was wrong. Saturday's *Times* carried a major story telling me and everyone else what I did not know. Here is the lead: "Federal auditors at Columbia University reported yesterday that important records accounting for more than $60 million in Federal research costs in 1986 have been destroyed, even though Columbia knew the government might need them to determine the extent to which inappropriate expenses had been charged to taxpayers."[1]

The lead was accurate, though the implication that we might have been seeking to hide something was not. What happened was that the Office of Naval Research, the agency overseeing our research contracts with the federal government, had completed its audit for the year ending six years earlier but had not yet signed off. It had delayed that final step after Stanford was found to have overcharged the government millions in overhead costs for federally sponsored research, and a congressional subcommittee undertook an extended investigation into expenditures universities charged to the government. Under the circumstances the Office of Naval Research notified us that it might have to reopen the audit and that all records relevant to the audit should be preserved. That message was duly circulated to the appropriate university employees.

About one hundred and fifty cartons of records were stored in the basement of one of our apartment buildings, an arrangement that upset the residents. They feared a fire hazard and wanted the space to store their own things. An associate controller, forgetting the order to preserve the records, bowed to the residents' repeated complaints. The boxes were compacted and sent to a landfill.

As bad luck would have it, the Office of Naval Research did want to see those records, and a few days before my call from the *Times* our controller's office advised them that the records had been destroyed. Naval Research in turn informed the congressional subcommittee, which generated the *Times* story and was rewarded with ample space for its comments:

> "The subcommittee has been informed that there are problems with large and not properly justified overhead expenses at Columbia but it appears that the records associated with those charges were destroyed by the University," Representative John D. Dingell, Chairman of the subcommittee, said through a spokesman. "In all of the cases the subcommittee has examined, this is the only university where there has been a problem with record keeping and certainly with the destruction of records."

Whatever the faults of my subordinates, I had, however unwittingly, committed a cardinal sin: I had failed to protect Columbia's trustees from being surprised by bad news in the public press. I scrambled to catch up, beginning with an apologetic call to G. G. Michelson, our chairman.

To find out how much of the *Times* story was true and to decide on next steps, I summoned key administrators and the offending associate controller to a Sunday morning meeting. I learned that it was almost impossible to recover the lost records (though I did order a visit to the landfill to check) but that we could probably produce duplicates of almost everything. I was assured that we had no reason to expect the auditors to find any overcharges particularly as they had already worked through those records for eighteen months. That assurance was borne out by subsequent events. I was warned that Congressman Dingell and his staff were bullies, that we could expect no mercy from them, and that we should do everything we could to appease them.

We resolved to cooperate fully with the Dingell subcommittee, going so far as to retain a lobbyist for the sole purpose of helping us with the relationship. We also appointed an independent counsel to investigate Columbia's behavior.

We found the duplicates, the special counsel reported that we had been sloppy but not guilty of any wrongdoing, and the audit was concluded without further incident. After considerable reflection I decided not to fire the associate controller. Years later, after I had left the presidency, I called him for help with a minor matter. He was very responsive.

Year twelve brought trouble on another front. Not long into my second decade, financial pressures had begun to mount. New York State cut its support to us from more than twelve million dollars a year to less than three. The medical costs of our fringe benefits package were growing by leaps and bounds. The federal government was pushing back on the indirect costs of research, the amounts they paid to universities to help pay the overhead expenses we incurred in aid of research.

Our successes were breeding fresh strains. New buildings entailed new energy and maintenance expenses. Higher salaries increased fringe benefit costs. And, of course, the larger faculty brought all sorts of costs.

We were violating the spending rule I had initiated to keep the real value of the endowment from eroding, which it will do if expenditures plus inflation exceed the endowment's growth. (Gifts to endowment are expected to increase its value, so they are not counted toward merely preventing it from eroding.) Our peer schools were generally spending 5 percent or less of their endowment. That widely utilized 5 percent figure was and is thought to achieve the desired result over time. We adopted a version of the 5 percent rule too, choosing 5.5 percent.

During my first decade the capital markets were frequently quite good to us, giving us gains that exceeded expenditures plus inflation. As a result, we could violate our spending rule and not only preserve the real value of the endowment but actually add to it. Since we had many pressing needs, though I had recommended the spending rule, the trustees and I thought it prudent to exceed it. Several years of this gave rise to a lack of discipline; one year we spent over 10 percent instead of 5.5 percent.

That is not quite so profligate as it sounds because the percentage was applied to a three-year average. If the endowment is rising, 10 percent of a three-year average is obviously less than 10 percent of this year's value. And the endowment was continuing to grow faster than inflation. We never invaded the endowment, and we maintained a balanced budget every year. Nonetheless, it did seem that our spending was slipping out of control, so we decided that, over time, we would come into compliance with the 5.5 percent rule.

The budget pressures coincided with the coming of age of a new Columbia component, the Arts and Sciences Faculty. Our history in this area was peculiar. We originally had four schools in the arts and sciences: Columbia College; the Graduate School of Arts and Sciences; the School of International and Public Affairs; and General Studies, which was devoted mainly to older students. The faculties of these schools were almost identical, overlapping about 95 percent. Yet there was no arts and sciences faculty as such.

In the mid-1980s, I created the post of vice president for the arts and sciences with responsibility for the faculty in those four schools. (We later added the School of the Arts.) There was considerable opposition to creating a single faculty of arts and sciences for fear that it would subordinate Columbia College. It took me several years to persuade the trustees to create the Faculty of Arts and Sciences on condition that the College faculty and the faculties of the other schools be allowed to continue as well. Though the dean and faculty of the College with the strongest commitment to undergraduate education still opposed the idea, a substantial majority of arts and sciences professors favored it. I believed it would lead to more responsible governance. I was mistaken.

The new organization took hold just as our budget difficulties were coming to a head. The Arts and Sciences Faculty elected an executive committee chaired by a man I had passed over for provost: I had fired another of its members as dean of the College. As the old saying has it, friends may come and go, but enemies accumulate. My new creature gave me a hard time, complaining vociferously about the retrenchment we were imposing.

We were not, in fact, requiring any drastic remedies, no hiring freezes, no caps on faculty salaries. We simply slowed our annual rate of growth from the double digits of the 1980s to the 5 to 7 percent range. That was enough to upset some of the faculty.

Even as campus events were demanding my full attention, Joan's health was deteriorating. After a mastectomy, we had been told that no cancer cells had been found in her lymph nodes, so we had good reason to hope we had seen the last of her breast cancer. But four and a half years later, the cancer had metastasized to her brain.

We were blessed with extraordinary medical care in the combination of Bud Rowland, Columbia's chief of neurology, and Ben Stein, the chief of neurosurgery. They were later joined by a wonderfully caring oncologist, Martin Oster. Thanks to them and Joan's determination to live as full a life as she could, we managed surprisingly well. Joan attended Columbia events where I thought her presence would be helpful or where I thought she would have a good time. We continued to entertain, go to theater and concerts, even to travel.

But the cancer was spreading. She underwent brain surgery one more time. It may have slowed the disease, but it didn't stop it.

It was against this background that I had to deal with the complaints of the arts and sciences faculty. Jack Greenberg, who had become dean of Columbia College, and Jonathan Cole, the provost, advised me that I should spend more time meeting with individual or small groups of faculty to respond to the complaints. At one time I would have tackled that assignment with gusto, and I started to follow their advice. But I discovered that with a life-and-death crisis at home I had no patience with what by comparison seemed like the petty grievances of faculty. And I didn't want to take that extra time away from Joan.

A university president who cannot empathize with the problems of his faculty has no business in the job. After giving the matter a great deal of thought, I decided the time had come for me to retire from the presidency. My decision was reinforced by a growing tension between my original goals in joining the university and the demands of the presidency. It is thrilling to be leading an enterprise that aspires to transmit the heritage of civilization, to prepare tomorrow's leaders in virtually every field of human activity. It is exciting to go to work each day knowing that you are contributing, in however modest a way, to the work of scientists and scholars who are exploring the cosmos, seeking an understanding of our past, pursuing answers to the mysteries of life itself.

Yet . . . I became a professor in the first place because I believe in the value of helping others to learn and grow and contributing something to knowledge and understanding. While making it possible for others to do that at the highest possible level can be very satisfying, it remains the case that one's original purposes now lie at a remove. Though the presidency is indeed a bully pulpit, it is a pulpit without intimacy, without the sustained dialogue of the mutually nourishing teacher-pupil relationship.

As is the custom, I gave a year's notice, announcing in June 1992 that I would leave at the end of the next academic year. The trustees, though sorry to see me go, understood and adopted a generous resolution, including these passages:

> A restless engagement with the world is as characteristic of this man as his humanist imagination, his profound commitment to justice, and his insistence on excellence. . . .
>
> In sum, we are indebted to Michael I. Sovern for his lifetime of service to Columbia. He has been a leader, educator, and colleague of the highest order, a man who helped shape this institution and leaves it, strengthened, to a rising generation.

I could not have hoped for a more appreciative sendoff. Even the *Columbia Spectator*, the student newspaper that often served as an ex officio critic of Columbia's president, devoted an editorial to my accomplishments and bid me a fond farewell.

29

THE LAST YEAR

There is no better way to learn something than to teach it.

G reg Fusco would refer to the 1992–1993 academic year as my victory lap, but it was anything but relaxed.

In September we dedicated the Morris A. Schapiro Center for Engineering and Physical Science Research. The building was named for the very same donor who had given us the residence hall that completed our drive to make housing available to all Columbia College students. Fundraisers take heed: treat your donors well, and they will keep on giving.

A few days later I left to visit alumni in the Far East. We started in Taipei, where I made a new friend in Douglas Hsu, who seemed to know everyone in Taiwan. He brought us to meet President Lee and arranged a special visit to the Palace Museum, the home of a superb collection of Chinese art and artifacts that Chang Kai Shek had taken when he and his Nationalist forces fled the Communist mainland. Douglas would become a generous supporter of Columbia and would later join me on the board of the Asian Cultural Council and help support arts exchanges between Asia and the United States.

After I spoke to the Taiwan Alumni Association, we moved on to Hong Kong, where I met with the Hong Kong United States Economic

Cooperation Committee, of which I was a founding member; spoke at an Asian Cultural Council luncheon; addressed the Asia Society; and was feted at a beautiful party hosted by the Hong Kong Alumni Association. I also had the pleasure of meeting Peter Woo, a leading businessman who would later join the Columbia trustees.

On to Seoul, where the Korea Alumni Association turned out in force for my talk, and then to Tokyo, where I addressed the Japan Alumni Association. Our ambassador to Japan, Michael Armacost, a Columbia Ph.D., hosted a reception for us at his residence. While I was on the receiving line, a Japanese guest I didn't recognize handed me a small package. When I opened it later, I found an expensive camera. I searched for an accompanying card, but there was none. I never found out who my mystery benefactor was.

When I returned I addressed dinners for Harlem Hospital, the Horwitz Prizes, and the Alexander Hamilton Medal. I told the guests at the dental school's seventy-fifth anniversary dinner how happy I was to be able to talk to them without something in my mouth. And there were the inevitable sad occasions: eulogies for Bob Christopher, the former *Newsweek* editor and Pulitzer Prize administrator; and for Ward Dennis, the beloved dean of the School of General Studies.

The story of *Babar the Elephant*, a book I had read to my children, provided a delightful interlude. Frances Poulenc had set the work to music, and the Columbia University Orchestra wanted to perform it at a children's concert. Would I serve as narrator? Synchronizing with the orchestra proved harder than I anticipated, but the children loved it, and so did I. The performance was recorded and, I note with pride, is still available from Arabesque Records.

On the fiscal front we managed to make a real dent in our fringe benefit costs, addressing both pensions and health benefits. Our pension plan was grossly excessive. Before I became an administrator, I knew that under Columbia's deferred contribution plan I would actually retire at considerably more than I was making as a full-time faculty member. That was when the mandatory retirement age was sixty-eight. When the retirement age moved to seventy, with two more years of university funding and two fewer years of benefits, the plan became even richer.

With the elimination of mandatory retirement, faculty who chose to stay much past seventy would reap a bonanza. It obviously made sense to redirect some of the assets going into pensions. But faculty regarded the existing plan as an entitlement. Provost Jonathan Cole and Joe Mullinix, our vice president for finance and administration, held countless meetings to explain what we planned to do, and their efforts helped calm everyone. And anyone objecting to the changes couldn't call upon me to resign: I had already announced my retirement.

Our proposal was not harsh. Under the old plan, when I reached the age of fifty-five with twenty-five years of service, the university would increase its contribution each year to 15 percent of my salary up to the Social Security base and 20 percent of my salary above that. We simply shaved 2.5 percent off those numbers so they would become 12.5 percent and 17.5 percent. Though contribution levels were lower for younger faculty with fewer years of service, the plan was still a very generous one after our cuts. The change would ultimately save millions of dollars.

Our initiative on health benefits was better received. It took advantage of the fact that we have a large and distinguished medical faculty, many of whom were already the doctors of choice for our colleagues. We entered into an agreement with a point-of-service health care organization to add our medical faculty who wished to be included to their roster for the sole purpose of serving Columbia faculty who opted for that program. Then we made the program financially more attractive than the old indemnity plan. More than half the faculty with an indemnity plan elected to move into managed care, generating substantial savings in our health care costs.

One of my fantasies while president was that some day I would teach the College's Humanities course. There is no better way to learn something than to teach it, and while I learned a great deal when I took Humanities as an undergraduate, the books are virtually inexhaustible, and I thought it would be great fun to return to them as a teacher.

I found a way to bring that fantasy closer to reality by conceiving of a TV series that took as its theme a key premise of the study of the humanities—that the great works of the past have something to teach us about the present. With Jerry Greene's financial help, I brought that series to life during my last year as president.

Each program had a major topic—for example, war and peace, leadership, natural law. I would lead a conversation with two guests, one a Columbia professor well versed in the great works of the past and the other someone with a special connection to the topic. On war and peace, Robert McNamara, America's secretary of defense during the Vietnam War, who had just written a *mea culpa* book, proved to be the perfect guest. Fritz Mondale was my outside guest for the leadership program. Justice Antonin Scalia joined Professor Charles Larmore and me for natural law.

The series, entitled *Leading Questions*, ran on Channel 13 in New York and on a number of other Public Broadcasting System channels. I can safely say it was one of the most intellectual series ever to appear on television and almost certainly one of the least watched. But my belief that teaching is a great way to learn was confirmed yet again. Along with a handful of viewers, I learned a great deal.

Early in the spring of 1993 I played a small role in helping persuade President Clinton to appoint Ruth Ginsburg to the Supreme Court. Here is how her husband, Martin Ginsburg, would later describe my bit part:

> I went looking for academics who knew and admired Ruth and would be pleased to confirm in writing. High on my list was Michael Sovern, President of Columbia University who, twenty-two years earlier, as Dean of Columbia Law School, hired Ruth as the first tenured woman law professor in that institution's long history. In April Mike wrote a really great letter to President Clinton urging Ruth's nomination. . . .
>
> Toward the end of April I received, out of the blue, a telephone call from Senator Moynihan. He had just flown to New York City on Air Force One with President Clinton. During the ride the President

had asked if he, Pat, had recommendations for the Supreme Court vacancy. . . . He had only one recommendation, Ruth Bader Ginsburg. . . .

What I did not yet understand was why Senator Moynihan, uninterested in early February, had metamorphosed into so grand a champion at the dawn of May. But I learned later. When Mike Sovern wrote the President, he sent a copy of his letter to the Senator with the briefest covering note—which read simply, "Pat, She's the real thing. Mike." I had not known this, but Pat and Mike had been close and mutually admiring friends for decades, and that brief note from a highly regarded friend did it.[1]

When the time came for me to be honored at a moving farewell dinner, for the first time since Salman Rushdie's appearance I heard several hundred people gasp in unison. The cause was John Kluge's announcement that he was pledging sixty million dollars to Columbia in my honor.

John's pledge was the high point of an evening that included tributes from Henry King, chairman of the trustees; Pamela Harriman; Kitty Carlisle Hart; and Franklin Thomas. Speaking for the faculty, University Professor Tsung-Dao Lee, a Nobel laureate in physics, touched on what I believe a university is all about:

Michael Sovern knows how to attract the world's best scholars to Columbia and what it takes to support such a world-class faculty. . . . Thanks to him, Columbia is one of those rare places where the most exceptional scholars and the best teachers are one and the same.

In some sense this should come as no surprise, since Mike himself is an outstanding legal scholar and great teacher.

30

A BACKWARD GLANCE

We tried to maintain a community of civility,
to treat all with decency and respect.

A common refrain of departing executives is that it's time for me to go because I have accomplished what I set out to do. No retiring university president can honestly say that unless his or her goals were insufficiently ambitious. There will always be needs unfulfilled, challenges unmet, more to be done.

As I remember with pleasure the moment we admitted women to Columbia College, I must also remember that the women we were admitting would be taught by an overwhelmingly male faculty. And despite my earnest efforts that was still largely true when I left office.

Until World War II, America's elite professoriate was essentially the preserve of white Protestant men. The late Milton Handler, one of the law faculty's greats, told me that he had originally wanted to be a professor of English but had been warned off: Columbia did not appoint Jews to its English department. The odds were stacked even more heavily against women. Columbia never granted tenure to the great Margaret Mead.

The virtual bar against Jews is long gone, as my own career attests. And the doors are generally open to women and minorities, although other factors still operate to slow them down. Prominent among these are inadequate public schools for minorities and science education that fails to inspire girls and young women.

With few tenured women faculty to teach our newly admitted women students, we set out to recruit established scholars and to fill the pipeline with promising young women who might one day receive tenure. The process was painfully slow. I was able to strengthen that process by appointing women to key academic posts—deans of the Graduate School of Arts and Sciences, the journalism school, the law school, and, of course, nursing. Still, when all is said and done, the most I can claim is that I helped lay the groundwork for my successors to build a more diverse faculty.

Another notable failure was our attempt to generate greater cross-disciplinary collaboration. We created a small fund to support the effort, but not a great deal happened. Intellectual walled gardens continued to dominate. Much more has happened in recent years, especially in the sciences.

And I have already acknowledged that we never solved the problem of rewarding dedicated teachers sufficiently.

I can claim with pride that we were true to our values. We never wavered in our commitment to free speech, need-blind admissions, and affirmative action. To the best of my knowledge we remained free of the taint of hypocrisy. And we tried to maintain a community of civility, to treat all with decency and respect, including our neighbors.

We set out to repair Columbia's financial base and succeeded more than we dared hope, culminating in a triple-A credit rating. The sale of the land under Rockefeller Center, the development of a policy to make the most of our intellectual property, and the building of a fundraising engine took us from nearly broke in 1980 to an endowment of two billion dollars in 1993, the foundation of an eight-billion-dollar endowment today.

Those steps also enabled us to strengthen the university in other ways. We invested well over half a billion dollars to repair our decaying physical plant and add new facilities. With John Kluge's help in preserving the College's need-blind financial aid program, our support for keeping the College's rigorous core curriculum intact and our success in funding new residential halls to assure all of the College's students a place to live on campus, complemented by our making the College co-ed, we enabled the College to become one of the most selective undergraduate institutions in the country.

We were also able to endow 120 new professorships, restore the real value of faculty salaries, create a host of new academic centers, and add a million books to our libraries. Will I be the last Columbia president to boast of how many books we bought? I doubt it, but we hedged our bets, helping develop the Internet and building our own technological capability.

Though I felt I had left more than enough for my successors to accomplish, I was, of course, pleased by the *New York Times'* appraisal: "Columbia owes Mr. Sovern a lasting debt. When he took office in 1980 Columbia was adrift both financially and academically. The University's ailing physical plant was rebuilt and its academic reputation recovered."[1]

Letting go is hard. I am sure I was not unique in thinking my immediate successor was making some bad decisions. Predecessor-successor relations can be difficult. And for a time they were for George Rupp and me. But we got over it, and then I had the special pleasure of seeing one of my best students chosen as Columbia's nineteenth president. Under Lee Bollinger's visionary leadership, Columbia is enjoying one of its best eras ever.

31

THERE IS LIFE AFTER
A PRESIDENCY

*Anyone could pick a class of very bright people from a pool of
seven thousand applicants, but our admissions office also does a
good job of choosing attractive human beings. I tell my colleagues
that if these terrific young people turn into the sons of bitches we
sometimes encounter in the profession, it will be our fault.*

Three months after I left the presidency, my wife, Joan, died. I
needed to keep busy. My experience suggests that a successful
university president who looks as though he has a few good years left in
him can expect a welter of invitations. I accepted several.

I joined the board of the Kaiser Family Foundation, which does
outstanding work in the health policy field and has become the gold
standard for reliable data in health policy debates. I was attracted by
the quality of its board, the vision of its president, the importance of its
work, and the fact that its headquarters near San Francisco meant that I
could visit my son Doug whenever I attended a board meeting.

Cy Vance asked me to succeed him as chairman of the Japan Society.
I was so flattered by his invitation that I hardly even considered declin-
ing. The society was founded in 1907 by influential Americans who were
persuaded by Japan's victory in the Russo-Japanese War that Japan had
become important enough to learn about. During World War II the
society naturally went into hibernation. It was revived after the war with
the help of John D. Rockefeller III.

Supported by charitable contributions from both Japanese and Americans, the society seeks to foster mutual understanding, appreciation, and cooperation between the two countries and their peoples. Located in a beautiful building near the United Nations, the society offers art exhibitions, film showings, language instruction, and a host of lectures and symposia on issues of importance to the United States, Japan, and East Asia.

By the time Cy Vance called on me, I had visited Japan several times and had talked on and off with some of Columbia's great experts on Japan. But I could claim no more than passing familiarity with its politics and culture. While that left me underqualified to be chairman, my interest in learning more moved me to accept the assignment.

During the eleven years I served as chairman, I visited Japan thirteen times, meeting many of the politicians and business leaders of the day, including Prime Minister Junichiro Koizumi and Shoichiro Toyoda. When we spent some time with former prime minister Miyazawa Kiichi, I couldn't bring myself to ask whether the story I had heard about him and the first President Bush was true. Bush, in a widely publicized event, had become ill and, seated next to Miyazawa, had thrown up in his lap. The story had it that Miyazawa, who spoke excellent English, responded by saying, "I guess I can call you George now."

My standard trip to Japan would entail a week on the society's affairs and a week for my new wife, Pat, and me. Pat and I met after I realized I had very few copies of a lovely book about my late wife, Joan, and her work as a sculptor. I telephoned the publisher to order more. I discovered that the head of the firm had died; I was speaking to his widow. She offered to drop some books off, I gratefully accepted and found myself greeting a beautiful woman. We talked for hours and agreed to meet again. We were living together six months later.

Pat shared my taste for travel. On our trips to Japan we visited Kyoto, tourist sites like Nara and Kamakura and places that few Westerners ever try to see, including a monastery on Koyasan, where we spent the night, were kindly invited to morning prayer, and ate a lifetime's supply of tofu.

On my last visit to Japan as chairman, as we headed for the airport, I told Pat, "I am getting dangerously close to the illusion that I know what is going on here." The Japanese conferred a gorgeous medal on me—the Order of the Rising Sun, Gold and Silver Star. I am still awaiting an appropriate occasion to wear it.

On this side of the Pacific I had the pleasure of spending an evening with Yoko Ono when the Japan Society put on a hugely popular exhibition of her work. She told me that John Lennon called her the most famous unknown artist in the world.

Shortly after accepting the Japan Society invitation, I was visited by Adele Chatfield-Taylor, president of the American Academy in Rome, and Andrew Heiskell, chairman of its executive committee and one of New York's great citizens. I had first met Andrew when he was part of the ruling triumvirate of the Time-Life empire, and we would see each other occasionally when he was chairman of the board of the New York Public Library, but we didn't know each other very well, and I didn't know Adele at all.

They had come to ask me to be chairman of the American Academy in Rome. Each year the academy awards the Rome Prize to more than two dozen scholars and artists who are invited to spend most of a year working at the academy's campus on the Janiculum, the highest of Rome's seven hills. Some of America's leading painters, composers, architects, scholars, and writers have called the experience among the best in their lives.

Though I was beginning to worry about overload, I ultimately found this invitation irresistible too. I became chairman just in time to participate in the academy's celebration of its centennial at the White House, the Library of Congress, and the Vatican's museums. I remained in this role for twelve happy years, visiting Rome at least once a year, marveling at Adele Chatfield-Taylor's extraordinary leadership, and enjoying the company of my fellow board members and the exciting Rome Prize winners.

I was still serving on the boards of the Asian Cultural Council and the NAACP Legal Defense Fund, which I had joined back in my decanal days. I had also helped found the Puerto Rican and Mexican-American Legal Defense Funds and served on their boards. I am perhaps the only person to have been a board member of all three civil rights organizations.

After convincing the Gannett Foundation to establish its Media Studies Center at Columbia, I agreed to serve on its National Advisory Council, ultimately as its chairman. The center closed down when the foundation, after having changed its name to the Freedom Forum, decided to redeploy its resources. Its main new investment was the Freedom Forum Newseum in Washington, D.C., a state-of-the-art museum of news that celebrates the First Amendment. I thought its name was too cute by half, but the conception was worthy and the execution was outstanding, so I became a member of its board.

I had long regarded Channel 13, the New York area's prime public television station, as a terrific educational institution. That, plus the fact that the person who headed its nominating committee and invited me to join its board was my old friend Jerry Greene, led to a quick acceptance.

I also agreed to join the board of Atlantic Philanthropies, where I served for eighteen years. Atlantic is committed to disbursing all of its assets in an effort to bring about "lasting changes in the lives of disadvantaged and vulnerable people." The focus is on aging, children and youth, population health, and reconciliation and human rights. Atlantic Philanthropies was created by an act of unparalleled generosity. Chuck Feeney, who had made a fortune as one of the founders of Duty Free Shoppers, gave it all away. That has enabled Atlantic Philanthropies to make gifts and grants of more than five billion dollars so far. The remaining two billion are to be committed by 2016 and the lights turned out several years later.

No foundation Atlantic's size has ever spent itself out of existence, so it has been working its way through some challenging issues. For example, how do you attract and retain people to staff an organization that is going to disappear? And how do you prepare grantees who depend upon you for support for the end of that critical help?

During my presidency of Columbia I had joined the boards of Chemical Bank (which later merged with Chase and J. P. Morgan) and AT&T. When Comcast acquired AT&T's broadband business in 2002, the agreement called for five AT&T directors to move to Comcast. Since I was past AT&T's retirement age, I agreed to be one of the five. I joined the board of Warner Lambert shortly after leaving the presidency, and when it was taken over by Pfizer I joined that board. In addition, my friend Norman Alexander had pressed me for years to join the board of his company, Sequa Corporation, and I finally yielded.

I was also continuing as a director of the Shubert Foundation, which supports nonprofit music and dance companies all over America, and the Shubert Organization, which owns eighteen New York theaters and turns the profits over to the Shubert Foundation to give away. In 1996, I became president of that foundation.

But most rewarding to me was my return to the classroom. As a young member of the law faculty, I had taught part of the Legal Methods course, an introductory offering that prepares Columbia's students for the curriculum they are about to encounter. The dean granted my request to teach a section of that course, and I have been teaching it ever since.

I regard it as a teacher's dream. The students are highly intelligent: about seven thousand applicants vie for four hundred places in the entering class. Anyone could pick a class of very bright people from that pool, but our admissions office also does a good job of choosing attractive human beings. I tell my colleagues that if these terrific young people turn into the sons of bitches we sometimes encounter in the profession, it will be our fault.

In addition to being bright and attractive, the group may well be the most highly motivated cohort in the galaxy. They have seen movies and television shows that lead them to expect to be terrorized in the classroom, an expectation I try not to meet, though I do call on them. They know they are competing against other outstanding young people. They have come to work.

Because it's introductory, our course begins in August and finishes before the rest of the semester begins. We convene for three hours a day, five days a week for just under three weeks. When my hundred or so students are not in class, they are spending most of their time preparing for class. No teacher could ask for more.

And I'm good at it. I shall resist the temptation to quote from my students' evaluations, but I can't resist recounting a story that David Leebron, former dean of the law school and now president of Rice, liked to tell. He was teaching a class in torts, and the issue was the liability of a wrongdoer to someone he didn't intend to harm, for example, by shooting someone other than his intended victim. David asked a student hypothetically if he would mind stepping between him and a gunman shooting at him. According to David, the student replied, "I would take a bullet for Professor Sovern, but not for you."

Pat has suggested that in my various postpresidential activities I have managed to recreate most of the range of a university. For medicine, the Kaiser Family Foundation; for the arts and humanities, the American Academy in Rome, the Asian Cultural Council, and the Shubert Organization and Foundation; for science and technology, AT&T, Pfizer, and Sequa; for journalism, the Newseum and Channel 13; for international affairs, the Japan Society; and for the business school, my corporate boards.

I also took on one ad hoc assignment. President and Mrs. Clinton were incurring millions of dollars in fees to defend themselves on a number of legal fronts. I joined Theodore Hesburgh, Barbara Jordan, Nicholas Katzenbach, John Whitehead, and others as trustees of the Presidential Legal Expense Trust to help the Clintons meet their legal expenses.

Several years after that, the Pritzker family approached me to serve as their arbitrator to resolve disputes arising under agreements they were making to distribute their multi-billion-dollar empire among the family. I thanked them for their confidence but explained that I already had more than enough to do. After several importuning phone calls from their lawyers and the offer of a generous compensation package, I yielded. My pay ultimately found its way to my grandchildren's college tuition.

32

SHUBERT—A GREAT GIG

*The Shubert Foundation's principal activity is giving
away the money the organization earns.*

B ernard Jacobs was a graduate of the Columbia Law School, which turned out to be lucky for me. Until his death in 1996, Bernie was the president of both the Shubert Organization and the Shubert Foundation. We met at a reunion of his law school class, where he invited me to be his guest at a performance of the Broadway megahit *A Chorus Line*. Joan and I happily accepted. More invitations followed, and we became good friends with Bernie and his wife, Betty.

Bernie had probably never been prepossessing in appearance. By the time I met him, his most prominent features were the deep circles under his eyes, which may well have been earned during the many years he and Gerald Schoenfeld labored as in-house lawyers for the Shuberts. Their boss, J. J. Shubert, bullied them mercilessly, even firing them from time to time. But Bernie had endured it, and now he was one of the bosses, a titan of Broadway. A first-rate lawyer and tough negotiator, he was a decent, generous man who inspired affection and trust throughout the ranks of those who dealt with him, ranging from union representatives and employees to performers, writers, directors, and producers. I joined the legions of his admirers.

Bernie was president and Gerald Schoenfeld chairman of the Shubert enterprises, a relationship that is usually hierarchical, with the
chairman on top. But Bernie and Jerry were equals. I am not a fan of
two-headed organizations, but their partnership was a great success for
them personally, for Shubert, and for Broadway.

Al Hirschfeld's caricature of Jerry shows him with a grin broader
than his bald head. A gregarious man with an infectious smile and a
lively sense of humor, Jerry seemed a natural for the endless schmooz-
ing of the theater world. But like Bernie, he was no pushover and, also
like Bernie, he was very smart. He had a strategic sense, an awareness of
context that helped him think beyond the limits of Shubert's business
to what was good for the neighborhood and for New York City, and so
ultimately for Shubert.

When Bernie invited me to dine with him and Jerry, I suspected they
might be vetting me for a seat on the Shubert boards. (The Shubert
Organization and the Shubert Foundation each has its own board of
directors, but the membership is identical.) That evening marked the
beginning of a close friendship with Jerry that lasted until his death
more than thirty years later. John Kluge was also a member of the board.
With his, Bernie's, and Jerry's support, my election to the seventh seat
on the boards was a foregone conclusion.

The Shubert Organization had a checkered history. It was founded
by three brothers, Sam, Lee, and J. J. Shubert. Starting from scratch, they
built an empire that by the 1920s owned and operated 104 theaters in
twenty-nine American cities. Sam died early, but that enormous base of
theaters enabled Lee and J. J. to become dominant producers and booking agents as well as landlords. The Great Depression forced them into
receivership, but that proved to be just a pause for breath. They emerged
from the receivership still the dominant player in American theater. Too
dominant, the U.S. Department of Justice ultimately decided.

In 1950, the government began a civil antitrust action against the
Shuberts that culminated in a consent decree in 1956. Shubert was
forced to sell a number of theaters in New York, Boston, Philadelphia,
Detroit, and Cincinnati and to promise not to acquire any more theaters. By this time Lee Shubert had died, leaving J. J., a vicious tyrant,

as the sole owner of the Shubert enterprises. The only person he seemed to trust was his son John, with whom he shared more and more responsibility as he declined mentally and physically. But John died suddenly, the victim of a heart attack.

With John dead and J. J. incompetent, Shubert was headless. John had left written instructions that in the event of his death his cousin Lawrence Shubert Lawrence Jr. should be put in charge. But J. J. was still alive, so John's wishes had no legal effect. That J. J. was still alive did not keep the executors named in his will from accepting responsibility for the succession. They picked Lawrence Shubert Lawrence Jr. He proved to be a disaster. Under his drunken leadership, the business staggered along for nine years. At the nadir of his tenure most of the Shubert theaters were dark.

J. J. was oblivious to the mess his company had become. But by dying at the end of 1963 he opened the door to recovery. Upon his death the ownership of the Shubert Company passed to the Shubert Foundation, a charitable entity the brothers had founded some years earlier. It was now up to the foundation's board to choose the company's leadership.

The board tolerated Lawrence for a long time. But diminished by deaths, it was ultimately down to two members—John Shubert's widow, Eckie, who hated Lawrence, and Lawrence himself. They agreed that each would appoint two new members. Eckie chose Bernie and Jerry.

When Lawrence alienated one of his two appointees, Irving Goldman, the anti-Lawrence faction had the votes to depose him. In 1972, Goldman, Bernie, and Jerry were elected executive directors of the Shubert Corporation, with Jerry as chairman and Goldman as president. Bernie soon replaced Goldman as president, who remained on the board and oversaw the maintenance department until he was forced to resign three years later when he was charged with taking kickbacks and other offenses.

Jerry later described how he and Bernie divided the work:

Bernie would be responsible for the booking and for negotiating certain union contracts. I would be responsible for the financial and real-estate side, for theater and property maintenance and restoration, for negotiating certain other union contracts, and for governmental relations and insurance matters.

Despite these divisions of responsibilities, Bernie and I agreed that we both would be involved in all decisions, and that if one of us objected strongly to any matter, it would not be pursued.[1]

Thanks to the quality of both men, that arrangement proved enormously successful.

Bernie and Jerry's accession to the leadership of the Shubert Organization in 1972 could have served as an example of "Be careful what you wish for." The company was nearly broke, the theater business in general was in decline, Times Square and the theater district seemed an urban cesspool, and New York City itself would soon require a financial rescue.

All of that would change, much of it because of Bernie and Jerry. Nobody bats a thousand on Broadway, but their astute selection of shows both for investment and for booking into Shubert theaters helped turn the company around. Their cultivation of creative talent and influential agents and producers would assure Shubert a continued flow of offerings. Their success helped lift the theater business in general. And their leadership in restoring Times Square and the theater district helped bring that area back to the vibrant life it enjoys today.

By the time I joined the Shubert Organization, the revival was well on its way. And I had the fun of piggybacking on Bernie and Jerry's many fascinating friendships. When Joan and I joined Bernie and Betty for dinner with another couple, the other couple turned out to be the great director-choreographer Michael Bennett and Donna McKechnie, who won a Tony for her role in *A Chorus Line*. When Pat and I gave an intimate dinner at our home to celebrate Jerry and Pat's fiftieth wedding anniversary, the guest list included Steve Sondheim and Beverly Sills. When Pat and I joined Jerry and Pat for an evening of theater in London, the evening included drinks with Andrew Lloyd Webber.

But for all its glitz and glamour, the theater business is a cottage industry. The total revenues of all of Broadway's theaters add up to less than half of Columbia's annual operating budget.

The Shubert boards meet about eight times a year. At the Shubert Organization we receive reports on the current and planned productions in our eighteen New York theaters and our Philadelphia venue, we review our finances, and we take up a variety of other topics relating to the organization.

The Shubert Foundation's principal activity is giving away the money the Shubert Organization earns. If you pay a high price for a hit show, take heart: some of your money will be recycled into support of creative activity—at least if you are attending a Shubert theater. The Shubert Foundation currently gives away about $20 million a year, the lion's share to nonprofit theater and dance companies all over America. That number has increased every year for the last thirty years, and we expect it to keep right on rising.

We are currently helping well over three hundred theater companies performing for more than twenty million people each year. I know of no other institution—public or private—that regularly supports as many theaters as we do. Their leaders particularly appreciate our mode of giving. Our grants take the form of general operating support. In other words, they help pay the bills rather than funding special projects that leave management scrambling to keep the lights on.

We try to be especially generous to companies offering risk-taking work that challenges audiences, believing that such efforts are vital to the intellectual and artistic life of our nation. In the words of the Arena Stage's nomination of the Foundation for the National Medal of Arts, "The Foundation directly contributes to America's artistic legacy. . . . The performing arts are vibrant in the United States in no small part due to the Shubert Foundation."

A foundation staff of three, headed by the peerless Vicki Reiss, studies the performance activity and finances of hundreds of prospective grantees and prepares reports on those they believe worthy of support. As president of the foundation, I review these reports along with a summary of applicants turned down and suggest whatever modifications I think appropriate. The reports are then forwarded to the members of the foundation board for action.

It is often said that the choice of a chief executive is a board of directors' most important responsibility. And succession planning should not be left until a vacancy actually arises. While Bernie Jacobs was alive, the board could relax: if anything happened to either him or Jerry, we would still have the other to run the business. But after Bernie died, it became important to plan for what we might do if anything happened to Jerry.

Jerry was not interested. It is not unusual for a CEO to resist choosing a successor. Sometimes the resistance is born of a reluctance to consider one's own mortality or the end of his or her time as chief, sometimes of a fear of creating a competing power center. To some leaders keeping one's subordinates guessing seems a good motivational tool.

We needed Jerry's judgment of his subordinates. In desperation at one point I suggested to Jerry that as an interim step he write a long letter to the board setting forth his views of possible successors and lock it in his safe for opening after his death or incapacitation.

All of us on the board continued to press him, both privately and in board meetings. Finally, he relented. He began reporting periodically on what he saw as the strengths and weaknesses of Phil Smith and Bob Wankel, the only credible internal candidates to succeed him, and on what he was doing to round out their readiness. From time to time he also shared his views on possible candidates from outside the Shubert Organization.

After conversations among ourselves and separate sessions with Phil and Bob, the board tentatively concluded that if anything happened to Jerry, our best move was to return to the joint CEO structure that had served us so well under Bernie and Jerry. We would make Bob and Phil co-CEOs.

Phil Smith began work at Shubert in 1957, the same year Bernie Jacobs did. It was a good year for Shubert. Everybody liked Phil (they still do), and he was always good at what he did. From assistant treasurer at the Majestic box office, he rose through the ranks to become Bernie's right-hand man and good friend, working closely with him on booking shows. When Bernie died, Jerry proposed that Phil succeed to the presidency of the organization, and the board agreed. We also elected him to both boards. Believing his own relationship with Bernie to have been unique, Jerry proposed that Phil not succeed to Bernie's role as co-CEO. The board concurred. Jerry would be our sole chief executive. Nor did Phil become president of the foundation, as Bernie had been. Jerry asked me to fill that role, and I happily acquiesced. Phil, a naturally gracious man, seemed entirely comfortable with the arrangement.

Bob Wankel was executive vice president of the organization. He had come up the financial side of the business and led the computerization of Shubert's ticketing, a major contributor to the company's profits. Jerry told us that Bob, like nature, abhorred a vacuum. Whenever Bob saw a need, if no one else was filling it, Bob would. A highly intelligent man who got things done without leaving a lot of broken glass behind, he inspired confidence.

And so when the awful moment came and Jerry died suddenly, we were ready. The boards met over dinner and concluded that Bob and Phil would be co-CEOs of the Shubert Organization, with Bob as president and Phil as chairman. And Phil would also succeed to Jerry's position as chairman of the Shubert Foundation.

A few years earlier, Jerry's wife, Pat, had said to several of us, "Instead of doing something to honor Jerry after he dies, do something now—name a theater for him." Pat is not a woman to whom it is easy to say no. Besides, it was a good idea. Jerry and Bernie were leaders in bringing Shubert and Broadway back to life. They deserved to be recognized.

We decided to rename two theaters close to each other on Forty-fifth Street—the Plymouth and the Royale. The dedication was a characteristic Broadway event. Forty-fifth Street was closed to traffic, a stage was erected in front of the theaters, and Bernie and Jerry's virtues were extolled by Hugh Jackman, Mayor Bloomberg, and me. Dame Edna (né Barry Humphries) added her huzzahs from a balcony across the street. Jerry responded gracefully. And then the theater marquees were lit. Bernie and Jerry's names were up in lights.

Shubert board members are invited to all the openings of shows in Shubert theaters. Pat and I attend as many as we can both because that's

the heart of the business and because it's usually fun. Some of our grantees also invite me as president of the foundation to their openings, and
we take in a sampling of those as well.

Each year we see a handful of plays and musicals that strike us as
special, a number that offer a pleasant evening of theater but are quickly
forgotten, and a few that cause us to ask what could possibly have made
the creators and producers invest their time and money in that. Year
after year, though, the number of actors whose performances are memorable far exceeds the number of shows that evoke that praise. The talent
pool in American theater is remarkably deep. And the British regularly
add to it. It's a rare opening in which we don't see an individual performance to admire.

Opening-night audiences also include a sprinkling of celebrities. On
one occasion, Pat and I arrived only to find our seats occupied. The occupants and I politely compared tickets, and they apologized for their
error and moved over two seats. It wasn't until we had settled in that I
realized I had just evicted Harrison Ford and Demi Moore. For a moment I felt like a star-struck kid again.

On another occasion Hugh Jackman and his wife were sitting behind us. Since Hugh and I knew each other from the dedication of
the Jacobs and Schoenfeld theaters, we introduced our spouses at the
intermission and chatted for a bit. He told me that he hoped to return
to Broadway in a Shubert theater, a hope I naturally encouraged with
great enthusiasm. One of his projects was a musical based on the life of
Harry Houdini. I voiced the first thought that came to mind: "Women
would go crazy for you in chains."

Theater people and movie stars are not the only notables to turn up
at openings. At various times I've had the pleasure of introducing Pat
to Justice Breyer, Mayor Bloomberg, and Tom Friedman (to whom I
presented a Pulitzer Prize years earlier), among many others.

And then there are the parties after the openings. Once in a rare
while the producers will opt for a lavish affair. More commonly, the offering is a simple buffet with ample alcohol served in a hotel ballroom or

party venue. These producers have figured out that the main attraction is the chance to stargaze and, for some, to network.

The producers, the director, the playwright, the cast, and just about everyone else involved in the evening's production attend. We've been to a lot of them. At the opening night party for *Sunset Boulevard* in Hollywood, Glenn Close, clearly mistaking Pat for someone else, embraced her warmly and said they really had to get together. We never figured out who she thought Pat was.

At the opening-night party for *Equus*, Pat and I did something we have never done before or since. We asked for an autograph. Daniel Radcliffe was starring, and we knew that two of our granddaughters were mad about him from the Harry Potter movies. We left that evening with two *Playbill*s signed by Radcliffe, a very agreeable young man.

We always attend the Tony awards unless we're out of the country. The acting nominees are all in the first few rows where they are assigned to aisle seats so they can easily move to the stage if need be. We usually have seats next to them or nearby. When the winner is announced and joyously bolts from his or her seat, we often look at those who didn't make it. Knowing that the television cameras may also be looking, they typically applaud politely. No dismay or disappointment shows. These are actors, after all.

Except for that moment when a winner rises, there are no empty seats on a Tony telecast. Members of the audience are only allowed to leave their seats during commercial breaks. And if you don't make it back in time your seat is taken by one of a corps of seat fillers who remain there until you return, presumably at the next commercial break.

When *La Cage Aux Folles* was a nominee for best musical revival, I was waiting in the rear of Radio City Music Hall for the next commercial break. I suddenly realized that the people waiting in front of me were not others returning from a restroom visit. They were the gay chorus line from *La Cage*, in full regalia. As the orchestra broke into "The best of times is now . . ." they set off down the aisle dancing and singing. I love the song and had to resist the impulse to step off with them.

Though Shubert has had its share of dark moments, the bright ones are thrilling. In addition to housing countless hits, the Shubert Organization has produced and coproduced wonderful theater, including *Cats*, *Sunday in the Park with George*, *The Grapes of Wrath*, *The Heidi Chronicles*, *The Life and Adventures of Nicholas Nickleby*, *Amadeus*, *Passion*, *Passing Strange*, and *Dance of Death*. Being even a very small part of all that is, as one friend put it, "a great gig."

33

ALMOST A JUSTICE

*Looking back, I am sorry to have missed the chance
to play a part in the shaping of one of the greatest
documents our species has ever produced, but I have been
extraordinarily lucky in the life I have led instead.*

When the counsel to the president of the United States calls
and asks you to join him for breakfast, you oblige. The call
came in the spring of 1994 while I was in Washington helping celebrate
the hundredth anniversary of Congress's grant of a charter to the American
Academy in Rome, the organization I had recently agreed to chair.

Lloyd Cutler, a very wise Washington lawyer, had taken leave of his
law firm, Wilmer, Cutler, and Pickering, to serve as President Clinton's
counsel. We were old friends, our paths crossing both professionally and
socially over the years. We came together most notably when we served
together on the arbitration panel convened to resolve a dispute between
the Rolling Stones and their former manager.

The morning after his call, I met Lloyd in a quiet corner of a Washington hotel dining room. After we exchanged greetings, he said: "I'm
sure you know why I asked you here." I hadn't a clue, but I saw no point
in admitting that, expecting that Lloyd would tell me. I didn't have long
to wait.

"Will you accept appointment to the Supreme Court?" At just about
any other time in my life, my answer would have been a swift and sure

yes, despite my initial surprise. But Lloyd was catching me at a moment of particular disarray. My wife, Joan, had died less than a year earlier, and I had only recently met Pat, the woman who would become my wife. It was also less than a year since I had left the Columbia presidency, a post that had been the center of my professional life for thirteen years. I was doing fine, but my life was not exactly a model of calm and stability.

I answered my old friend: "Lloyd, since you're not offering me the job, I don't have to decide." He came right back: "Yes, you do." And so I did. It never occurred to me to say, "May I think about it?" Perhaps I knew instinctively that no amount of reflection would change my answer. "Yes," I replied.

Lloyd then asked me whether there were any skeletons in my closet, and I assured him there weren't. He also warned me to avoid any publicity about this, and I assured him on that score as well. Our business had taken roughly two minutes. We spent the rest of breakfast, as friends will, chatting about a variety of subjects.

I left that breakfast excited but conflicted. When I was president of Columbia, I would occasionally be asked whether the Columbia presidency had been my ambition. I would answer, only half-jokingly, "No, I wanted to be Chief Justice of the United States." After all, one of my predecessors as dean of the law school—Harlan Fiske Stone—had made it. But I knew that the chances of being appointed to the Supreme Court were roughly equivalent to the chances of being struck by lightning.

Yet here I was—a serious candidate. My conflict arose not only from the unsettled state of my life, not an ideal time to be striking off in a new direction, but also from the daunting prospect of working out my approach to a whole range of constitutional issues in public. I had been out of the law for more than fifteen years. While I had kept up with the court's handling of the big questions, even had views on most of them, I had never been responsible for actually deciding them. Still, as my answer to Lloyd suggests, I felt I could handle the challenge.

Several days later Al Connable, my friend and favorite editor, called: "Do you know you are being considered for the Supreme Court?" "Yes,

I do, but how do you know?" It turned out that an old friend of Al was the brother of Attorney General Janet Reno, and he had learned that the FBI had been ordered to do the background checks on me and one other candidate. Sure enough, phone calls from friends who had been interviewed confirmed that the FBI was on the job.

After a few suspenseful weeks, President Clinton appointed Stephen Breyer, chief judge of the Court of Appeals for the First Circuit, to the vacant seat. I couldn't help thinking: why him and not me? Several factors came to mind. Before his appointment to the bench, Judge Breyer, then a distinguished member of the Harvard law faculty, had served as counsel to the Senate Judiciary Committee, where he earned the respect of Orrin Hatch, a leading Republican senator. Senator Hatch would presumably help Judge Breyer avoid a confirmation contest. He would be aided by the fact that the Senate had previously confirmed Breyer to his Court of Appeals seat. Judge (now Justice) Breyer would also be more attractive than I because he is seven years younger, which would presumably give him a longer, perhaps more influential tenure on the court. And I had to acknowledge the possibility that he was the better man for the job. I admired him as scholar and judge and continue to admire him as justice.

I was disappointed, of course, but also slightly relieved. Looking back, I am sorry to have missed the chance to play a part in the shaping of one of the greatest documents our species has ever produced, but I have been extraordinarily lucky in the life I have led instead.

34

SOTHEBY'S

When news of the Justice Department's antitrust allegations
became public, the race to the courthouse was on.

I was working in my study on a winter's day in February 2000 when
the call came: Would I be interested in becoming chairman of
Sotheby's? Another improbability.

Sotheby's and Christie's dominated the worldwide auction scene. Sotheby's had over ninety offices in thirty-six countries and held roughly
750 auctions a year. Over the centuries it had sold countless master-
pieces, Napoleon's library, the collections of the Duke and Duchess of
Windsor, property from the estate of Jacqueline Kennedy Onassis, and
the Declaration of Independence—not to mention Sue, the Tyranno-
saurus Rex fossil.

But now Sotheby's was in serious trouble. Its chairman, Alfred Taubman, and its CEO, Diana (Dede) Brooks, had just resigned in the wake
of antitrust accusations. The journalist Christopher Mason called the
Sotheby's-Christie's conspiracy "the most devastating scandal ever to
befall the art world."[1]

But why call on me? I had bought prints at auction, though never
at Sotheby's, but that was the limit of my exposure to the auction
world. Nor could I claim any art expertise: a generous appraisal would

rate me an interested amateur. The *New York Times* offered an answer: "[Mr. Sovern's] appointment is evidence of the desire of Sotheby's board to bring in a respected figure who can help the company preserve its image and deal with whatever integrity problems may arise from the inquiry."[2] The fact that I was, as another newspaper account would have it, squeaky clean was an important qualification.

So was the happy accident of mutual trust. My caller was Ira Millstein, head of the law firm that had represented Sotheby's for years. Ira and I were good friends who had worked together before. A key member of Sotheby's board of directors was Henry Kravis, the brilliant founder of Kohlberg, Kravis, and Roberts and a Columbia alumnus with whom I had become friends during my time as Columbia's president. Henry and I talked at considerable length on the telephone on my way to accepting the invitation to the chairmanship. Sotheby's board also included the redoubtable Max Fisher, a vital nonagenarian, with whom I became acquainted when the Securities and Exchange Commission had appointed me to monitor overseas payments by the United Fruit Company. Max was part of a group that took over that company after the misconduct that led to my appointment as monitor.

Though I was not privy to the discussions, I'm sure the call from Ira would never have come if Ira, Henry, and Max had not assured Sotheby's board that I was the man they needed. And no one could ask for better supporters than that triumvirate.

The question remained: Did I want the assignment? My wife, Pat, argued forcefully that my life was full enough. What did I need a new headache for? But I was intrigued. One friend, remembering some of my Columbia days and my labor mediation efforts, accused me of being a "crisis junkie." And there's no doubt that I respond well to high stakes and high pressure. I have always been able to focus on tasks requiring immediate attention, temporarily shutting everything else out. Crises simply sharpen my focus. As the old aphorism has it, the prospect of being hanged concentrates the mind.

I enjoy challenges and, as I approached seventy, it was good to know that they weren't all behind me. I must confess that I was not indifferent to the prospect that I would receive considerable public attention as a man of integrity riding to the rescue of a prestigious company with origins even older than Columbia's.

But none of those reasons was enough to cause me to embark on a suicide mission. I needed to know more. Ira and Henry had been forthcoming, so the basic facts were clear. Al Taubman and Dede Brooks had been accused of violating the antitrust laws by agreeing with their counterparts at Christie's to fix prices. The allegations included agreements not to compete in other ways as well, but price-fixing was the heart of the matter.

Among the questions I asked: Is there a management team ready to function? Who are its key members? How strong is the board of directors? Tell me about each of them. And will the litigation bankrupt the company? I also asked, and received, Henry Kravis's assurance that he would remain on the board for as long as it took to get the company back on track.

An especially critical question for me was whether anyone other than Taubman and Brooks was involved in the conspiracy. If any member of Sotheby's board of directors so much as knew what was happening and had done nothing to expose it, I would be volunteering for a messy assignment, working with a board I would have to purge. If there was a real possibility that the conspiracy had been implemented by Sotheby's employees other than Brooks, the assignment would entail a continuing investigative effort to identify them and root them out, a task for which my experience had not prepared me.

Ira Millstein's law firm, Weil, Gotshal, and Manges, had already looked into the charges. Both he and Henry Kravis were completely convinced that the board was clean, having acted promptly after learning of the allegations. Ira's partners had also questioned every employee who could conceivably have been involved and found only one employee who had had a conversation about prices with his Christie's counterpart, but that conversation had not been acted upon.

Ira also suggested I talk with Sotheby's general counsel, Donaldson Pillsbury, a respected former senior partner at the Davis, Polk law firm.

In our first long conversation he inspired my confidence in his judgment. He answered my questions fully, volunteered what he thought
might be helpful, and left no doubt in my mind that he would have
nothing to do with a cover-up. In the years that followed, I would spend
many hours working with Don Pillsbury, and he never failed to justify
my confidence.

I needed assurance on one more score. I had promised my daughter,
son-in-law, and three grandchildren a vacation at a ranch in Arizona, a
trip that was about to begin. Was the pace of events at Sotheby's such
that I could keep my promise? Yes, Ira assured me, there was no reason
I couldn't just take a briefcase full of background materials with me and
report for duty in a week. And so, elected on February 21, 2000, I began
my chairmanship of Sotheby's.

Several days into the trip, Ira called to let me know that Sotheby's
directors were about to gather, and didn't I think I should be there? I
treated the question as rhetorical. Commercial air connections couldn't
get me back to New York in time, so I asked Ira to arrange a charter
flight for Pat and me. I also asked him to have the materials for the
board meeting on the plane so I could prepare properly for the meeting
I was about to chair.

The plane didn't arrive until late evening, and the board materials had
missed the flight. I saw them for the first time in the car that met our
plane when we landed at Teterboro Airport in New Jersey a little after
one a.m. It was not the first time I was glad I'm a quick study.

Shortly before ten a.m., I arrived at Sotheby's glass-clad headquarters, an imposing building filling the block between Seventy-first and
Seventy-second Street on York Avenue. Appropriate to the dark mood
of its occupants, the neighbors to the immediate south are hospitals
treating cancer, physical impairment, and a host of maladies.

In the moments before Sotheby's board of directors convened for
the first meeting led by its new chairman, I met my new colleagues.
Max Fisher and Henry Kravis introduced me to the Viscount Blaken-
ham, former chairman of Pearson and the *Financial Times*; the Marquis
of Hartington, who would become the Duke of Devonshire upon his

father's death; Lord Black of Crossharbour, né Conrad Black, an author and chairman of a major publishing empire who would leave the board after his indictment for financial crimes unrelated to Sotheby's; Walter Curley, former American ambassador to France and Ireland; Jeffrey Miro, Alfred Taubman's long-time counsel; Sharon Rockefeller, CEO of WETA, the Washington, D.C., public broadcasting station; Robin Woodhead, Sotheby's executive vice president in charge of Europe and Asia; Deborah Zoullas, another Sotheby's executive vice president; and Bill Ruprecht, who had been elected CEO the same day I was chosen as chairman.

Corporate governance gurus are emphatic about limiting the representation of management on boards of directors in the interest of board independence. The CEO, yes, perhaps one other, but no more. Though Ira Millstein is regarded as America's foremost corporate governance expert, Sotheby's had three members of management on its board. Circumstances had overridden structural ideals. Deborah Zoullas, an executive vice president, had asked in the midst of the crisis to be added to the board, and if she were to join, Robin Woodhead, the head of Sotheby's London office, could hardly be passed over, and so they joined Bill Ruprecht, our freshly minted CEO.

The board meeting was not a joyful one. The directors received a full briefing on our legal exposure. Though Alfred Taubman maintained his innocence, there was no doubt that Dede Brooks had violated America's antitrust laws. It was equally clear that, as president and CEO of Sotheby's, her violation was the company's, which left us essentially defenseless to both civil claims and criminal prosecution. As far as the law was concerned, the fact that innocent employees and shareholders would suffer the consequences was irrelevant. How much that would cost was not yet knowable, but the numbers would surely be substantial. Under the circumstances, the board decided, it was only prudent to eliminate the dollar-per-share dividend the company had been paying. The board concluded its business over lunch and dispersed.

Bill Ruprecht and I posed for some publicity photos before meeting with counsel. The pictures were taken in front of a beautiful Modigliani portrait hanging in my office. I looked forward to seeing it again, but it was gone the next day. I learned that my office had been a conference room where special clients of Sotheby's would be invited for private viewings of the most expensive works of art. When I was not on the premises, I had no objection to its continued use for that purpose. That had a delightful side effect: I never knew what I might find on my walls. The surprises among many other extraordinary pieces included two seductive Matisse odalisques, a stunning Monet, a Fabergé egg, and Picasso's *Boy with a Pipe*, a picture that ultimately sold for 104 million dollars, at the time the highest price ever paid at auction.

Before settling into the first of many meetings with our team of lawyers from Weil Gotshal, I returned a phone call from Ron Baron. A mutual fund he ran owned millions of shares of Sotheby's stock. It was not hard to anticipate his mood. Sotheby's stock had peaked at a price above forty. On this day one could buy it for fifteen dollars a share. We exchanged greetings, and he asked, "You know I'm your largest shareholder?" "Yes," I replied, "and you have some of my money." My wife Pat had a small investment in one of his funds. Having gotten us off on the right foot, I accepted his invitation to lunch.

Baron posed an unexpected challenge for me. Sotheby's had two classes of stock outstanding. The B stock had ten votes per share, the A but one. Though Taubman had resigned as chairman, he and his family still owned enough B shares to assert majority control over Sotheby's. Baron's fund owned a majority of the A shares, but they could be outvoted by the Taubmans' B shares. The A shares had only one feature the Taubmans could not control: they had the right to elect 25 percent of the board of directors. Since Baron controlled a majority of the A shares, he alone could choose a quarter of the board. In the past, Baron had been content to go along with the slate of directors nominated by the board, but he was not a happy shareholder now. Would I be able to persuade him to go along in the board election that was only a few months away?

We lunched in his office in an ultramodern suite, complete with a gym for his employees, near the top of the General Motors Building. Ron Baron is an intelligent, knowledgeable business leader with a sense of humor, and we became friends almost at once. (Years later he would invite me to join his board of directors.) But for a time he was a pain in the ass. To be sure, having lost many millions of his shareholders' money because of Sotheby's misconduct, he had every right to be. But that didn't make my job any easier.

For several weeks I thought I had him persuaded that the board had been on the job but had been artfully deceived by Dede Brooks. In the end he decided he no longer had confidence in the existing board and wanted to elect his own representatives. That posed two problems. First, the annual meeting at which shareholders elect directors was already scheduled and didn't allow enough time for Baron to come up with a slate of new directors and for Bill Ruprecht and me to vet them. Technically we had no such right, but we all agreed that the graceful way to proceed would be for the board to nominate all the directors, including Baron's. This was more than a matter of form. I did not want our board to be riven by factions. We could function most effectively if Baron's directors were welcomed as full-fledged colleagues. The answer was simple: postpone the annual meeting. That's a potentially embarrassing step, but we managed it well enough and no harm was done.

The second problem was more serious. With Al Taubman and Dede Brooks gone and Al's son Bobby slated to join the board, Sotheby's had thirteen directors. That would entitle Baron to five, making the board an unwieldy eighteen. If one of the existing directors gave up his seat, the thirteen would become twelve and Baron's 25 percent of the board would become four, yielding a more manageable sixteen. Fortunately, I had just the right assignment for Walter Curley: he would make the perfect chairman of our International Advisory Committee, a prestigious organization composed of leading collectors from around the globe. After consulting with Bill Ruprecht, I invited Walter to accept the chairmanship in lieu of his board seat, with the assurance that he would continue to be invited to meetings of the board of directors. He graciously accepted my proposal and gave up his seat on the board.

Bill and I proceeded to meet with each of Ron Baron's nominees. There was one exception we thought ill suited to the role. We persuaded

Ron to withdraw that man's name. We accepted the other four; they were duly nominated and ultimately welcomed to the board.

That eased Ron Baron's pain but did not eliminate it. He still had a huge loss in the stock and was outraged that the Taubmans, who had a smaller economic stake in the company than he, retained the majority voting interest. But as much as he might fulminate, and he did, there was nothing anyone could do about that disparity. The structure was there when Alfred Taubman took the company public, it was fully disclosed, and everyone who bought stock knew what they were getting into. The arrangement could only be changed if the Taubmans agreed to the change, and they were not about to do that at this time. Years later we were presented with an opportunity to end their multiple voting rights, and we took it.

Ron Baron required, indeed deserved, attention, but he and I both understood that the center ring at Sotheby's lay elsewhere. Under the Sherman Anti-Trust Act, price-fixing by competitors is deemed sufficiently egregious to warrant both a criminal prosecution and the recovery of damages in a civil action by anyone the conspiracy has injured. And to deter as many would-be offenders as possible, the measure of damages in the civil action is unusually punitive—three times the actual damage suffered. It was not hard to imagine a worst case in which a jury could levy damages against Sotheby's that would put it out of business.

Sotheby's and Christie's basic business entails two kinds of prices— a seller's commission and a buyer's premium. Under the Sotheby's-Christie's agreement, if you sold a painting at a Sotheby's auction for five million dollars, you would pay Sotheby's a non-negotiable commission of 2 percent, or $100,000. (Consignors of works of lesser value would pay a higher percentage based on a sliding scale that for the most part topped out at 10 percent; museums and dealers were offered preferential rates.) If you sought a better deal from Christie's, you would hit a stone wall: Christie's would offer you the same price.

If Sotheby's and Christie's had not conspired, they might have competed with each other for your business, lowering the commission to get your painting in the hope of making their profit on what the buyer paid.

In fact, before the conspiracy, both companies, seeking a painting of this value, would sometimes waive their commission altogether. The remedy offered by the antitrust laws gave every seller during the allegedly seven years the collusion lasted the right to recover three times any damage suffered. The payout could total two hundred million dollars or more.

That was the lesser part of the problem. The purchaser of the five-million-dollar painting also has to pay a fee. Back in 2000 Sotheby's buyer's premium was 20 percent of the sale price up to $15,000, 15 percent on the next $85,000, and 10 percent of any remaining amount over $100,000. On a five-million-dollar painting, that sums to a handsome $505,750. Christie's and Sotheby's typically maintain the same or similar buyer's premium schedules. If that is the product of competition—neither wanting to charge more than the other for fear of losing business—the outcome is perfectly legal. But if their parallel pricing is the product of agreement between them, the law is violated, and treble damages can be recovered by those harmed.

Because the buyer's premium is so much larger than the seller's commission, if Sotheby's and Christie's colluded on it, the treble damages recoverable would also be much larger, enough in fact to do what two and a half centuries of wars and financial panics had never done—close Sotheby's down.

When news of the Justice Department's antitrust allegations became public, the race to the courthouse was on. Lawyers signed up Sotheby's and Christie's clients as plaintiffs and sought to be designated as counsel for the whole class of those who had been damaged. The class action is a procedural device intended to streamline litigation: instead of hundreds or thousands of individual lawsuits each claiming the same violation, all the claims are handled in a single, sometimes massive class action. The law firm designated lead counsel for the class is the biggest winner of all.

Sometimes the fact that counsel started suit well before anyone else will help him win the coveted designation from the judge assigned the case. Sometimes counsel for the client with the largest claim will win the prize. Judge Lewis Kaplan thought he had a better idea, one that had been used a few times before. He invited counsel to submit bids.

How much was counsel prepared to agree would have to be paid to plaintiffs before counsel was awarded a penny in fees?

The winning law firm would then get one-quarter of everything recovered in excess of its bid. The winning bidder was David Boies, a brilliant advocate who later that year would earn a footnote in American history books by losing *Bush v. Gore* in the Supreme Court of the United States. That Boies would be representing the plaintiffs was not good news. The amount of his bid was worse—$405 million. That told us that unless Boies was to self-immolate and serve without payment, Sotheby's and Christie's could not settle the case short of trial for less than $405 million.

The bad news did not end there. We learned that Boies had already reached a tentative agreement with Christie's that could leave Sotheby's with the choice of going to trial or paying the lion's share of the settlement. As later summarized by Boies in his book, *Courting Justice*, Christie's would pay $160 million and cooperate with Boies in prosecuting the case against Sotheby's in return for a share of what Sotheby's paid.

Boies was beautifully positioned. To go to trial Sotheby's would have to bet the company. And in the months and years that might take, Christie's would have put the problem behind it while we would have a Damoclean sword over our heads, frightening away both clients and staff.

We believed, and the evidence generally supported our belief, that the price-fixing agreement extended only to the seller's commission. If we could go to trial on that issue alone, the only question would be the amount of damages, and we could live, however unhappily, with the outcome. But there was enough evidence on the buyer's premium for that issue too to be part of any trial. And while we might persuade a jury of our innocence on that score, we would have to manage that even as we admitted our guilt on the seller's commission, not a terrific tribute to our trustworthiness. And if we lost on the buyer's premium, the company was gone.

We were due for some good news, and we got it. Boies agreed to abandon his deal with Christie's after we offered the same $160 million that Christie's had and persuaded Boies that he had a better case against Christie's than he had against us.

Our success was short-lived. The next day Boies told us he had told Christie's of his deal with us. They had countered with a higher offer. At that point we contacted Christie's lawyers and persuaded them that unless we worked together Boies would continue to play us off against each other. From then on it was clear that whatever sum Boies was able to extract from us would be divided equally between Christie's and Sotheby's.

The next question was where would we find the funds to pay our share. Though Alfred Taubman maintained his innocence, he too was a defendant in the class action. As a very wealthy man, he shared our interest in avoiding a devastating judgment. Moreover, his shares in Sotheby's were worth many millions of dollars, obviously an investment worth protecting.

By late summer of 2000, we were negotiating on three fronts—with Boies on how much he would take, with Christie's on how much to offer Boies, and with Alfred Taubman on how much he would contribute to the settlement. All were inextricably linked. Boies squeezed us hard, we transmitted the pressure to Taubman, and managed to hold ranks with Christie's.

Finally, the deals were done. Sotheby's and Christie's would each pay $256 million, for a total of $512 million. Alfred Taubman would contribute $186 million to Sotheby's half.

Though we settled with Boies in September 2000, it took until March of the following year for Judge Kaplan to approve the settlement and then until July 2002 for an essentially frivolous appeal to be disposed of. But Boies had done so well for his clients that virtually no one expected the settlement to be overturned. A great weight had been lifted from our shoulders.

We were still embattled on a number of other legal fronts, and we had yet to conclude a settlement with Dede Brooks. Once perhaps the most influential female executive in America, a trustee of Yale, a director of Morgan Stanley and a sought-after prospect for other prestigious boards, she was now a disgraced, reviled figure.

As CEO of Sotheby's Brooks had dangled the prospect of future wealth before Sotheby's employees by a heavy reliance on stock options in their pay packages. The plunge in the value of the company's stock in the wake of the antitrust revelations left virtually all of those options worthless. Alfred Taubman accused her of seeking to avoid punishment by falsely accusing him of having directed her to work with Christopher Davidge, the CEO of Christie's. (She in turn testified that Taubman had conspired with the chairman of Christie's, Sir Anthony Tennant, the former chairman of Guinness, the brewing giant and sponsor of the book of records.) And she was, of course, an admitted felon.

When we met for the first time, at her request, I saw a tall, slender, well-dressed woman, not quite fifty. (When HBO considered making a movie about how the mighty had fallen, Sigourney Weaver was regarded as the favorite for Dede's role.) The air of command I had heard about was gone, but she had not lost her dignity. She wanted me to know that she would help us in any way she could and hoped we would not treat her harshly. I just listened.

We got down to business at a later meeting with her and her counsel, one of whom I remembered well as a former student of mine at Columbia. They were eloquent advocates, but Dede had caused Sotheby's shareholders enormous harm, and, as a director, I owed my loyalty to those shareholders. We were not being vengeful, I explained, but the shareholders' claim on her assets had to be met. We would have to take almost everything.

She would not be left in poverty. Her husband was a successful investment banker, and we stopped short of trying to take their apartment. We stopped there for two reasons. First, it was not clear whether her husband could claim the apartment was his, not hers. And second, we did not want to turn Dede against us by seeming to be seeking vengeance.

The story Dede was telling the Justice Department and ultimately would tell in court was critically important to us. She had been steadfast in maintaining that the price-fixing agreement covered only the seller's commission, not the buyer's premium. The Justice Department pressed her hard on the point. If she were to yield, our exposure to civil damages would soar, and our criminal culpability would swell. And by yielding she might get a better deal from Justice.

By pleading guilty and cooperating with the Justice Department, culminating in her testimony against Alfred Taubman at his trial, Dede won special consideration from the department. It would not urge the judge to send her to prison. But it would not urge him not to either. That invaluable recommendation might have been forthcoming if she claimed that the price-fixing agreement covered the buyer's premium. But she never did. She stuck to the truth: there was no such deal. Brooks avoided prison nonetheless. Because of her cooperation, the judge sentenced her to six months of house arrest.

With the David Boies, Alfred Taubman, and Dede Brooks settlements wrapped up, our next big challenge was the criminal prosecution. We were undeniably guilty of an antitrust violation, and the Justice Department was not going to settle for anything less than a plea of guilty to a felony. But what would that mean? A corporation obviously can't be sent to prison. How substantial a fine would Justice demand?

We offered two arguments for a modest fine that seemed to us to carry considerable weight. The first, commonly advanced in circumstances like these, was that we had cooperated fully, holding nothing back. The second was special to our circumstances. A heavy fine on top of all our other costs could easily put us out of business. Ironically, in the name of protecting competition the Justice Department would then have severely damaged it, leaving Christie's standing virtually alone in the worldwide auction business. (Christie's was not fined at all because it had come forward to reveal the conspiracy to the Justice Department.)

We didn't get much sympathy from Justice. The fine they demanded was an onerous $45 million. The one break we did get was permission to pay in installments over five years without interest. The last act of our settlement with Justice included a bit of gallows humor. To conclude the matter we had to plead guilty to a felony in open court. There was no stampede of volunteers for the assignment. As general counsel, Don Pillsbury agreed that he was an appropriate representative. The picture of Don, the epitome of integrity, pleading guilty to a felony, struck a few of us, including Don, as ruefully funny.

There is an old French curse that goes: "May you be involved in a lawsuit in which you are in the right." At Sotheby's we found a worthy companion: "May your wrongs expose you to multiple classes of plaintiffs." In addition to the main antitrust action, we also had to confront two less costly sets of claims and two nuisance actions.

A class action brought on behalf of buyers and sellers in auctions conducted outside the United States was initially dismissed by the trial judge, but the Court of Appeals reinstated it. We thought we could ultimately win this one, but it would take years, victory was by no means assured, and it was important for us to dispel the lingering clouds hovering over Sotheby's. We settled it for $20 million.

Another clutch of lawsuits alleged violations of the securities laws harming purchasers of Sotheby's stock who would not have bought the stock at the prices they paid if the conspiracy hadn't been kept secret. We settled this too, agreeing to pay $30 million in cash and $40 million in stock. Alfred Taubman agreed to fund the $30 million in cash. The court approved this settlement on February 16, 2001, just days before the first anniversary of the scandal's breaking.

We had yet to deal with a particularly parasitic segment of the bar. (No, I do not think that redundant.) When a publicly held corporation has misbehaved and its misdeeds have been brought to light by one group of lawyers, a second group may allege those same wrongs in what is known as a shareholders derivative action, demand that the board of directors take corrective action, and ask for a fee for their service to shareholders. To get rid of this nuisance, we paid the lawyers a million and a half dollars, most of which was covered by insurance.

The prize for creativity went to the lawyers who brought six California class actions alleging that California residents who purchased from a dealer who in turn had purchased from an auction house might have paid prices that were inflated by Sotheby's and Christie's agreement on sellers' commissions. Yes, you read that summary correctly. It was cheaper to buy this one off for $192,500 than to litigate it.

There was more unfinished business abroad. Since our price-fixing agreement covered the auctions Christie's and we conducted in Europe, the European Union had to exact its pound of flesh. We ultimately paid them a fine of just over $20 million.

Managing our way through all the litigation was indispensable to our survival, but it was not enough. There was still a business to be run. Bill Ruprecht, our new president and CEO, was the key actor on that front. Bill had spent virtually his entire adult life at Sotheby's, starting in the rug department, where he became a leading expert. He became an auctioneer, was promoted to be head of marketing and then executive vice president and managing director of Sotheby's North and South America, the position he held when he was named CEO. An obviously talented man, physically imposing and well respected, he was untested as a leader of a complex company in crisis.

The challenges we faced would have been daunting for a seasoned CEO, but our novice never flinched, at least not so anyone could see. Consignors had to be reassured they could entrust their valuable objects to us, that we were not going under. We needed to renegotiate our bank credit agreement to help pay for our settlements and provide the liquidity our business required. Key staff had to be retained even as hundreds were being laid off. Then a new poacher appeared on the scene.

Bernard Arnault, the head of LVMH Moet Hennessy, decided he'd like to have an auction house just like his business rival Francois Pinault, the owner of Christie's. Having had his offer to buy Sotheby's rejected by Alfred Taubman some time before, he decided to invest heavily in what had been a small auction house, Phillips, combine it with a firm led by Simon de Pury, a former Sotheby's employee, and try to fill out its staff with recruits from Sotheby's.

At the same time we were fighting off those raids, we had to cope with Phillips's extravagant efforts to win business from both Christie's and us. A key competitive weapon in this contest was the guarantee. To persuade a potential seller to consign a painting, an auction house will on occasion guarantee the consignor a minimum price for that work of art. If the painting fails to sell at auction, the consignor will still receive the guaranteed amount. The auction house will, in effect, buy the painting.

Similarly, if the picture does sell but for less than the guarantee, the auction house will make up the difference. On the other hand, if the picture sells for substantially more than the guarantee, the typical guarantee agreement will award the auction house a portion of that overage. In sum, a guarantee shifts the risk of a disappointing sale from the seller to the auction house but rewards the auction house if the sale is highly successful.

This is no game for amateurs. Knowing when to guarantee and for how much requires not just negotiating skill but a thorough knowledge of both art and the art market. In this arena restraint is often the wisest course. That was not the path chosen by Phillips. In the almost four bruising years before Monsieur Arnault abandoned the field, we lost a number of important consignments to Phillips, and Phillips lost well over half a billion dollars on rashly generous guarantees.

We were also trying to salvage our attempt to auction valuable objects on the Internet. Begun by Dede Brooks during the dot-com mania, the Internet business would eat up over $100 million in badly needed capital before we shut it down.

Soon we were joined in our misery as the economy sank into recession. And then came the unimaginable events of September 11, 2001, which made our troubles seem less than cosmic.

As the new millennium wore on, we were lucky in one important respect. New collectors were appearing. American tech tycoons and hedge fund managers were amassing great wealth. So were Russian oligarchs and a new class of Chinese capitalists. Like the Middle Eastern elite, they wanted to acquire art, and price was hardly an issue. Their willingness to buy at almost any price prompted owners to sell.

But we did not turn a profit again until 2004. In the meantime Ron Baron continued to seethe over the Taubmans' control of the company. At one point he enlisted Carl Icahn to consider joining our board as a Baron nominee. Sometimes referred to as a corporate raider, sometimes simply as an activist shareholder, the mere mention of Icahn's name has been known to fill management hearts with terror. He and I had several polite conversations in which we fenced over the possibility that he and his uncle would become Sotheby's directors. But we never really had to engage: with the help of the Taubmans' investment banker, who helped Baron sell his position, and Ariel Capital, who bought much of it, the Carl Icahn threat disappeared.

Ron Baron was not alone in disliking our dual-class stock structure. Many investors shun stocks that permit weighted voting. And the arrangement limited Sotheby's ability to raise capital. Because the company's charter provided that the Taubmans would lose their multiple votes if their voting power dropped below 50 percent, they would not agree to Sotheby's engaging in any stock transaction that would have that effect.

Not surprisingly, Alfred Taubman had lost his zest for Sotheby's. Even after he had served his sentence—originally a year and a day—he obviously could not involve himself in the affairs of the company. His son Bobby, who joined Sotheby's board a few months after me, is an effective and influential director. But Bobby is the CEO of the family's main venture, the publicly traded Taubman Centers, a multi-billion-dollar real estate company, and has other interests of his own.

It made sense for the Taubmans to sell their position, but until Sotheby's became profitable again, no buyer was going to offer a price acceptable to them. By 2005, Bill Ruprecht and his management colleagues thought the moment had arrived for the company itself to buy the Taubmans out. The benefits to Sotheby's would be considerable: increased financial flexibility; a larger pool of potential investors; enhanced liquidity for the company's shares; and, with a substantial reduction in the number of shares outstanding, increased earnings per share for the remaining shareholders. And management would be happy to eliminate the risk that the Taubmans might sell to a third party with a different vision or agenda for the company.

Only one factor needed to be weighed against these advantages: money. Controlling positions in a stock generally command a premium over the market value of the shares. The question for the board of directors was whether a price fair to all the shareholders could be agreed upon.

A world of complexity attends that simple question. Plaintiff's lawyers love deals between a company and its controlling shareholder. In deciding to go forward, I thought it highly likely that we would be sued if we concluded a deal with the Taubmans. The claim would be that a subservient board disserved the interests of the other shareholders in order to unfairly enrich the Taubmans. Nonetheless, if we could arrive at terms that benefitted all the shareholders, going forward made sense. To be sure we would prevail if we were sued, we needed to proceed as porcupines do when they make love—very carefully.

The first step was for the board to appoint a committee composed exclusively of independent directors—directors who were neither part of management nor affiliated with the Taubmans. I chaired it and was joined by Allen Questrom and Don Stewart, recent additions to the board, and Steve Dodge, one of Ron Baron's original nominees. Next, to buttress our independence, we retained our own counsel and our own investment bankers to advise us.

The first issue for us was whether Sotheby's could afford to go ahead. The Taubmans owned over fourteen million Class B shares. Sotheby's stock was trading around sixteen to seventeen dollars a share. A premium of 20 percent would take the price to roughly twenty dollars per share. If the stock moved up or if a 20 percent premium wasn't enough, the cost could be even greater. Could Sotheby's afford over a quarter of a billion dollars in cash to buy the Taubmans' stake?

The answer was no, but the solution was obvious: pay for the B shares with a combination of cash and A shares, each of which carried just one vote. That approach would also eliminate the possibility that others might infer that the Taubmans, with their inside knowledge of the company, had decided that Sotheby's was no longer a good investment.

We faced a number of other issues and potential stumbling blocks. What if, having taken stock as part of the purchase price, the Taubmans turned around and sold that stock on the open market? The mere possibility that they might could weigh on the stock price. We sought and obtained reassurance in the form of an agreement that they would not sell on the open market for at least two years.

Getting through the subsidiary issues was relatively easy. The big issue was, of course, price. We met frequently with our investment bankers, the late Bear Stearns, as they developed a mountain of data to help us decide on a fair price. They in turn, along with our lawyers, a team from Simpson, Thacher, and Bartlett, skirmished with the Taubmans' counterparts in the quest for agreement. I also called periodic meetings of the entire board, often on the telephone, to keep them informed of the state of the negotiations.

In the end it came down to Bobby Taubman and me. In a series of phone calls, spaced so he could consult with his father and their advisers and I could consult with my committee and our advisers, he and I agreed on a price.

On September 7, 2005, Sotheby's board of directors met to approve the transaction in all its details along with a new financing agreement that would provide funds to help us pay for the deal. The total price was approximately $168 million in cash and 7.1 million Class A shares, which meant that each share of Class B stock would be exchanged for cash and stock worth almost $21 a share, a 20 percent premium over the closing price on the New York Stock Exchange of Class A shares on August 3. In addition to ending the dual-class stock structure, the deal reduced the total number of shares outstanding by 11 percent, boding well for future earnings per share.

We seem to have done it right. The stock promptly rose and so, despite my initial apprehension, no one sued. The head of our Simpson Thacher team asked if I'd like to join any other boards; he'd be only too happy to recommend me to his other clients. (I declined with thanks.) And Ron Baron called to congratulate me.

Over the years, in addition to managing crises, handling special negotiations, advising management, and presiding at meetings of the board and various committees, I would occasionally help with efforts to obtain consignments from collectors who were friends of mine or estates whose lawyers were friends or former students. And I would put in occasional appearances at auctions and special events. I was typically joined by my wife, Pat, who repented of her having urged me to decline the chairmanship.

In the years that followed the Taubman transaction, our profits grew, we began paying a dividend again, our stock price soared, cresting at over fifty, and dozens of artists' works sold for record prices. Watching two bidders going after a painting with abandon is a great spectator sport. "I have fifty-one million. Will you say fifty-two million?" our auctioneer would ask. Seeing bids rise in million-dollar increments was enough to make our salesroom crowd almost giddy. And when the victor emerged, they might actually applaud.

Among the sales that provoked applause: Rothko's *White Center (Yellow, Pink, and Lavender on Rose)*—$72.8 million; Rubens's *Massacre of the Innocents*—$76.7 million; and Picasso's *Boy with a Pipe*—$104 million.

All of us knew, however, that the auction business is cyclical and that the good times could not last. And they didn't. The reckoning came toward the end of 2008. The world economy slid into crisis, and the art market suffered accordingly. Sotheby's laid off hundreds and reduced the compensation of senior executives. Then we waited for the wheel to turn again.

And it has. In 2011, Sotheby's generated the second best financial results in its history. Despite the difficult challenges facing the world economy, the art market looks promising. But how we will fare in this unusually volatile world remains to be seen.

35

AMERICA'S CHALLENGE

*The older generation, whose own educational expenses
were aided by previous generations, has let their
children and grandchildren down.*

I could retire as Columbia's president, but I cannot help continuing
to care about the fate of higher education. Its value is inestimable.
Its central role in America is undeniable. Its future is at risk. To allow
this irreplaceable asset—still the best in the world—to continue to deteriorate would be a shame.

The generations that preceded us appreciated the importance of universities. At different times and different places they recognized them
as engines of upward mobility, generators of scientific advances and
technological breakthroughs, sources of greater understanding of ourselves and the world around us, proving grounds for the development of
tomorrow's leaders, shapers of an informed citizenry, developers of the
knowledge needed for a successful foreign policy, and still more.

Those generations bequeathed us a thriving enterprise—a healthy
mix of the public and the private. Though public colleges and universities are state run, national policy has been supportive since 1862, when
Congress awarded the states large tracts of federal land to be sold with
the proceeds dedicated to the support of state colleges.

The next big bursts of national support were triggered by World War II, which for the first time caused our national government to recruit and organize academic scientists in pursuit of national goals. Radar and the atom bomb were the most dramatic results. The potential uses of the symbiotic relationship between universities and government were not lost on some wise observers. Federal support of academic research would become a lasting legacy of the war.

The war also yielded an unprecedented expansion of the student population. The instrument of that expansion was the GI Bill, a compendious law that rewarded those who had served in the war with a variety of benefits, including the payment of tuition and living expenses of any military veteran who wished to attend college. At a stroke, access to America's universities was opened to millions, many of whom hadn't even contemplated a university education before.

After the war the booming economy enabled many states to invest heavily in their public universities. Inspired by regional pride, a belief that a strong public university was good for the local economy, and the wish of tax-paying parents to be sure their children could attend a good university, state legislatures poured funds into facilities and faculty. Before long, the best of the state universities—the University of California at Berkeley is a prominent example—were as good as the great Ivy League institutions.

By the middle of the twentieth century one could observe an implicit undertaking by each generation to pay for the education of the next. In the state schools that payment was made in the form of taxes. Public universities were supported with taxpayer dollars, and students paid nominal fees to attend. In the case of private universities the generational support was more complex and less complete, but still substantial. Part of the cost was borne by an endowment built up over generations, part by gifts from alumni and others, and in most instances part by parents of students. Tuition charges could be met by middle-class families. Columbia charged $600 per year when I entered in 1949. Modest scholarships were available for families without means.

All that has changed. The generational compact has been breached. Millions of students are forced to go into debt if they wish to attend college. Tuition at private universities has soared far beyond the ability of most families to pay. Columbia is currently charging approximately $60,000 (including room and board). That is for a single year. With rates rising every year, a student who has just begun at Columbia will spend roughly a quarter of a million dollars for the four-year program.

The challenge for America's elite private institutions is to keep from becoming the exclusive preserve of the wealthy. About two dozen of them meet that challenge by following what is known as a need-blind full-need policy. At many of those colleges most students are receiving financial aid. Students are admitted without regard to their ability to pay, and the college helps them meet the cost of tuition and living expenses from its scholarship funds. Those funds come from endowments, gifts, and a portion of the revenues from the tuition paid by other students.

The problem is that America's elite universities can admit only a very small proportion of those who wish to attend. Columbia College is currently receiving almost 29,000 applications for roughly one thousand places.

Most students never even seek a place in a private university. Though public universities now also charge tuition, they charge less, and many students from especially poor families can receive enough from state and federal programs to cover the tuition expense. As a consequence, public institutions now educate roughly three-quarters of America's university students.

I should be more careful. All we really know is that approximately 75 percent of college students attend public universities. Some, I fear, do not receive much of an education.

And that brings me to the heart of the problem. The issue of access is not principally one of access to a college education, although that too is becoming a problem. The issue is access to a *quality* education.

The belief of many Americans that their taxes are too high has sapped the willingness of state taxpayers to invest heavily in their universities.

To some extent the taxpayers' reluctance has been offset by increases in tuition, mitigating the damage to quality at the expense of diminishing access.

Public universities have also sought and found another source of revenue. With alumni numbering in the hundreds of thousands and the fundraising model of the private sector to imitate, public universities have enjoyed considerable success in supplementing taxpayer support with gifts.

But tuition and donations have rarely proved an adequate replacement for taxpayer support. The path of least resistance for politicians is procrastination. Maintenance or replacement of the physical plant can always be put off for a little while, a temporary cap on faculty salaries won't lead to an immediate exodus to better-paying institutions, and offering courses every other year instead of annually doesn't hurt all that much. And so the quality of public institutions has begun to erode.

Well-endowed universities are hovering like buzzards over the best public institutions, urging their faculty to move. Students complain that they cannot finish their education in four years because the required courses are not offered often enough or because they are unable to enroll in overcrowded classes. America's best public universities are on a glide path to mediocrity.

A community college in California recently considered charging extra for certain courses.[1] In theory, applying the market approach to deal with heavy demand may sound brilliant. In practice, it may well prove an abomination. Imagine attending a school where those with money can take the courses they want and need while their frustrated classmates look on with envy.

The daunting task is to turn the tide of taxpayer resistance, to renew our citizens' conviction that great universities are worth the pain in their pocketbook.

I should acknowledge that neither public nor private universities are models of efficiency. And I would not wish to be understood as maintaining they could not do well with less. But the savings that could be realized would not nearly make up for the cuts being imposed.

The federal government is already a major source of support for both public and private universities. The GI Bill has been resuscitated for war veterans. The National Institutes of Health, the National Science Foundation, and a number of other federal departments and agencies support university research. Pell grants are available to low-income students, but they cover only a portion of their costs. Students can also take advantage of federally subsidized loans.

But then we run into the aphorism that "the cause of problems is solutions." The ready availability of loans, subsidized and otherwise, has taken the outstanding debt of students past and present to unprecedented heights—surpassing one trillion dollars, more than America's outstanding credit-card debt. Ninety-four percent of students who earn a bachelor's degree borrow to pay for their education.[2] The burden represents an unforeseen drag on the economy, warps career choices, and demonstrates dramatically how the older generation, whose own educational expenses were aided by previous generations, has let their children and grandchildren down.

I am not naïve about the prospects for increased funding at both the state and federal levels, but this is our future. We must speak out. I was an advocate for support for the private sector when I thought that right, but now it's the public sector that needs advocates—especially from those for whom such advocacy is not self-interested.

We desperately need a reordering of our national priorities so that investment in future generations moves higher on the agenda. The simplest way to do that would be to expand the Pell Grant program by extending it to reach middle-class families and increasing the level of support to $10,000 a year per student, indexed for inflation. That would put a public university education within reach of almost everyone and give a modest boost to private-sector financial aid packages as well. What shall we ask of universities in exchange for the billions this would cost? No more tuition rises in excess of inflation. New students at a college or university that raised tuition in excess of inflation would be ineligible for Pell grants.

Despite its superficial simplicity, this is a very complicated idea. The premise is that for many, perhaps most, institutions the prospect that students would take their Pell money elsewhere would be enough to put an effective cap on tuition hikes. Before a school would find a tuition rise in excess of inflation worthwhile, it would have to take into account the lost Pell money.

Even institutions for which that calculation proved attractive would have to reckon with the effect on the composition of their student body. No respectable college wants to be in the position of teaching only the children of the rich and upper middle class. A college could, of course, offer disadvantaged students financial aid packages that made up for the lost Pell money, but that information might never make it to potential applicants from poor families. And that means fewer minority applicants as well, students that colleges are also seeking.

Deterred by financial, political, and social pressures, institutions of higher education would presumably choose to moderate tuition increases, push back against parsimonious legislatures, increase their fundraising, and take a closer look at their cost structures.

Some see online courses as an answer to rising costs. Perhaps, but I am old enough to remember when the advent of television was hailed as promising a new era in education. Online courses hold real potential, but I would not count on their solving our cost problem.

There could be dispensations from the rule I propose. I can think of one. If a university committed all the tuition funds produced in excess of inflation to financial aid, it could continue to welcome Pell grant recipients.

That might also have the effect of making my proposal less draconian than it at first appears. Tuition rises already include a financial aid component. If colleges and universities were permitted to take their tuition higher to fund financial aid, they might feel free to shift the financial aid funds already embedded in their tuition increase to meet other expenses.

I recognize the risks in my proposal. If state legislatures continue to cut college and university budgets, the institutions' inability to replace the lost dollars with new chunks of tuition revenue could accelerate the very decline I am decrying. My hope is that if elected officials know their parsimony cannot be replaced by effectively taxing the young and diminishing access, they will behave more responsibly.

If I am wrong, we will have entered a Darwinian world in which some states see their public colleges and universities decline, their bright young people go elsewhere, and their economic vitality seep away. In contrast, states whose legislatures behave responsibly will enjoy the benefits of thriving institutions of higher education open to all who can benefit from them.

I see another potential problem. If colleges and universities seek many exceptions to the cap on tuition, a regulatory system could evolve: universities would have to justify their expenditures in excess of inflation before an administrative agency. That is an unattractive prospect, though public oversight of state college and university budgets already exists.

Given my proposal's rich potential for unintended consequences, I suggest that the cap on tuition rises be enacted for a limited time—say ten years. In that period experience should enlighten us as to whether renewing the limitation makes sense.

It is hard to be optimistic about the prospect of any of this happening. But it surely won't happen if we don't try.

36

WHAT NEXT?

The three ages of man: youth, middle age, and "You look terrific."

Of the eight survivors who returned for the sixtieth reunion of the Columbia Law School Class of 1918, which I attended as dean, seven seemed to be in terrific shape. Though they would never see eighty again, they were still engaged in the practice of law and seemed to be enjoying life. The eighth alum was doddering: he had retired. Yes, I know the difference between causality and concomitance. His retirement may have had nothing to do with his deterioration. Still, I like the possibility.

But I do not need that lesson to keep retirement at bay. As much as I enjoy theater, music and dance, travel, reading, hiking, and friends and family, I still like the action of work in my life.

An old joke has it that if you are past the age of sixty and you wake up in the morning and nothing hurts, you're dead. I have a new hip, my cataracts have been removed, and so has a melanoma that did not spread. The remaining aches and pains are bearable and do not keep me from working out five times a week. Most importantly, I see no diminution in my mental ability and perhaps even a little improvement in my psychological state. On his ninetieth birthday, the late Harold Medina told me, "You can't scare a ninety-year-old man." And I think it is generally true that past a certain age one worries less about what other people may think of you.

I would be less than candid if I did not admit that the threat of Alzheimer's is frightening. Some of the ablest people I know have succumbed to it. But so far at least I have no sign of it.

Another relevant quip says that there are three ages of man: youth, middle age, and "You look terrific." I am frequently told that I look terrific, and nobody gives voice to the unspoken "considering your age." But my (relatively) youthful appearance and my still quick mind have not spared me from "ageism," the practice of treating the aging differently from younger people. Many boards of directors have mandatory retirement ages. (I prefer term limits as a fairer way of making room for fresh perspectives on a board.) And though throughout my life people have sought me, sometimes out of the blue, to help them solve a problem or resolve a crisis, that doesn't happen nearly so often now.

But please don't think me an object of pity. I am in no danger of lacking things to do. I will continue to teach as long as I can lurch to the lectern. I love the exchanges with my brilliant students. They help keep me vital.

When my selection as chairman of Sotheby's was announced, my friend Schuyler Chapin called to congratulate me. At the time I had been president of the Shubert Foundation for several years. As befits a man who had once been in charge of the Metropolitan Opera, Schuyler's congratulations were positively operatic. "Mike," he said, "You stand astride the arts." A bit bravura certainly, a considerable exaggeration surely, but I enjoyed the characterization nonetheless. And I have never ceased to treasure the good luck that blessed me with the chance to spend part of my time focused on theater and dance and another part focused on painting and sculpture and a miscellany of beautiful objects. The businesses underpinning those heavenly activities turned out to be fascinating as well.

Finally, at least for now, I have piles of books still to read, essays still to write, and a juicy slice of life yet to be lived.

ACKNOWLEDGMENTS

Memory is fallible, so it has been a great help to check mine with friends who shared experiences with me. Those kind enough to read and react were: Harold S. H. Edgar (chapter 7); Diana Phillips and Jon Olsoff (chapter 34); Joel Klein (chapter 33); Vicki Reiss, Amy Dorfman Wine, Phil Smith, and Bob Wankel (chapter 32).

Jonathan Fanton and Norman Mintz provided wise counsel on the ideas advanced in chapter 35.

I inflicted the entire manuscript on Alfred Connable, Margaret Montana, and my wife, Pat, and their suggestions were invaluable.

I am grateful for research help to Jocelyn K. Wilk, public services archivist at the Columbia University Archives; my son Professor Jeff Sovern and his St. John's colleague Professor John Q. Barrett for leading me to the archive containing my correspondence with Justice Felix Frankfurter; the Columbia *Spectator* for making their archives available; and to my research assistant Tim Shenk.

My assistants Mary Mygatt and Kathleen Grace Vanden Heuvel earned my warm thanks, cheering me on as they typed and retyped innumerable drafts and obtained needed permissions.

The Rockefeller Foundation was my gracious host at their Bellagio Center, offering a gorgeous environment that also managed to be amazingly conducive to thinking and writing.

Finally, this book would not have been written nor the life lived as it has been without the countless Columbians—my teachers, my colleagues, my students, and the wonderfully generous alumni and friends who supported Columbia and me. My gratitude is boundless.